Divine Wisdom and Warning

Decoded Messages from God

Nicholas Gura

Hamilton Books

An Imprint of
Rowman & Littlefield
Lanham • Boulder • New York • Toronto • Plymouth, UK

Copyright © 2011 by Nicholas Gura

First published in 2015 by Hamilton Books
4501 Forbes Boulevard, Suite 200, Lanham, Maryland 20706
Hamilton Books Acquisitions Department (301) 459-3366

Unit A, Whitacre Mews, 26-34 Stannary Street,
London SE11 4AB, United Kingdom

Library of Congress Control Number: 2015932571
ISBN: 978-0-7618-6572-8 (pbk : alk. paper)—ISBN: 978-0-7618-6573-5 (electronic)

Cover art by Catherine Gura

∞™ The paper used in this publication meets the minimum requirements of American National Standard for Information Sciences Permanence of Paper for Printed Library Materials, ANSI/NISO Z39.48-1992.

To my two heroes

the Honorable Reverend Dr. Martin Luther King, Jr.

Beate Klarsfeld

Contents

Acknowledgments

I want to thank my wife, Catherine, for her many contributions to this book, including her original painting for the cover, editing, interpretations of the material, myriad suggestions, and her support. I would also like to thank Marilyn Horowitz, Barb Burg, Arielle Eckstut, Sharon Goldinger, and Michael Levin, for their encouragement and help. I am grateful to Rabbi Aron Mathless, Rabbi Binny Freedman, and Rabbi Elie Weinstock, for sharing their wisdom and knowledge. Thank you to Rabbi Haskel Lookstein, Congregation Kehilath Jeshurun, and the Ramaz Yeshiva, for providing the foundation for my love and understanding of Judaism. Additional thanks to Esther Kustanowitz, for reading the manuscript and for her wonderful editing and contributions. Many thanks to my copy editor, Adam Nadler, whose erudition and style made an enormous difference. Thanks to my friend Bertrand Laurent and to my family, who provided me with a well-rounded education. Many thanks to Hamilton Books, especially Julie E. Kirsch and Nicolette Amstutz for their great help. I am extremely grateful to Marsha Brooks for her expert guidance. And thanks to Bruce Bleecker, for his wisdom and friendship.

Dr. Nicholas Gura

I want to express my deepest gratitude to my husband, Nicholas, who welcomed my contributions to both the editing and the cover painting of this book. Additionally, I would like to thank the School of Visual Arts, in New York City, whose talented faculty has been a guide and inspiration, in particular Elizabeth Sayles, Shelley Haven, and Melanie Marder Parks. And a special thanks to Joyce Grossbard, for her wisdom, warmth, and encouragement.

Catherine Gura

I

Divine Messages: Real or Random?

Chapter One

The Discovery

After 9/11 we all searched for answers. Some demanded government action, others focused on apprehending the evildoers, and many suffered the emotional and physical fallout of that terrible day. I, too, sought answers, but by using a method 3,200 years old and deeply embedded in the Jewish tradition. Gematria, most commonly referred to as Jewish numerology, is the tradition of assigning specific, traditionally prescribed numbers to Hebrew letters in order to convert text into a number. This practice allows words and phrases with identical numerical values to be compared. When two phrases share the same numerical value, it reveals a hidden relationship between them that teaches us deeper meanings and associations. For example, the Hebrew word for "soul" (*Neshama*) has the numerical value of 395, and a phrase from Psalm 46:6: "God is within her" (*Elokim B'kirbah*) has the same value, revealing that God resides within the soul. A second example: a phrase from the Book of Esther 2:2: "beautiful of appearance" (in Hebrew *Tovote Mareh*) has the numerical value of 669, and a phrase from Leviticus 26:6: "peace on earth" (*Shalom B'aretz*) has the identical numerical value. Therefore, Gematria reveals the hidden wisdom that "peace on earth" is the true "beautiful of appearance."

The earliest reference to Gematria is found in the Book of Genesis Chapter 14:14, when Abraham's servant, Eliezer, is referred to as "318 servants." The Talmud (the ancient authoritative book of Jewish law) explains that 318 is the Gematria (or numerical value) of the name Eliezer. Gematria is used throughout the Talmud to explain biblical text, and has been used by biblical commentators for over 2,000 years to enhance their interpretations. Others have been fascinated with Gematria, including Sir Isaac Newton, who dedicated much time to using it to search for the key to unlock hidden biblical wisdom. He was not successful.

I was first introduced to Gematria in the third grade at the Ramaz Yeshiva in New York City. After the Israeli Six-Day War, my seventh-grade Bible teacher, Mr. Rappaport, told the class that the total number of Israeli soldiers killed in the war was 679. He wrote the number on the blackboard and said, "Using Gematria, the Hebrew letters that correspond exactly to 679 can be used to spell the Hebrew word *Ateret.*" *Ateret* is defined in the Hebrew dictionary as the "crown or glory of [victory]." Although I didn't grasp the significance of Mr. Rappaport's comment that day, many years later I incorporated his insight into my own, new gematrial technique.

The events of 9/11 rekindled my interest in the hidden meaning of numbers and letters. I wondered if 911 was a random number or if it had any greater significance. Eventually, I discovered that the numbers 9 and 11 are associated with three other tragic and horrific events. According to historical accounts, approximately 2,600 years ago, in 586 B.C.E., on the 9th day of the 11th month of the Jewish calendar (the Ninth of *Av*), the Holy Temple in Jerusalem was destroyed by the Babylonians. The Temple was soon rebuilt, but in 70 C.E., also on the 9th day of the 11th month, the Romans destroyed the Second Holy Temple.

The numbers 9 and 11 appear again in 1938 Nazi Germany. On November 9, the 9th day of the 11th month of our modern calendar, thousands of Jewish stores were looted and destroyed, hundreds of synagogues burned, and over 20,000 Jewish citizens were sent to concentration camps. That day, known as *Kristallnacht* (Night of Broken Glass), should have been a wake-up call to the world that Nazi Germany was a major threat.

These discoveries encouraged me to continue exploring Gematria. It was a very natural fit. I have an undergraduate degree in bioengineering from the Columbia University School of Engineering and Applied Science and a D.D.S. from the New York University College of Dentistry. After graduating from dental school, I worked on Wall Street for over 20 years, trading stock options on the floor of the American Stock Exchange. I am also a lifelong enthusiast of puzzles and games, and an expert in backgammon. Each of these areas of study prepared me for my work with Gematria.

Then one night in 2006 my wife showed me page 484 of the book *The Joys of Yiddish,* by Leo Rosten. It was a brief chapter on Gematria, which I read with great interest. Then she turned on the television and began watching the annual Scripps National Spelling Bee in Washington, D.C. The judge announced the next word, "gematrial," and continued with the definition: "Of, or pertaining to, the study of Gematria." My wife and I looked at each other. What was the probability that she would turn on the TV at that exact moment, to that channel, to the word "gematrial," immediately after I had read the Gematria chapter? It could have been a coincidence, but to me it was a sign that I needed to continue with my work.

After two more years of intensive research, I devised a new gematrial technique, easily verifiable and reproducible without the use of a computer, that revealed messages of wisdom and warning embedded in Hebrew words and phrases. These revealed messages were both profound and metaphorical, and appeared to answer timeless questions and mysteries such as: Why does the world exist? Who wrote the Old Testament? Is the Bible true? Was Jesus actually a messenger of God? What is the secret to being with God? Is there a conflict between science and the Bible? Why is quantum theory so strange? And what are the minimum requirements for entry into heaven?

My first discovery came in 2008, a month before Passover. I had been thinking about the upcoming Seder, a ceremonial dinner held on the first and second nights of Passover to commemorate the Children of Israel's exodus from Egypt in approximately 1,250 B.C.E. After having attended Seders for over 40 years, I wanted to contribute something new to the dinner conversation. The Hebrew word for Passover is *Pesach*. Each letter in the Hebrew alphabet has a certain, specific numerical value, ranging from *Aleph's* 1 to *Tav's* 400. So, I took the three Hebrew letters that spell *Pesach*, used Gematria to assign the appropriate number to each letter, and added up their values (80 + 60 + 8). This yielded a total numerical value of 148. I then converted the number 148 into the three specific and unique Hebrew letters that correspond exactly to it. This is a simple and straightforward exercise. Here are the steps required to transform the 148 numerical value of Passover (*Pesach*) into letters: 100 generates the specific letter that corresponds to 100 (*Koof*); 40 generates the specific letter that corresponds to 40 (*Mem*); and 8 generates the specific letter that corresponds to 8 (*Chet*). This yields a new set of three letters, which together spell the Hebrew word for "flour" (*Kemach*). Flour is the key ingredient of matzah, the unleavened bread central to the Passover holiday. (Chapter 2 of this book contains the complete step-by-step mathematics of this technique.)

After attending many years of classes, sermons, and lectures on the topic of Passover, I thought I had heard it all. But this was a new insight and I found the discovery exciting. Because of my engineering education and my trading experience, I also understood the odds. Because the Hebrew word for Passover was over 3,200 years old, the probability was low that after all this time, I had actually decoded a hidden message. Could it really be that I had devised a new technique that revealed a hidden embedded message, possibly even divine in origin?

I decided to test the technique with five significant Hebrew biblical words. Using my Gematrial technique the Hebrew word for "peace" (*Shalom*) generated the hidden word "make" (*Asu*), which I interpreted as conveying the directive "to make peace." The word "Israel" generated the hidden message "I shall watch over" (*Eshmor*), interpreted as: "I God shall watch over Israel." The word "Zion" generated "His [God's] nest" (*Keno*).

The Hebrew word "Torah," the biblical term for the "Old Testament," generated "awe of" (*Yirot*). And the Hebrew word "Menorah" (candelabra) generated the word for "fire" (*Aish*).

I had studied enough probability theory to know that if a scientific technique or theory works perfectly with five random samples, there is a strong probability that the theory has validity. Still, while I was confident that I had uncovered something intriguing, I remained cautious about proclaiming my discovery. So many others have studied and used Gematria, why had no one else ever discovered this? According to Jewish tradition, the Torah (The Five Books of Moses) was transcribed by Moses on Mount Sinai. Why would these embedded messages be revealed now?

Then I realized something so profound that it finally convinced me my discovery was valid: The new letters generated by my method could be rearranged to spell multiple words, and each word described an aspect of the original topic. For example, embedded within the Hebrew word for "Passover" are the three Hebrew letters that spell "flour," but these letters (*kuf, mem, chet*), can also be rearranged to spell five other words, each one describing a different aspect of Passover. In addition, I often found that the new letters spelled a word that could be interpreted as a positive directive, but if the directive is ignored, the same letters rearranged spelled a warning. For example, embedded in the Hebrew word for "peace" is the directive "make." But rearrange the Hebrew letters of "make" (*Asu*) and they spell the word for "cry out" (*Shiva*). This I interpreted as a warning for what will happen if the directive "to make peace" is ignored: "You shall cry out." A second example is that embedded in the Hebrew phrase for "human rights" (*Mishpat Gever*), found in the Book of Lamentations 3:35, are the hidden Hebrew letters that spell the directive "For [all] generations" (*L'Dorot*). But when those same hidden letters are rearranged, they also spell the word for "to descend" (*Laredet*). This is interpreted as a warning: "If you do not provide for human rights for all generations, you shall descend." This warning may be taken metaphorically or literally.

When I began to share my discovery, both Jews and non-Jews, were moved by the mathematically generated messages. I also sought out and received acknowledgment from many rabbis and scholars that my techniques and results were original. This included a Ph.D. in linguistics; a professor of Hebrew; and outstanding rabbis from America and Israel.

After testing thousands of other Hebrew words and phrases, I made a second discovery applicable to every Hebrew word or phrase: that each number, or numerical value, represents a specific theme. (The principle of "themes," and the process by which they are identified and confirmed, is explained and expounded upon in the next chapter, and is applied in each of the succeeding chapters.) In short, it seems as if God created the world with numbers. Convert any Hebrew text into a number and that number represents a specific principle or topic.

For example, after studying and analyzing all known Hebrew text with the numerical value of 355, I concluded that 355 represents a philosophical question, found in Psalm 36:8: "What is valuable?" (In Hebrew, *Ma Yakar*). Every Hebrew word or phrase that has the numerical value of 355 can therefore be interpreted as referring to the issue of: What is valuable? Two basic sets of answers were revealed: "to attain power and wealth at any cost," with the "Pharaoh" (a numerical value of 355) as the symbol, and "to help repair the world," with "Oprah" (also a numerical value of 355) as the symbol. In Hebrew, the words "Oprah" and "Pharaoh" consist of the identical letters.

The number 281 has been identified as the theme of "Russia." Written in Hebrew letters, it is pronounced the same as in English, and its numerical value is 281. The Hebrew words and phrases with that numerical value have been found to reveal aspects of Russia. This includes its past, present, and even its possible future: "heal," "glory," or "ashes"?

The number 356 represents America (again spelled with Hebrew letters but pronounced the same as in English). An analysis of the word and the value of its letters reveal insights about America's purpose, why some countries hate America, and the specific actions necessary to shift the perception of the haters.

The number 353 represents the theme of "happiness;" 486 represents the commandment "Thou Shalt Not Steal"; 357 "humanity"; 138 "success"; 661 "gossip"; 911 "September 11th"; 614 "freedom"; 458 "daughters"; 788 "harmony in the home"; and so on.

These techniques and principles when applied to biblical or Talmudic text, or even to text from the Hebrew dictionary, have consistently uncovered what appear to be hidden, embedded messages. After converting less than 1 percent of the Bible into numbers, and then applying my methods, I uncovered thousands of messages of incredible beauty. Sometimes the embedded messages state profound wisdom, and sometimes they are directives, such as "make peace" or "human rights for all generations." But often they simply provide perfect summaries of the text. This supports the idea that the messages are not a coincidence and, to me, implies that God may actually be their author.

Here are nine examples of embedded messages:

1. From the story of Moses and God at the Burning Bush, the Book of Exodus 3:4 states: "God from amidst the bush" (*A-donai Metoch Hasneh*). This phrase has a numerical value of 672, and the specific and unique Hebrew letters that correspond exactly to 672 spell the Hebrew word for "burns" (*Bo-eret*). "Burns" is the exact same verb used in the

previous biblical sentence describing the Burning Bush, thus suggesting that the embedded message is not a coincidence.

2. Exodus 34:28 recounts the story of Moses meeting God on Mount Sinai. It states: "Forty days and forty nights" (*Arbaim Yom V'arbaim Lailah*). This phrase has a numerical value of 783, and the specific and unique Hebrew letters that correspond exactly to 783 spell "you shall meet" (*Tifgosh*).

3. The Book of Judges contains the history of the judges of ancient Israel. Deborah was the sole female judge. Judges 5:12 states: "Arise, arise, Deborah" (*Oori Oori Devorah*). This phrase has a numerical value of 789, and the specific and unique Hebrew letters that correspond exactly to 789 spell "female judge" (*Shophetet*).

4. In the Jewish mystical tradition, the most famous example of hidden wisdom is the Kabbalah (widely disseminated in the 13th century C.E.). The Gematria of the term "hidden wisdom" (*Chachma Nistarah*) is 788, and the specific and unique Hebrew letters that correspond exactly to 788 spell the word for "you shall search for" (*T'cha-pace*).

5. "Kindness and compassion" (*Chesed V'Rachamim*), Psalm 103:4, has a numerical value of 376. The Hebrew letters that correspond exactly with 376 spell the word for "do" (*Asu*).

6. The word "life" (*Chaim*), from Genesis 2:7, has a numerical value of 68. The Hebrew letters that correspond exactly to 68 spell "have compassion" (*Chas*). Compassion is the essential element for a meaningful and beautiful life.

7. From the Book of Malachi 2:10, the phrase "Did not one God create us all?" (*Halo E-L Echad Brah-anu*), has a numerical value of 345. The unique and specific Hebrew letters that correspond exactly to 345 spell the word used to refer to God (*Hashem*). This is literally "The Name" of the one God that created us all.

8. This method can also be applied to examples from modern Hebrew. Here is an example of text from *The Complete Hebrew English Dictionary,* by Reuben Alcalay. The term for "greed" (*Ahavat Betza*) has a numerical value of 570. There are two sets of Hebrew letters that correspond exactly to 570. One set spells "evil" (*Resha*) and the second set spells "arrogance" (*Ah-tak*).

9. Here is an example from the Midrash (an ancient commentary, originally peserved orally, written down beginning in the 2nd century C.E.). In discussing God's annual decrees on the Day of Atonement (Yom Kippur), of who lives and who dies, the Midrash refers to God's: "ledgers of life and ledgers of death" (*Sifray chaim V'sifray maytim*). "Ledgers of life" (*Sifray chaim*), has a numerical value of 418, and the three specific Hebrew letters that correspond exactly with 418 spell the word for "you shall live" (*T'chee*). "And ledgers of

death" (*V'sifray maytim*), has a numerical value of 846, and the four specific Hebrew letters that correspond exactly with 846 spell the word for "you shall die" (*Tamoot*).

These examples illustrate the beauty that the new techniques and methods reveal. But these techniques do not apply only to ancient biblical text—it seems that they can be used to predict current events and even reveal the more distant future. For example, in 2011, the government of Israel faced a difficult decision. Should they give up 1,027 Palestinian prisoners for one kidnapped Israeli soldier, Gilad Shalit? There were excellent arguments pro and con, and no one knew for sure what to do. However, Gematria seemed to predict, or at least suggest, the answer! The numerical value of the Hebrew letters of "Gilad Shalit" is 456, and the unique and specific letters that correspond exactly with 456 spell the word for "You shall give" (*T'nu*).

My first discovery, which reveals messages directly embedded in Hebrew words and phrases, works most of the time. But my second discovery, which identifies the "themes" of numbers, works all of the time.

As you will see in each chapter, my techniques mathematically generate messages of wisdom and warning that will benefit individuals, families, and nations. The revealed wisdom ranges from powerful coaching for relationships to disclosing what may happen after death.

The mathematically generated messages can often be interpreted as literal or metaphorical and are similar to poetry in that, with only a few words, they condense multiple layers of meaning.

The power and clarity of the messages made it mandatory for the title of this book to contain the words "divine" and "God." But let me be clear: I am not a Messiah or even a messenger of God. Consider me equivalent to the person who framed Picasso's paintings. The paintings are incredibly valuable and treasured by all, but no one cares about the framer. He just wanted to do a good enough job so that the frame would not distract from the greatness of the art.

But is it possible that, thousands of years ago, the messages were embedded by some brilliant person and not by God? To make each distinct word, phrase, and verse add up to a numerical value that has profound meaning is incredibly complex and seems unlikely to be the work of a human being. In addition, my techniques, when applied to modern Hebrew text, continue to reveal powerful messages embedded within them. It is hard to believe that this is a coincidence.

For example, the Hebrew word for "Karma," a concept from the Hindu religion, was only recently added to the Hebrew dictionary (pronounced the same as in English but spelled with Hebrew letters). It has a numerical value of 345, and the three unique Hebrew letters that correspond exactly to 345 spell the Hebrew word most commonly used to refer to God, *Hashem* (literally translated as "The Name"). If you rearrange the Hebrew letters of the word "Karma," you spell the word for "chance" or "fate" (*Mikreh*). Therefore, the Hebrew word for chance also has a numerical value of 345, and generates the same three unique and specific Hebrew letters that spell the Hebrew word used to refer to God. This suggests the notion that the guiding force beneath both karmic and chance events is The Name of God.

While this book is complete, it is not finished. Hundreds of messages have not been included. Simply too much material has been generated. Nevertheless, when you read any chapter or page of this book, it is my hope that you will see the wisdom and beauty of the messages. But as you read, ask yourself this question: Are the messages actually from God or are they mere numerical coincidence? Read on, and after considering what I have put forth, decide for yourself.

Chapter Two

Gematria

God's Math or Numerical Coincidence?

This chapter confronts the fundamental question: Does using Gematria un-cover knowledge divine in origin or just numerical coincidence? First, let us briefly review the history and definition of Gematria.

On the wall of every classroom where Hebrew is taught hangs a chart that shows the 22 Hebrew letters and their corresponding numerical values rang-ing from 1 to 400 (see Table 2.1). According to Jewish tradition, these numerical values, or Gematrias, have been passed down from generation to generation, for over 3,000 years, since the time of Moses on Mount Sinai. Simple addition is used to calculate the numerical value of a Hebrew word or phrase: assign the prescribed value to each letter, and then add up all the values. This converts a word or phrase into a number, and this number, the sum total of all the letters, is called its Gematria. An example of this exercise, familiar to many, is that the Hebrew word *Chai,* defined as "life" or "lives," has the numerical value of 18. Therefore, the number 18 is considered to be a lucky number.

The Talmud teaches that the first recorded use of Gematria appears in the Book of Genesis 14:14. All classic Jewish commentators on the Bible, in-cluding the famous, Rashi (1040-1105 C.E.), used Gematria to varying de-grees. The word "Gematria" has a Greek root, due to the Greek presence in Israel from approximately 250 B.C.E. to 30 B.C.E., during which time the Old Testament was translated into Greek.

The purpose of Gematria is to convert Hebrew text into numbers so that words and phrases of identical numerical values can be compared. When words or phrases share the same numerical value, hidden relationships be-tween them are revealed that teach us new meanings and associations. The

Table 2.1.　Gematria Table of Numerical Values of the 22 Hebrew Letters

Letter	Hebrew	Numerical Value
Aleph	א	1
Bet	ב	2
Gimmel	ג	3
Dalet	ד	4
Heh	ה	5
Vav	ו	6
Zayin	ז	7
Chet	ח	8
Tet	ט	9
Yod	י	10
Kaph	כ	20
Lamed	ל	30
Mem	מ	40
Nun	נ	50
Samech	ס	60
Ayin	ע	70
Peh	פ	80
Tzadi	צ	90
Kuf	ק	100
Resh	ר	200
Shin	ש	300
Tav	ת	400

discoveries presented here have been accessed through this ancient practice of assigning prescribed numbers to Hebrew letters.

Many doubt that God wrote the Bible, and these people certainly do not believe that hidden divine wisdom is embedded in the text. Yet even those who do believe should be skeptical of anyone claiming to reveal hidden messages from God. Therefore, be skeptical, and let Gematria and the new techniques introduced in the first chapter prove themselves.

For example, the first sentence of the Bible states: "In the beginning God created the Heavens and the Earth." In Hebrew, the first word in that sentence (*Beraishis*) is defined as "In the beginning." If the Bible were indeed written by God, and if my work is valid, then the result of applying my techniques to "In the beginning" may reveal mathematically generated answers to the timeless question: What was God actually thinking about at the beginning of time? At the very least, we could expect some new information regarding the universe: Is it random or is there purpose? Perhaps we can even learn what God wants from us. What follows is but a partial look at the results of a gematrial analysis of "In the beginning."

After assigning the appropriate number to each Hebrew letter and adding up each value, the total numerical value of "In the beginning" is calculated to be 913. As it turns out, 913 is also the numerical value of the phrase "Do no evil" or "Do no wrong" (*Lo Ta-asu Avel*), from the Book of Leviticus 19:15. That these two phrases share the identical numerical value reveals a hidden relationship between them, and suggests that intrinsic to the creation of the world, the command to do no evil has primary importance.

In the Book of Genesis, Chapter 5 discloses the genealogy of the human race, and the names of the ancestors from which we all have descended are listed. Genesis 5:1 states: "This is the account of the history of mankind, on the day that God created a person, He created him in the image of God." The Hebrew phrase "Created in the image of God" (*B'dmut Elokim Asah*) has a 913 numerical value. Because all text with a 913 value can be understood as referring to something of primary importance, this phrase teaches us an essential lesson. It reminds us that because each person has been created in the image of God they are holy and hence deserving of dignity and respect. Imagine if we all behaved according to that idea. The hidden wisdom here is that, while most people claim to love and respect God, it is actually how we treat each other that determines our relationship with God.

The Bible can be described as the instruction manual for life, the definitive guide to what is permitted and what is forbidden. The numerical value of the Hebrew words for "permitted" and "forbidden" (*Mutar Asur*), taken from Talmud *Avodah Zarah,* page 34a, also add up to 913. This section of the Talmud deals with the laws pertaining to the prohibition of idolatry. According to the sages of the Talmud, the prohibition of idolatry is a universal law that applies to every human being.

When the Bible introduces the concept of monotheism to humanity, in the story of God appearing to Abraham (at that time known as Abram), in the Book of Genesis 17:1, it states: "And God appeared to Abram and said to him I am God," (*Vayera A-donai El Abram Vayomare Elav Ani E-L*). This phrase also possesses the identical numerical value of 913 and emphasizes that monotheism is a primary law of creation.

Another phrase with a 913 Gematria seems to reveal the core and essence of monotheism: "The two tablets of stone" (*Shnay Luchot Avanim*), found in the Sabbath Morning *Shemoneh Esreh* prayer, and in Exodus 34:4-5 (*Shnay Luchot Avanim V'*). According to the Bible, Moses inscribed the Ten Commandments upon two tablets of stone on Mount Sinai. And to underline the primary importance of the Bible and the Ten Commandments, a phrase stating that Moses "received the Torah [Old Testament] from Sinai" (*Kebale Torah Me-Seenai*), found in Mishnah *Avot* 1:A, has the same numerical value of 913. (The Mishnah is the Jewish Oral Law, also believed to have been received by Moses on Sinai, and was transcribed between 200 and 500 C.E.)

Incredibly, if we rearrange the Hebrew letters of "In the beginning," it spells the actual birth date of the world: "The first of *Tishrei*" (in Hebrew "*Aleph B'Tishrei*). This is the date of the Jewish New Year, *Rosh Hashana*, which celebrates the birth of the world.

Traditionally, Gematria has been used only to convert words into numbers, thus revealing text of identical values, as with the "In the beginning" example. While this process has traditionally revealed beautiful and compelling associations, this book introduces a new technique: using numbers to generate letters. In other words, after converting a word or phrase into a number, that number is used to generate the specific and unique letters that correspond exactly to it. Thus, with this new method, introduced in the first chapter and described below in greater detail, biblical text of multiple words is transformed into a few new letters that can be arranged to spell other words. These words can then be interpreted as divine messages of wisdom or warning.

Here is the result of applying this technique to 913 (the numerical value of "In the beginning"). The five Hebrew letters that correspond exactly with 913 (תשריג) can spell the Hebrew word for "I chased" (*Garashti*), interpreted here as a description of God chasing Adam and Eve out of the Garden of Eden. With the expulsion from Eden, Earth and Heaven became split. But rearrange the Hebrew letters of "I chased" and they spell the word for "I made a bridge" (*Gasharti*). This reveals that, although God created the world separate from Heaven (or the Garden of Eden), He made a bridge between them. When these same letters are rearranged again, they spell the secret to crossing the bridge back to the Garden of Eden: "That the 613" (*Sheh-Taryag*). This refers to honoring and observing the 613 commandments of the Torah (The Five Books of Moses).

The rest of this chapter consists of various examples of divine wisdom and warning accessed through my new use of Gematria. For those who are interested, the following example provides the step-by-step mathematics of applying my technique to the Hebrew word for "peace," *Shalom. Shalom* consists of four letters: *Shin,* which has a value of 300; *La-med,* which has a value of 30; *Vuv* which has a value of 6; and *Mem,* which has a value of 40. When the numerical value of each letter is added up (300 + 30 + 6 + 40), the total value is 376. Therefore, the Gematria, or the numerical value of the word *Shalom,* is 376. Whereas traditional Gematria ends here, my technique goes a step further. I use the number 376 to generate a new set of letters, the unique and specific Hebrew letters that exactly correspond to 376. The specific letter that corresponds exactly to 300 is the letter *Shin*; the specific letter that corresponds exactly with 70 is *Ayin*; and the specific letter that corresponds to 6 is *Vav*. These three new letters can be used to spell the Hebrew word for "make," *Asu*. This is interpreted as the divine directive "to make peace." In addition, these new letters rearranged spell the Hebrew word for "cry out," *Sheeva*. This is interpreted as the warning for what will happen if you do not make peace. Therefore, directly embedded in the Hebrew word for peace is the hidden message: "Make peace or you shall cry out."

(Note: Those of you who are familiar with the field of differential equations may notice that this technique is analogous to the Laplace transform, used to simplify the solution of a differential equation by converting the equation from calculus into an algebraic polynomial equation. This allows the equation to be solved algebraically and then transformed back into calculus.)

I have mentioned, that after converting thousands of ancient and modern Hebrew words and phrases into numbers, I made a second discovery: that every number represents a particular theme, such as a principle, an idea, or a major event. For example, all Hebrew text with a numerical value of 911 can be interpreted as referring to an aspect of the 9/11 attack! This includes the significance of the date, details about the perpetrators, the dust and ashes of the fallen towers, the family members searching in vain for survivors, the directive to respond, specific prayers that should be recited, the holiness of the victims, and prophetic messages about the ultimate outcome. (See the chapter on 9/11 for the complete discussion.)

These new techniques reveal powerful new information, including wisdom that resolves the conflict between the Bible and science, incredible messages regarding Jesus, and the connection between charity and success. Simply take any word or phrase, biblical or otherwise, write it in Hebrew, and calculate its Gematria by converting the letters into numbers. Then add each number and calculate the total. This sum represents a theme. Once you identify the theme you can understand the hidden meaning of all words and phrases that have the identical numerical value. This concept of themes has been tested with tens of thousands of examples, and it has consistently been validated. Can this really be a coincidence?

Identifying and confirming a theme is usually simple. Major concepts, such as peace and free will leap out as examples, as do major events, such as the Holocaust. But without identifying the theme, the embedded messages may be impossible to understand. What follows is the story of the identification of the theme of the number 751.

In 2008, I noticed that the Hebrew phrase "make peace" (*Aseh Shalom*), from Isaiah 45:7 and from the *Kaddish* prayer, had a Gematria of 751. But the four specific unique letters that corresponded to 751 spelled the Hebrew word for "hatred of" (*Sin-ot*). This seemed very confusing; what did "hatred of" have to do with "make peace"? The two phrases are almost opposites.

This led to a search for a 751 theme: a word or phrase whose letters were also valued at 751, that would give rise to these two possible responses or choices: the choice to make peace and the choice to promote the hatred of someone or something.

Sections of the Bible, the Jewish prayers, and the Hebrew dictionary were mathematically analyzed looking for the answer to the mystery of 751. By consulting the Website Biblewheel.com (an excellent site dedicated to Gematria), I could see the list of all words in the Old Testament that have the numerical value of 751. I read each one. The first entry was "to greet you" (*Likratcha*), from Genesis 32:7. This phrase didn't seem to help nor did the other entries. After six months of looking for the theme, I stopped and continued to work on other numbers. A few weeks later, in the mail, I received a letter from a charity that collects money to help pay for proper burials for those who cannot afford them. The letter was in Hebrew, and one sentence translated as: "On the merit of the dead the world exists." The phrase "the world exists" (*Ha-Olam Mitka-yame*) was intriguing, so I calculated its Gematria. It equaled 751. Immediately it was clear: the world exists to give us a choice to make peace or to promote the hatred of others. The theme of 751 is "The world exists." More than a year later, attending synagogue for the two-day holiday of Rosh Hashanah, the Jewish New Year, I heard a prayer recited: "Today the world is born." The phrase "The world is born" (*Harat Olam*), found in Jeremiah 20:17, had a Gematria of 751. This was further confirmation that the theme of 751 had been correctly identified.

Armed with this insight, take another look at the phrase "to greet you," from the Book of Genesis 32:7. Earlier in Genesis, Jacob tricked his blind father and stole the blessing of the firstborn from his older brother, Esau. Esau became furious and wanted to kill Jacob. Jacob's mother sent him away. After 20 years, Jacob returned home hoping that his brother was no longer angry. Jacob sent messengers to tell Esau that he had returned and that he had brought gifts for him. Genesis 32:7 states: "The messengers returned to Jacob, saying, we came to your brother, Esau, and he is coming to greet you and four hundred men are with him." Jacob did not know if Esau and his 400 men were coming to greet him in peace or in hatred. The phrase "to greet you" (a 751 Gematria) occurs here because this story is about the choice to make peace or to promote hatred. The phrase "to greet you" is located in several other places in the Bible, and present in all cases is the choice to respond in peace or with hatred. The chapter "Why does the World Exist" will show that all Hebrew words and phrases with a 751 Gematria relate to the theme "The world exists."

As of today, the themes of approximately half the numbers from 1 to 1,091 have been identified. Each chapter in this volume covers one theme and consists of a list of messages of identical numerical value that refer to that specific topic. The messages were generated either by the techniques introduced here or were found in the Old Testament, the Hebrew prayers, the Talmud, the ancient biblical commentaries, or the modern Hebrew dictionary. Because the spelling of Hebrew words and phrases determines their numerical value, the exact spelling found in the particular source is used. When there is no source attributed to a particular message, that message is a combination of part scripture and part Hebrew dictionary.

The math of the messages is accurate. The messages exist. The questions for the reader are: Where do they come from? Are they random or divinely embedded? While I believe the messages are of a divine origin, the brief comments that have been added for clarity are mine alone. Different interpretations may be entirely valid, and in no way do I claim to speak for God.

Analyzing the Gematria of biblical names reveals beautiful wisdom. For example, the Hebrew spelling of David, the name of the most famous king of Israel, has a Gematria of 14. The number 14 generates two specific and unique Hebrew letters that spell the word for "hand" (*Yad*) as well as the word for "enough" (*Dai*). David's hand was enough to slay the Philistine giant, Goliath, with his slingshot. The word "hand" also provides a summary of David's life. With his hand, David played the harp and wrote and compiled the Book of Psalms. And in approximately 1100 B.C.E., he conquered Jerusalem, established it as the capital of Israel, and instructed Solomon, his son, to build the Holy Temple there. David also gathered and prepared the raw materials for its eventual construction. In addition, according to Jewish tradition, the Messiah will be a descendent of David. Therefore, it could be said that when the Messiah comes and ushers in world peace, it will have been by the hand of David.

The Hebrew name Abraham has a 248 Gematria. The number 248 generates three specific, unique, and new Hebrew letters that spell several words, including the word for "compassion" (*Ra-chame*). Abraham is known for his exceptional acts of compassion. This includes welcoming the stranger, feeding the hungry, and even arguing with God to save the inhabitants of the evil city of Sodom. Also, the Hebrew word for "womb" (*Reh-chem*) can be spelled with these letters. This can be interpreted as metaphoric, that from Abraham's "womb" came monotheism. Abraham is the father to three of the world's great religions: Judaism, Christianity and Islam. The three letters can also be rearranged to spell the word for "destruction" or "disgrace" (*Cheh-rem*). This can be interpreted as the consequences of discarding the teachings and values of Abraham.

Here is another example of Gematria facilitating a direct experience of being, literally, in the presence of God's genius. There is a phrase in Deuteronomy 18:13 that states: "You shall be with God" (*Te-heyeh Im A-donai*). The Gematria of this phrase is 556, and the four specific Hebrew letters that correspond exactly to 556 spell the word *Tikkun,* meaning "repair." To teach us to repair the world with charity and acts of kindness is the purpose of the

Bible, of the entire Jewish tradition, and of virtually all religions. This suggests that the secret to being with God is to do the work of *Tikkun*. But rearrange the letters of *Tikkun* and they spell what will happen if we do not do this work: we will feel "removed" and "cut off" from God (*No-take*). And if we rearrange the letters yet again, we find that they spell the Hebrew word for "You shall purchase" or "You shall acquire" (*Tiknoo*), which describes what we often do when we feel removed from God. This illuminates what drives our consumerist society: an attempt to compensate for feeling removed from God. This insight, which uses only four letters to delve so deeply into the universal desire to connect with God, seems proof that Gematria is truly God's math.

There are other examples of God's genius. The Hebrew word *Torah,* defined as the Five Books of Moses, transcribed by Moses over 3,200 years ago, has a numerical value of 611. Yet, the four specific and unique letters that correspond exactly to that number spell the word for "My Website" or "My place" (*Atari*), interpreted as God's Website or God's place is the Torah. The Hebrew word for Website was only recently added to the Hebrew language. Who could have known the word for "My Website" 3,200 years ago?

The mathematically generated messages in this chapter—and in each chapter of this volume—were found after converting less than 1 percent of the Bible from text into numbers. Most likely, the Bible contains an infinite number of hidden messages. The techniques introduced here can be applied to any word or phrase in the Bible or in the Hebrew language. Therefore the title of this volume is *Divine Wisdom and Warning: Decoded Messages from God.* It may sound arrogant to claim to have decoded messages from God, but who else could have written the Bible, the best seller of all time, and simultaneously have hidden mathematically coded messages within each word, phrase, and sentence of the text?

II

Divine Wisdom and Warning
for Timeless Questions and Mysteries

Chapter Three

Why Are We Here?
Why Does the World Exist?

THE WORLD EXISTS = 751

Why did God create the world? Was this the first time the world was created? Is the Bible an essential element of creation? What is the secret formula for happiness on earth? This chapter consists of mathematically generated words and phrases that seem to answer these mysteries. Other questions are answered as well, some that seem unrelated, such as: Why do those who promote hatred always end up shamed and humiliated? And why does a man's mistreatment of a woman guarantee his ultimate failure?

The research for this chapter was different than all the others. Usually, a topic (peace, for example) was first chosen and then its numerical value was analyzed. After that, the embedded messages were uncovered. But with the topic of "The world exists," the research began with the number 751 and not with a specific topic. I had noticed that the Hebrew phrase for "Make peace" and the Hebrew word for "Hatred of" both had the same numerical value of 751. What I did not know was the topic for all words or phrases with a 751 numerical value. After much research, the number 751 was identified as representing "The world exists" (in Hebrew *Ha-olam Mit-ka-yame*). (The process of how this was discovered was explained earlier in Chapter Two.) Therefore, every Hebrew word or phrase with a numerical value of 751 can be interpreted as referring to an aspect of "The world exists." A biblical version of this term was found in the Book of Jeremiah, and it also has a numerical value of 751. The biblical term is listed as the first message.

Message 1: "World was created" or "World was born" (*Ha-rot Olam*), literal translation of Jeremiah 20:17. This phrase is recited on Rosh Hashanah, the Jewish New Year, considered in Jewish tradition as the day the world was created.

According to the Talmud, the Jewish New Year commemorates the date that Adam, the first person, was created. But it appears that God did not just create the world for our enjoyment. He had a further plan. It seems that the world was designed to test humans, measuring us to see if we are friends or enemies of God. Whether we pass or fail this test is based on two criteria, listed as the following two messages.

A TEST WITH TWO POSSIBLE CHOICES

Message 2: "Make peace" (*Aseh Shalom*), Isaiah 45:7. There is no doubt that this is the choice that the Bible and God recommend we make. Just look at the subtext of the Ten Commandments: each one is consistent with an aspect of peace, whether it is peace with God, ourselves, our families, our neighbors, our workers, or even with our animals. When we choose to make peace, we are friends of God.

Message 3: "Hatred of" (*Sin-ot*) or "You hate" (*Sa-nay-tah*), two possible translations of a term in Psalm 5:6. It appears that there are two basic ways of being in the world: we can either make peace or promote hate. We have the free will at every moment to choose either path, but if we choose to promote hate then we are God's enemy and may face consequences.

The rest of this chapter consists almost entirely of the consequences of our choice between peace and hatred.

MESSAGES DIRECTLY EMBEDDED WITHIN
THE HEBREW PHRASE FOR "THE WORLD EXISTS" (751)

There are four specific and unique Hebrew letters that correspond exactly with the number 751 (תשנא). These four letters have the following values: *Tav* (400) *Shin* (300) *Nun* (50), and *Aleph* (1). Together, they add up to 751, because 400 + 300 + 50 +1 = 751. These letters can be used to spell seven words: the previous message, "Hatred of," and six others (listed below). Each word seems to refer to the choice to either make peace or promote hate. All other messages in this chapter also have a numerical value of 751 but those words and phrases consist of a variety of different letters that add up to 751.

Message 4: "That I shall provide" (*Sheh-eh-tane*), from the *Milog Hebrew Hebrew Online Dictionary*. This may suggest that, if we choose to make peace, God will provide us with a beautiful and bountiful world that offers us everything we need.

Message 5: "Carry" or "laden" (*No-sote*), Genesis 45:23. This section of Genesis tells of donkeys carrying gifts of grain, bread, and provisions. On a mystical level, that the word "carry" is found in this particular section of Genesis could be interpreted as comparing human beings to donkeys or asses, because, although laden with divine gifts, we all too often choose to act with hatred, giving in to our baser, more animal instincts. The word "carry," with the same numerical value as "The world exists," may also indicate that at all times we carry both possibilities with us: the ability to respond with hatred or to make peace.

Message 6: "That you shall weep" (*Sheh-ta-ahn*), alternative translation of Talmud *Pesachim* 108b. When we weep it is often the result of hatred. However, "That you shall weep" may also be prophetic: If we choose to promote hate, a consequence may be that we will ultimately weep.

Message 7: "Discouraged" or "hopeless" (*No-eshet* or *No-a-shote*), alternative spelling as found in *The Complete Hebrew English Dictionary*, by Reuben Alcalay. This message suggests that hatred may be the ultimate cause of much of the suffering and hopelessness on the planet.

Message 8: "Misled" or "deceived" (*Ni-sase*), *The Complete Hebrew English Dictionary*, by Reuben Alcalay. This may suggest that if we choose to promote hatred of others, perhaps out of some conviction or belief that we will benefit, we have been deceived.

Message 9: "High" or "exalted" (*Ni-sase*), *The Complete Hebrew English Dictionary*, by Reuben Alcalay. When we choose to make peace, we will be exalted, literally or metaphorically.

WAS THIS THE FIRST TIME THE WORLD WAS CREATED?

Message 10: "The tenth test" (*Nee-sah-yone Asarah*), a variation of a phrase in Ethics of the Fathers 5:4. This may reveal that this is the 10th time the world has been created.

Message 11: "Do not call this the first" (*Lo Yi-ko-reh Achat*), Esther 4:11. Out of context, this seems to further support the notion that our present world is not its first incarnation.

MESSAGES OF WISDOM

The following messages are Hebrew words or phrases consisting of a variety of different letters with the numerical values of 751. Each message refers to an aspect of the world exists.

Message 12: "There is truth" (*Yesh Emet* or *Emet Yesh*), Talmud Yevamot 105a and Midrash Rabbah Deuteronomy 1:10 (words not consecutive). This suggests that inherent to the creation of the world is the existence of truth, that there is such a thing as right and wrong. This is in contrast to postmodernism that believes that there is no such thing as truth and that everything is relative.

Message 13: "It's your question," "It's your request," or "It's your wish" (*Shay-lah-techah*), Esther 5:6. Simply said, this message reveals that the purpose of our life is up to us. At each moment of our lives, we have the free will to choose between hatred and peace. It is we who determine the answer to the question: Why does the world exist?

Message 14: "Truck" or "lorry" (*Mah-saw-eet*), *The Complete Hebrew English Dictionary,* by Reuben Alcalay. This tells us that, just as a truck can carry equipment to use for peaceful purposes, or carry weapons to promote hatred, we too have that choice.

Message 15: "Maiden voyage" (*Haflagot B'chorah*), *The Complete Hebrew English Dictionary,* by Reuben Alcalay. The first time a ship leaves the shore is a lovely metaphor for the creation of the world, the first launch of God's big project into the universe.

Message 16: "Ground wire" (*Teel Ha-arakah*), *The Complete Hebrew English Dictionary,* by Reuben Alcalay. The literal definition of a ground wire is a wire from an electrical source connecting to the earth or ground. Metaphorically, this describes the creation of the world as a connection between the heavens and earth.

As discussed earlier, the world was considered born with the creation of Adam, the first human being. The following four messages refer to the creation of human beings.

Message 17: "He fashions the human being" (*Yatzar Et Ha-adom*), from the daily prayer of appreciation of our bodily functions, recited by observant Jews after using the bathroom.

Message 18: "The dust" (*Et Aphar*), Genesis 2:7 (words not consecutive). This verse states: "And the Lord God formed the human being of the dust from the ground." This reminder of where we came from is intended to make us more humble. Realizing that we were created from dust may decrease our arrogance. When a person forgets that he or she is human, and behaves as if they are God, they take the law into their own hands. This is at the source of almost all of our problems.

Message 19: "Who placed you as a person" (*M'Som-cha L'eesh*), Exodus 2:14. In the context of the Book of Exodus, Pharaoh is questioning Moses, the best example of someone who chose to promote peace: amongst his people, between God and the Israelites, and ultimately by bringing peace to the entire world in the form of the Bible and the Ten Commandments.

Message 20: "Womb" + "Offspring" (*Rechem Sheger*), nonconsecutive words but found in the same verse of Exodus 13:12. Womb and offspring are two elements that create a system for reproduction that enables birth and reproduction, allowing the world to continue from generation to generation.

WHO CREATED THE WORLD?

Message 21: "King of the Universe the True Judge" (*Melech Ha-olam Dayan Ha-emet*), from the traditional prayer recited upon hearing of the death of a loved one. This is the answer to the question: Who created the world? God the King of the Universe and the True Judge created it.

Message 22: "God His way is perfect" (*E-L Tamim Darko*), 2 Samuel 22:31 and Psalm 18:31. While this principle may be understood by those with faith that God's perfection is embedded in the world's existence, often we cannot understand why a particular path is perfect.

Message 23: "My Name" (*Et Sh'mee*), Numbers 6:27. "My Name" refers to God's Name and comes at the end of an incredibly beautiful prayer blessing Israel. Because this phrase has the numerical value of 751, it is also related to the choice between promoting hatred and making peace. The hidden wisdom here may be that God's Name will bless any person or nation that chooses to make peace their priority.

WHAT DID GOD GIVE TO THE WORLD
TO HELP IT MAKE THE RIGHT CHOICES?

In this chapter the terms: Torah, Bible, Five Books of Moses, and Old Testament are used interchangeably.

Message 24: "God [that] teaches Torah" (*A-donai Mila-made Torah*), from the daily blessings of the Torah (the letter symbolizing the word "that" has been deleted). God teaches the Bible to us so we can make the correct decision to make peace. The Talmud and ancient biblical commentators have even gone so far as to say that the Torah is the reason the world exists.

Message 25: "Torah to people" (*Torah L'Am*), from the daily blessings of the Torah. The Torah seems to be the instructional manual for humanity.

Message 26: "The Torah is for elevation" (*Ha-Torah La-olah*), literal definition of Leviticus 7:37. This clearly suggests that the Torah is for spiritual and, possibly, material elevation.

Message 27: "To whom shall He teach knowledge?" (*Et Me Yo-reh Day-ah*), Isaiah 28:9. This may imply that God created the world in order to teach His knowledge to us.

Message 28: "To wisdom" or "To keen discernment" (*L'too-she-yah*), Job 11:6. The Bible is intended to help us make the right choice. This suggests that when we choose to make peace we choose wisdom.

Message 29: "With intelligence [he maneuvered]" (*See-kale Et*), Genesis 48:14. Out of context, the hidden message here may be that when we make peace we have acted with deliberate intelligence.

FUNDAMENTAL ELEMENTS OF CREATION: MONOTHEISM, THE TEN COMMANDMENTS, AND THE BIBLE

The Bible introduced the world to monotheism primarily by recounting the story of Abraham in the Book of Genesis. Approximately 3,800 years ago, Abraham, the first Jew in history, took the initial steps in the dissemination of monotheism to the entire world. The following message heralds Abraham's breakthrough.

Message 30: "God to Avram: Go yourself from your land" (*Adonai el Avram Lech Lecha Me-artzecha*), Genesis 12:1. In this part of Genesis God sends Avram (later God renames him Abraham) to leave the idol-worshipping place of his birth and to bring monotheism to the world. As *The Stone Edition* of the Bible comments on this verse: "This chapter begins a new birth of mankind: the story of Abraham and his descendents. . . . With Abraham there began a profound change in the spiritual nature of mankind." This reveals that monotheism was a fundamental principle embedded in the creation of the world.

Message 31: "This God spoke to your entire congregation on the mountain" (*Eleh De-bare A-donai el Kal K'halchem Ba-har*), Deuteronomy 5:19. Here Moses has just repeated the Ten Commandments to the Children of Israel and is reminding them that they first received the Commandments at Mount Sinai after the Exodus From Egypt. The hidden wisdom here seems to be that the Ten Commandments (and all the 613 commandments of the Torah) were a major reason the world was created. In addition, the Bible and Commandments teach us the elements of peace.

Message 32: "The essence is peace" or "The foundation is peace" (*Ha-ekar Shalom*), words are not consecutive but were found in the *Breslov Machzor Rosh Hashanah,* by Mohorosh of Heichal Hakodesh Breslov. Peace is the key to solving every problem that confronts humanity, whether it is an issue with a family member, neighbor, co-worker, the environment, or with another country or people.

MESSAGES OF WARNING AND THE CONSEQUENCES FOR MAKING HATRED YOUR PRIORITY

Message 33: "Money will answer everything" (*Ke-seff Ya-aneh Et Ha-kol*), from Ecclesiastes 10:19. The person who believes that money is always the answer also believes that any behavior is acceptable in the pursuit of it. This attitude leads to hatred of others and hatred of the law.

Message 34: "You have destroyed" or "The devastations" (*Ha-she-mo-tah* or *Ha-Shaymot*), alternative translations of Job 16:7. When we choose hatred we cause destruction. Devastations such as the Holocaust, 9/11, and the Armenian, Rwandan, Cambodian, Bosnian, and Darfur genocides are consequences of the choice to pursue the hatred of others.

The following two messages are metaphors that seem to reveal God's disappointment in humanity for so often choosing the path of hatred.

Message 35: "Prehistoric period" (*T'kufah Hak-dumah*), from *The Complete English Hebrew Dictionary,* by Reuben Alcalay. This reveals God's opinion of us when we choose hatred as our guide. It is as if we are living in prehistoric times, when we were concerned only with our basic survival.

Message 36: "The uncircumcised" (*Ah-ray-lim Et*), Ezekiel 32:30. Referring to someone as uncircumcised is a biblical insult. As this verse states: "They were broken from their might in shame, the uncircumcised lie with those slain by the sword, bearing their shame with those who descend to the pit."

EXAMPLES OF HATRED

In the Book of Exodus we learn that, after 200 years of Jews being slaves in the land of Egypt, God decided to intervene and save them, choosing Moses as their leader. The following two messages make clear that God views slavery as a clear example of hatred.

Message 37: "And I shall send you to Pharaoh" (*V'esh-lah-cha-chah El Pharaoh*), Exodus 3:10. Here, God speaks to Moses from the Burning Bush, instructing him to go to Pharaoh and take the Israelites out of Egypt. Moses fears that Pharaoh will not respond with peace but with hatred. After meeting with Moses, Pharaoh orders the slaves to work harder. Indeed, Pharaoh has chosen to respond with hatred.

Message 38: "And my nation are the wicked ones" (*V'amee Ha-rish-amim*), Exodus 9:27. God has sent plagues upon Egypt to force Pharaoh to free the Jews. In the end, Pharaoh relents and admits that he and his nation are wicked.

Message 39: "Hadassah is Esther" (*Hadassah He Esther*), Esther 2:7. The Scroll of Esther is read on the holiday of Purim, which recounts the story of the Jews in the Persian kingdom in approximately 516 B.C.E. The phrase "Hadassah is Esther" reveals that Esther was her Persian name and that her real Hebrew name was Hadassah. She used a Persian name and hid her Hebrew name because she was afraid of the hatred of Jews. The word "Esther" in Hebrew can be translated as "I will hide." How often throughout history have the victims of hatred tried to hide their identities?

Message 40: "Design evil against me" or "Think evil against me" (*Choshvim Olai Ra-ah*), from "Prayer of the 18" and Talmud Berachot 17a. Plotting to do evil is another common expression of hatred, because hatred begins with thoughts and leads to actions.

The phrase "To meet you" is found in multiple places in the Bible: each time the term is used, it relates to a situation where there is the choice between reacting with hatred or with making peace. Here are three examples of its use.

Message 41A: "To meet you" or "To greet you" (*Lik-raht-chah*), Genesis 32:7. The full verse states: "Esau is coming to meet you and four hundred men are with him." Jacob is told that his brother, Esau, is coming to greet him. The last time they met, Jacob had stolen Esau's primogeniture, by pretending to be him in order to fool their blind father, Isaac, into blessing Jacob with the firstborn's blessing. Now, years later, Jacob is not sure if Esau comes to meet him in hatred or peace.

Message 41B: "To meet you" (*Lik-raht-chah*), Exodus 4:14. Moses has just witnessed the miracle of the Burning Bush and feels that he is unworthy of representing God and leading the Children of Israel. Moses has a speech impediment, but his brother Aaron speaks well and is the older of the two. When God tells Moses that Aaron is coming to meet him, Moses is not sure if Aaron will be jealous and feel hatred or if Aaron will make peace with God's choice of Moses as leader of the Jews.

Message 41C: "To meet you" (*Lik-raht-chah*), Numbers 20:18. Here, the Children of Israel are in the desert and arrive at the Kingdom of Edom. Moses sends messengers to ask the king of Edom for permission for the Israelites, the cousins of the Edomites, to peacefully cross through Edom, promising that they will pay for all water and produce they consume. The king of Edom tells them that if the Israelites pass through his land, "swords shall be sent to meet you." Again, there was a choice of how to respond, and the Edomite king answered Moses with hatred.

Message 42: "You shall only consume" (*Rok Tow-chahl*), nonconsecutive words found in the same verse in Deuteronomy 12:23. This may refer to many of us who live as if the reason the world exists is for us to consume. In addition, it reminds us that hatred is often not manifested by an outright hatred of a person or group but is driven by a commitment to profit without regard to the welfare of others.

Message 43: "You shall be inclined to the fire" (*L'Aish T'hiyeh*), Ezekiel 21:37. Out of context, this may refer to our tendency toward destruction and consumption. Almost always, we consume natural resources until the land is ruined. It is worth noting that the next words in this phrase are "to consume." As Ezekiel 21:37 states: "You shall be inclined to the fire to consume."

MESSAGES OF WARNING: FROM GOD TO ALL HATERS

Message 44: "[God] shall pour out His blazing wrath" (*Shaw-phach Charone Ah-po*), Lamentations 4:11. This tells us that if we continue on the path of hateful choices, God shall pour out His blazing wrath upon us. It is our choice.

Message 45: "His [God's] anger from above is sent" (*Ah-po Me-mah-rome Shalach*), Lamentations 1:12-13. This reminds us that if we choose hatred as our purpose, we will incur God's anger.

Message 46. "Dead man" (*Eesh Mate*), Sanhedrin 22:b. This suggests that when we promote hatred of anyone, we may be physically alive, even possess wealth and fame, but we will be spiritually dead. The Talmud in the tractate of *Rosh Hashanah* 16:b goes further. In a discussion of the High Holy Days (a period of repentance and of asking God that we be inscribed in the Book of Life), it mentions that there is a category of people who are already dead but whom God keeps alive because they serve more of a purpose that way. A hypothetical example could be a Holocaust denier, possibly rich and famous but featured in the news several times a year always shamed and humiliated. It could be said that God's purpose in keeping this person alive is to teach the world that a Holocaust denier will always be humiliated.

Message 47: "God is the Eternal King nations shall perish from His earth" (*A-donai Melech Olam Vah-ed Avdoo Goyim May-artzo*), Psalm 10:16. This is a warning to the nations of the world that if they promote hatred of others, they shall perish. History shows that every nation that has promoted hatred, whether of blacks, Jews, women, or any minority, eventually disappears or loses its influence.

Message 48: "He [God] shall cleanse His earth" (*Ki'pare Admato*), Deuteronomy 32:43. Eventually, God will eradicate all the haters from the world and from history. This verse states: "He [God] will bring vengeance upon His foes and He will cleanse His earth." This is a warning to the haters, because when we hate another person we become a foe or enemy of God. Hopefully, the haters will wake up and change their ways before it is too late.

HATRED OF JEWS AND OF ISRAEL: A DIVINE TEST?

More than any other issue, it seems, the state of Israel provokes strong reactions from the nations of the world. The United Nations, often silent regarding many of the world's serious issues, repeatedly speaks up critically about Israel. The next series of messages suggests that this fixation on Israel is not a coincidence. Since the Holocaust, it is no longer considered acceptable to hate Jews openly. However, this same hatred is now expressed as anti-Zionism or anti-Israel sentiment.

If it is true that God created the world, wrote the Bible, and chose Israel to be His partner in the repair of the world (*Tikkun Olam*), then it makes sense that the world should be so fixated on Israel. However, the hidden purpose of this fixation seems to be that, while each nation is free to declare their opinions and suggestions regarding Israel, they also are declaring whether they are on the side of making peace or on the side of promoting hatred.

The following message is found in the last chapter of the Bible, as the Children of Israel were about to enter the land of Israel, at that time called Canaan. As Moses finished his last speech, God said the following to Moses.

Message 49: "To him [Moses] this is the land" (*Ay-lav Zot Ha-Aretz*), Deuteronomy 34:4. The verse states: "And God said to him: This is the land that I swore to Abraham, to Isaac, and to Jacob, saying, 'I will give it to your offspring.'" Thus, God, by giving the land of Israel to the Jews, began 3,200 years of envy, hatred, conflict, and wars. The land of Israel seems to be a divine test, or measuring line, for every nation of the world. It is as if God is saying: "It's your choice, relate to Israel with hatred or with peace, but there may be consequences to your choice."

Message 50: "According to the nations of the world" (*K'goyay Ha-arat-zot*), found in the *Aleinu* prayer. This reiterates that each nation has the freedom to choose to promote hatred or to make peace with Israel and the Jewish people.

Message 51: "Each nation Jerusalem" (*Kal Ha-ahm Jerusalem*), 2 Samuel 12:31. Like Israel, the city of Jerusalem is an issue that constantly generates arguments and disputes. Every nation seems to have a strong opinion about it. "Each nation Jerusalem" seems to suggest that this is not a coincidence: but that the discussion about Jerusalem has been embedded into the creation of the world. In the context of the choice to make peace or to promote hatred, Jerusalem becomes another litmus test for the world: Will you relate to Israel and Jerusalem with hatred or to make peace?

Message 52: "The Middle East" (*Hamizrach Ha-tee-chone*), from *The Complete Hebrew English Dictionary,* by Reuben Alcalay. More than any other region on earth, the character and history of the Middle East hinges on people's choices between peace and hatred.

Message 53: "Our Holy Land" (*Eretz Kad-shay-nu*), from the prayer for the Peace of the State of Israel. This emphasizes that each person and nation of the world will choose how to relate to Israel.

The following three messages were formed by combining the Hebrew word for "Israel" with another word. In each case, the two-word combination has a numerical value of 751, the value of "The world exists." All the words were found in *The Complete Hebrew English Dictionary,* by Reuben Alcalay.

Message 54: "Width of" "Israel" (*Row-chav Yisrael*). The boundaries of Israel are debated in virtually all the nations of the world. This is a topic of conversation often motivated by a desire to make peace or promote hate.

Message 55: "He chose" "Israel" (*Bah-char Yisrael*). The term "the chosen people" has several meanings. It seems that Israel—meaning the Jewish people—was chosen by God for two reasons: as the vehicle through which the Bible, the Ten Commandments, and monotheism would be spread throughout the world, and so that Israel and the Jews would be the primary litmus test for hatred in the world. (See the chapter on anti-Semitism for the complete explanation.) This suggests that God chose Israel as His proxy to call forth those who hate Him. (See Numbers 10:35.) When we look at history, each group or ideology that has sought to dominate the world invariably attempted at one time or another to destroy the Jewish people. Whether it was Pharaoh, the Roman Empire, the Crusades, the Spanish Empire, the Nazis, or Islamic extremists.

Message 56: "Friend of Israel" (*Yisrael Cha-vair*), Ezekiel 37:19. This suggests that people and nations of the world that choose to make peace with Israel seem to be considered as friends of God.

Message 57: "God takes note of Israel," "God remembers Israel," or "God counts Israel" (*A-donai Pah-kod Yisrael*), Exodus 4:31. These words are located in the same sentence but are not consecutive. As this verse states: "That God remembered Israel and saw their affliction." This may imply that God keeps track of how we relate to Israel.

BIBLICAL PROPHECY PROVEN TRUE

It seems clear that God considers Israel to be essential, but some people and countries consider it as different and separate and not part of the family of nations. Again, Israel is synonymous with the entire Jewish people.

Message 58: "Shall not be considered" or "Shall not be reckoned" (*Lo Yitcha-shev*), Numbers 23:9. As this verse states: "Behold, [Israel] is a nation that will dwell alone and shall not be considered among the nations." Incredibly, the Bible, transcribed approximately 3,200 years ago, contains this thought. Who could have predicted so long ago that this attitude would still be so prevalent today? Could it be just a coincidence?

HATRED OF WOMEN

The following three messages were formed by combining the Hebrew word for "women" with another word. In each case, the combination has a numerical value of 751, the value of "The world exists." All the words were found in *The Complete Hebrew English Dictionary,* by Reuben Alcalay. The first message refers to the hatred of women, and the other two seem like suggestions to men to marry women, treat them well, and accept their contributions.

Message 59: "Hate" "women" (*Saw-nay Nah-shim*). Hatred of women can take many forms: F.G.M., (female-genital mutilation), domestic violence, rape, honor killing, objectification of women, and the mistreatment of women in the workplace. This possibly suggests that hatred of women is another litmus test used to judge us as to whether or not we are friends of God.

Message 60: "Marry" "women" (*Naw-saw Nah-shim*). This seems to be a divine recommendation to men that they need to marry women, implying that women can help influence men toward the healthy choice to make peace. (See the chapter on the Torah for other examples of women helping men make better choices.) In Genesis 2:18–22, God clearly states that because man needs help, God will create a woman to help him. The problem is that, if women are not treated as equal partners to men, then marrying a woman may not help!

Message 61: "Elevate" "women" (*Nee-saw Nah-shim*). This is a directive that men elevate women and let them contribute equally to the family and the community. Numerous epidemiological studies have concluded that when women in a community are treated well, there is a marked decrease in the incidence of malnutrition and the infant-mortality rate. Unfortunately, many men mistreat and disempower women, thus negating the contributions that women could make.

Message 62: "A wife for you" (*L'cha Eshet*), Hosea 1:2. This tells us that having a good wife may be the most important indicator as to whether a man chooses a path of peace or of hatred. In addition, the man who values his wife will most likely also value his fellow man and promote peace. But the man who hates women will likely choose to hate others.

IF WE CHOOSE PEACE

Message 63: "Pleasure on earth" (*Nachas Ba-aretz*), Midrash to Kohelet 9:6. This suggests that pleasure on earth could be a reality if we make the right choice between peace and hatred.

Message 64: "The poet" or "The singer" (*Ha-M'sho-rare*), 1 Chronicles 6:18. This may refer to the purpose of poetry and music: to bring peace to others. In addition, when there is peace, more of our children can become poets.

Message 65: "Holy convocation and" (*Mik-rah Koh-desh Oo*), Exodus 12:16. Here, the term "holy convocation" describes the *seder* feast of the festival of Passover. The hidden message is that, just as Jews sit for a feast on Passover, if all of us were to choose peace, it would lead to a holy convocation of all nations coming together, as if for a banquet.

Message 66: "And a feast," "And a banquet," or "And a party" (*Ooh-mish-teh*), Ezra 3:7. This suggests yet again that, with peace, life could be like a banquet.

Message 67: "Banquet" (*Misht-yah*), Daniel 5:10. It is worth noting that, although this is an Aramaic term, the Gematria is still 751. This reinforces the previous message "And a feast."

Message 68: "Their voice shall sing of pride of God, they shall shout for joy more than [by the] Sea [of Reeds]" (*Ko-lom Ya-ro-new Big-oan A-donai Tza-ha-loo Me-yam*), Isaiah 24:14. This seems to be prophetic, that eventually the entire world will unite in a song to God and make peace. In that moment, human beings will have finally lived up to their full potential.

Chapter Four

Who Wrote the Bible?
Is the Bible Really True?

TORAH = 611

The Bible. The Old Testament. The Torah. The Five Books of Moses. Whatever we call it, the series of books that delineate the stories of the Old Testament, and (depending on your belief system) outline the code of conduct in matters both earthly and divine, is 3,200 years old. According to traditional teachings, the Torah was divinely rendered on Mount Sinai to Moses, who then transcribed these words of God and delivered them to the people.

In the Old Testament, the Hebrew word used to refer to the book itself is "Torah," defined as law, instruction, and teaching. Therefore, the numerical value of the word "Torah," 611, is analyzed here. All Hebrew text with a numerical value of 611 has been found to refer to some aspect of Torah. A gematrial examination of the number 611 reveals the messages directly embedded within the word "Torah" and generates a list of Hebrew words and phrases that have the identical value of 611. The messages appear to answer questions such as: Who wrote the Bible? Is the Bible really true? What is the purpose of the Bible? Who was the greatest historical enemy of the Bible? And what happens if we disregard the teachings of the Bible?

In addition, at the end of this chapter, the related term "Holy Scriptures" (*Kitvay Ha-Kodesh*), with a numerical value of 841, will be analyzed and its embedded messages disclosed. In this chapter, the terms Old Testament, Bible, and Torah are used interchangeably.

MESSAGES DIRECTLY EMBEDDED
WITHIN THE WORD "TORAH"

Because the numerical values of the Hebrew letters only go up to 400, there are two different sets of specific Hebrew letters that correspond exactly to 611:

A. The first set consists of the letters with the values 400 + 200 + 10 + 1 = 611: תריא.

B. The second set consists of the letters with the values 300 + 300 + 10 + 1 = 611: ששיא.

Each set of Hebrew letters will be used to spell the messages directly embedded within the word "Torah." The first set of Hebrew letters that corresponds exactly with 611 (תריא) can be used to spell the following 11 messages. All other messages in this chapter also have numerical values of 611 but consist of a variety of different letters.

Message 1: "My Website" or "My place" (*Atari*), *The Complete Hebrew English Dictionary,* by Reuben Alcalay. There are some who think that the Torah is outdated, but "My Website" shows that God is quite up to date. Remember, the word "Torah" was transcribed by Moses over 3,200 years ago, and yet, embedded within this ancient word is the modern Hebrew word for "My Website." Who could have known 3,200 years ago that Websites would even exist, or what term would be used to describe them? "My Website" is interpreted here as a divine, hidden message that the Torah is, in effect, God's Website. But to access God's Website we don't have to go on the Internet, just read and learn the Torah.

Message 2: "My shape," "My appearance," or "My form" (*Toe-ah-ree*), *The Complete Hebrew English Dictionary,* by Reuben Alcalay. This tells us that God's shape, appearance, and form are manifested on earth as Torah.

Message 3: "Shall shine" (*Tah-eer*), Psalm 18:29. This suggests that Torah shall shine light on the world, and possibly that we shall shine through the study of Torah.

Message 4: "Evidence of" or "Proof of" (*R'ah-yaht*), *The Complete Hebrew English Dictionary,* by Reuben Alcalay. This tells us that the wisdom and laws of the Torah are evidence of God.

Message 5: "Lungs" (*Ray-ote*), *The Complete Hebrew English Dictionary,* by Reuben Alcalay. This seems to be metaphoric: just as lungs are essential for breathing and for life, so too is Torah.

Message 6: "Shall mark a boundary" (*Yit-ar*), *The Complete Hebrew English Dictionary,* by Reuben Alcalay. The message here is that Torah shall mark a boundary for our lives.

Message 7: "Shall adorn" or "Shall enhance" (*Y'tay-air*), *The Complete Hebrew English Dictionary,* by Reuben Alcalay. This teaches us that the Torah enhances our lives.

Message 8: "You saw" (*Rah-ee-tah*), Deuteronomy 1:31. In the Book of Deuteronomy, Moses reminds the Israelites of the miracles and events they witnessed during the Exodus from Egypt and the ensuing years in the desert: the Ten Plagues, the Splitting of the Reed (Red) Sea, and how God protected them in the desert and gave them the Torah at Mount Sinai. Moses urges his people to keep the laws of Torah in order to prepare them for their entrance into Israel, and ultimately to prepare them for all millennia. This message seems to remind Jews that they actually saw the Bible being given to them on Mount Sinai.

Message 9: "Awe of," "Reverence of," or "Fear of" (*Yir-ot*), Genesis 20:11. In this verse, Abraham, speaking about the wickedness of Sodom and Gomorrah, says: "There is no fear of God in this place." A recurring theme in the Bible is the importance of loving God, but having awe and fear of God and the Bible are also essential.

The next message uses a more contemporary term to illustrate what can happen when there is no fear of God. In addition, it refers to the greatest historical enemy and threat to the Bible and the Jewish people.

Message 10: "Aryan" (*Aw-reet*), from *The Complete English Hebrew Dictionary,* by Reuben Alcalay. According to Nazi ideology, the Aryans were the "master race." However, the belief that any race is superior to any other is the exact opposite of what the Torah teaches: that every life is equally sacred and valuable. As Genesis 1:27 states: "And God created humans in His image, in the image of God He created them, male and female He created them." And the Talmud in Sanhedrin 37a reinforces this idea: "If you save one life it is as if you have saved the entire world." The message here tells us that the primary focus of Nazi Germany was not just to exterminate the Jews but to exterminate the Torah.

Message 11: "You shall curse" (*Tah-ohr-ee*), a slight change of Numbers 22:6. This refers to those who hate the Torah: they shall curse it.

The following two messages consist of the second set of four letters that correspond exactly with 611: ששי‎.

Message 12: "I shall rejoice" (*Ah-sees*), Isaiah 61:10. The verse states: "I shall rejoice with God." This implies that embracing Torah leads to rejoicing.

Message 13: "Foundation" (*Ah-shish*), a slight change of Isaiah 16:7. This suggests that Torah is or should be the foundation for our lives.

WHO REALLY WROTE THE BIBLE?

Many consider it naive to believe that God wrote the Bible while others insist unwaveringly in the text's divine origins. But, for many of us in the middle, some proof would be reassuring. Now, through the use of Gematria, it appears possible to identify the actual name of the author of the Bible!

It has long been a Jewish custom for the author of a text or a prayer to embed his name in a concealed way within the written material. I have discovered that the actual author of the Torah seems to have "signed" his name within it in such a way that the total numerical value of his name equals 611—the identical numerical value of the word "Torah."

The phrase "God Lord of Hosts" (*A-donai E-l-o-him Tzeva-ote*) has a Gematria of 611 and occurs three times in the Old Testament: in Psalm 59:6, Psalm 84:9, and 2 Samuel 7:26. "God Lord of Hosts" appears to be the name of the actual author of the Bible and, if true, would prove that God Himself is the true author.

Here are the three instances in which the phrase "God Lord of Hosts" appears. Note that each time this phrase occurs, the literal biblical text surrounding the phrase seems to comment either on those who honor the Torah or on those who are against it.

Message 14A: "God Lord of Hosts" (*A-donai E-l-o-him Tzeva-ote*), Psalm 59:6. This psalm tells of "evildoers," "bloodthirsty men," and "faithless men of violence"—those who are against the Torah or against those who embrace it—and warns the evildoers that they will be consumed by God's wrath.

Message 14B: "God Lord of Hosts," Psalm 84:9. This psalm speaks of "those who dwell in God's House" and "those whose hearts focus on upward paths," apparently referring to those who honor and cherish the Torah, promising that "God shall bestow favor and glory, and shall not withhold any goodness from them."

Message 14C: "God Lord of Hosts," Book 2 of Samuel 7:26. This verse states: "And may Your Name be great for eternity, saying God Lord of Hosts." A second translation of this phrase is "And may Your Name be great unto the world, saying God Lord of Hosts." This appears to be prophetic, predicting that the world will eventually embrace the value and wisdom of the Torah.

The next five messages also seem to attest to a Bible written by God.

Message 15: "God appeared to me" (*Shaddai Nirah Ay-li*), Genesis 48:3. (*Shaddai* is one of God's holy names.) This verse states: "God appeared to me in the land of Canaan and He blessed me." This teaches us that God appears as the Torah and the Torah itself is a blessing.

Message 16: "Where is the God of Justice? Here I Am" (*Ayey Elokay Hamishpat Hineni*), Malachi 2:17–3:1. Since this phrase has the same numerical value as the word "Torah," it seems that God's answer to the prophet Malachi's question is: "Here I am in the Torah." This is consistent with the earlier messages "My Website" and "My Place," which revealed that God's Website and place is the Torah.

Message 17: "Who performed and made" (*Me Pa-ol V'asah*), Isaiah 41:4. This verse states: "Who performed and made, from the beginning it was I

God." The hidden message here seems clear: It was God who wrote the Torah.

Message 18: The property of God (*R'chush Ha-Elokim*), formed by rearranging the Hebrew letters of the phrase *Elokim K'Sarah,* found in the Blessing of the Children prayer. This describes the Torah as the property of God.

Message 19: "Mighty with holiness" or "Mantle of holiness" (*Eh-dar BaKodesh*), Exodus 15:11. This is a perfect description of the Torah.

The following two messages are found in the same sentence in the Book of Isaiah, with one phrase immediately following the other. The exact pattern is repeated in both Isaiah 29:11 and 29:12. The repetition of these phrases, each with a numerical value of 611, serves to emphasize their importance. This chapter of Isaiah rebukes the Children of Israel for not embracing the Torah and the commandments with their hearts but for only going through the motions.

Message 20: "The book says" or "The book expresses in words" (*Sefer Lay-more*), Isaiah 29:11 and 29:12. This message implies that the Torah expresses in words God's message to us.

Message 21: "Please read this and say" (*K'rah Na Zeh V'ah-mar*), Isaiah 29:11 and 29:12. Out of context, the hidden message here seems to be a divine request or suggestion: "Please read this Torah and talk about it."

IS THE BIBLE TRUE?

Did the miracle of the Splitting of the Red Sea (biblically, "Reed Sea") really occur? Were the Ten Commandments actually given to the Israelites on Mount Sinai by God? While the Torah is universally acknowledged as an ancient text, many people do not believe that all the events depicted in it actually happened. The following messages, however, and the analysis at the end of this chapter of the phrase "The Holy Scriptures," appear to suggest that they are wrong.

Message 22: "On the holy mountain" (*B'har Kodesh*), Ezekiel 28:14. This is a reference to Mount Sinai, the site where the Torah was given to the Jewish people after they left Egypt.

Message 23: "Truth from Sinai" (*Emet May-Sinai*), nonconsecutive words found in Rashi on Eruvin 4b. Here, the word "truth" refers to the Torah, which, according to Jewish tradition, was given to the Israelites on Mount Sinai.

Message 24A: "True before [God]" (*Emet Lifnay*), 2 Chronicles 31:20. The full phrase states: "That which was good, right, and true before God." The next verse, 2 Chronicles 31:21, states: "With the Torah or with the commandments to seek out his God." Therefore, "True before [God]" appears to refer to the Torah both as the truth and as the path to find God.

Message 24B: "In front of Me [God] is the truth" (*Emet L'fah-nigh*), alternative reading and translation of 2 Chronicles 31:20. This seems to be God's declaration that the Torah is the truth.

Message 25: "Before truth" (*Lifnay Emet*), nonconsecutive words found in Talmud Makkot 24a. According to the *Midrash Rabah* (an ancient collection of biblical studies and commentaries), God wrote the Torah 2,000 years before the creation of the world—hence the Torah was written a long time before the ancient Greek philosophers ever postulated or hypothesized about the concept of truth. God seems to be saying: "You ask if the Torah is the truth? Not only is it the truth, it is before truth."

Message 26: "Before all form" (*B'terem Kol Y'tzeer*), from the *Adon Olam* prayer, written in the 11th century C.E. by Shlomo ibn Gabirol. The message here is similar to that of the previous one, "Before truth," and appears to support the *Midrash* mentioned in Message 25, that God wrote the Torah before the creation of the world.

MESSAGES OF WISDOM

The following seven messages metaphorically describe the Torah.

Message 27: "Brings forth bread from the earth" (*Motzi Lechem Min Ha-aretz*), from the blessing over the eating of bread. This message tells us that, just as bread provides the physical sustenance for the entire world, Torah provides the spiritual. It follows that both Torah and bread are to be considered foundations for life.

Message 28: "Like the Nile of Egypt" (*K'y'or Mitz-ra-yim*), Amos 9:5. This metaphor, like the previous one, also describes the nourishment that the Bible provides. As the Nile of Egypt nurtures and sustains hundreds of millions of people, so too does the Torah.

Message 29: "Dance music" (*Musica L'Ree-kudim*), from *The Complete English Hebrew Dictionary,* by Reuben Alcalay. "Dance music" is music composed specifically to accompany dance, an appropriate metaphor for the Torah: the music for the dance of life.

Message 30: "Middle" or "median" (*Em-tza-eet*), from *The Complete English Hebrew Dictionary,* by Reuben Alcalay. Human beings are part physical, part spiritual, and these parts are often in conflict. The Torah represents the middle way, the path to balancing these two human attributes, as well as balancing a spiritual and religious life within the physical and secular world.

Message 31: "As a sign upon your arm" (*L'ote Al Yed-chem*), Deuteronomy 11:18. This phrase refers to the commandment of putting on phylacteries, or *tefillin,* and is found in the *Shema* prayer, which directs us to follow all the commandments. Deuteronomy 11:18 states: "Place these words of Mine upon your heart and upon your soul, and bind them as a sign upon your arm." This implies that Torah is not just intellectual but directs us to take concrete action.

Message 32: "Israel their Father" (*Yisrael Avoo-hone*), nonconsecutive Aramaic words found in the full Mourner's *Kaddish* prayer. The hidden message here is that the Torah is the father of Israel. As the role of a father is to protect, provide for, and teach his children, the word "Father" is an appropriate metaphor for Torah.

Message 33: "God is like Sarah" (*Elokim K'Sarah*), literal definition from the Blessing of the Children prayer, recited on Sabbath Eve. God is like Sarah, the first Jewish mother, because the primary concern of a mother is to make sure that her children are well fed and receive a quality education. This message reveals that, metaphorically, the purpose of the Torah is to serve as humanity's mother: to spiritually nourish and educate all of God's children.

The following message refers to the essential teaching of the Torah.

Message 34: "Acts of kindness" (*G'me-lut Chasidim*), Avot 1:2. The Bible states many times that God is most interested in our acts of kindness. That the numerical values of "Acts of kindness" and Torah are identical is not a coincidence but a clear statement that the two are equivalent and inseparable. This suggests that performing kind acts is the divine measure of reverence for and observance of the Torah.

WHY AND HOW HAS THE BIBLE SURVIVED FOR OVER 3,200 YEARS?

Many people believe that the Bible is a rigid set of laws. That is inaccurate. It is worth noting that the word for "law" in Hebrew is *Halachah,* literally defined as "walking" or "going," reflecting the Bible's inherent flexibility. It is the responsibility of rabbis and scholars to interpret and implement the Torah for each generation. This flexibility is what has allowed the Torah and the Jewish people to survive 1,900 years of exile, the Inquisition, pogroms, expulsions, and the Holocaust.

Message 35: "The teacher that walked with me" (*Moe-ree Sheh-hah-lach*), an alternative translation of the phrase "My teacher who has departed," found in the *Yizkor* prayer in memory of a deceased parent. The message here is that we should view the Torah as a scholarly companion who walks with us on the road of life.

Message 36: "Art" + "Science" (*Ah-mah-nute + Madah*), each word found separately in *The Complete English Hebrew Dictionary,* by Reuben Alcalay. This message reinforces the notion that the Torah encourages the middle way, that we can enjoy and benefit from religious study as well as from art and science. The Torah teaches us to perform acts of kindness and compassion in order to repair the world, but these principles will be communicated not only through the study of scriptures but also through the arts and sciences, whether in the musical *West Side Story* and its theme of racial harmony, or with modern medicine and its success in the eradication of polio.

Message 37: "Upon my head" (*Ahl Roshi*), from the bedtime prayer following *Shema*. This appears to be a divine suggestion: Keep Torah on your mind.

Message 38: "For everyone's mind" (*L'chal L'rosh*), alternative translation of Book 1 Chronicles 29:11. This emphasizes that the Torah should be or will be on most everyone's mind.

A REMINDER TO RELIGIOUS FANATICS

Because people sometimes use the Bible to justify violence or harassment, the next four messages are very important as they clearly state that the Bible emphasizes life, goodness, and peace.

Message 39: "For life and not for death" (*L'chaim V'lo La-mavet*), from the Prayer for Rain and Dew. The simple meaning here is that the Bible should be used only for life and not for death. This is clearly a rebuke to anyone who acts violently in the name of the Bible, whether against women, gays, those who are pro-choice, or those who worship differently than you.

Message 40: "For the sake of good perform" (*L'Tovah L'mah-an Aseh*), Genesis 50:20. This verse states: "God intended it for the sake of good perform." This implies that God intended Bible for the sake of goodness, and thus directs us not to use it to justify violence or harassment.

Message 41: "And for life and for peace Amen" (*Oo-l'chayin V'lishlam Amen*), from the ancient Aramaic prayer *B'rich Shmay,* written approximately 2,000 years ago and recited on the Sabbath and on festivals. This prayer proclaims Jewish faith in the truth of God and His Torah, and asks that God open our hearts to accepting the Torah's wisdom as the manual for life and peace.

Message 42: "Women" (*G'va-rote*), *The Complete English Hebrew Dictionary,* by Reuben Alcalay. In terms of gender stereotyping, women are often associated with nurturing, caring, healing, and contribution, each an element of repairing the world, *Tikkun Olam.* This is distinct from men, who are often associated with many of the problems in the world, such as violence, abuse, hatred, corruption, and war. Therefore the message "women" should serve as a reminder that women are at least equal to men in the eyes of God and can equally represent the principles of Torah.

OUR CONNECTION TO THE TORAH

Message 43: "Connected" or "bound" (*K'shurah*), *The Complete Hebrew English Dictionary,* by Reuben Alcalay. This is clear suggestion to keep oneself connected to the Bible.

Message 44: "That elevates you" or "That raises you" (*Ha-ma-aleh Etchem*), Leviticus 11:45. This message, in and out of context of this section of Leviticus, reveals that a major purpose of the Torah is to elevate us.

Message 45: "Parents unto the children" (*Avot Ahl Banim*), a literal translation of Deuteronomy 24:16. This reminds us to continue the 3,200-year-old tradition of transmitting the Torah from one generation to the next.

Message 46: "And dwell therein forever" (*V'yish-k'nu La-od Aleh-ha*), Psalm 37:29. The phrase states: "The righteous shall inherit the earth and dwell therein forever." The hidden message here is that the righteous shall dwell with the Torah forever.

Message 47: "Testimony" + "Decree" + "Justice" (*Aid* + *Chok* + *Mishpaht*), words found separately in *The Complete Hebrew English Dictionary,* by Reuben Alcalay. The Torah contains three types of laws: testimony, decree, and justice. The sum total of their numerical values (74, 108, and 429, respectively) add up to 611 (74 + 108 + 429 = 611), the same numerical value as Torah itself.

TORAH OFFERS DIVINE PROTECTION

The following five messages appear to show that divine protection is a hidden benefit of embracing the Torah.

Message 48: "For if you observe" (*Key Im Shah-more*), Deuteronomy 11:22. Deuteronomy verses 11:22–25 promise that, if we observe the commandments of the Torah, God will protect us.

Message 49: "You God are a shield for me" (*Atah A-donai Magen B'ahdee*), Psalm 3:4. This suggests that when we embrace the Torah it acts as God's shield for us.

Message 50: "God is waging war for them against Egypt" (*A-donai Nilcham Lahem B'Mitzraim*), Exodus 14:25. The purpose of the Exodus from Egypt was for Israel to receive the Torah and share it with the world. In return, God acted as Israel's shield and defeated the ancient Egyptians.

Message 51: "A defensive war" (*Mil-cheh-met Ma-gain*), from *The Complete Hebrew English Dictionary,* by Reuben Alcalay. While the Torah emphasizes the importance of performing acts of kindness, this message acknowledges that sometimes a defensive war is necessary and sanctioned by the Torah. In addition, the hidden message here is that to embrace and revere the Torah may itself be as protective as a defensive war.

Message 52: "God shall protect" or "God shall defend" (*M'shamrah A-donai*), nonconsecutive words found in the same prayer "My God the Soul" (*Elokai N'shama*). This seems to suggest that embracing the Torah and divine protection are connected.

THE TORAH AS A METAPHOR FOR LIGHT

Message 53: "And from darkness to light" (Oo-*may-cho-shech L'or*), from the 15th-century book *Archot Tzadikim.* Literally or metaphorically, this appears to be an implied promise to those who observe and honor the Torah that they will be brought from darkness to light.

Message 54: "To the earth and to those that dwell" (*La-aretz V'la-dah-rim*), from the daily blessings before the *Shema* prayer. The blessing states: "[God] in mercy You give light to the earth and to those that dwell upon it." The hidden message here is that the Torah is the light.

Message 55: "Law of light" or "Religion of light" (*Dot Ohr*), from *The Study of the Ten Sefirot,* by Yehuda Leib HaLevi Ashlag, based on the work of the Kabbalist known as the *Ha'Ari.* "Law of light" is the perfect description of the Torah: a book of law that also brings light unto the world by teaching kindness, compassion, and charity towards all living creatures.

The following three messages refer to some of the ways that the Torah contributes to everyday life.

Message 56: "To bear one's share in a hard task" (*Ah-dar Ba-ma-aracha*), from *The Complete Hebrew English Dictionary,* by Reuben Alcalay. This may be a metaphor for following the Torah, suggesting that its ultimate purpose is to assist us in the difficult task of repairing the world. In addition, this may suggest that the Torah helps us live in our world.

Message 57: "Long" + "short" (*Aroch Katzar*), words found separately in *The Complete English Hebrew Dictionary,* by Reuben Alcalay. This seems to refer to the Torah as being both a short-term and long-term strategy. It may also imply both short- and long-term benefits to the study and embracing of the Torah.

Message 58: "God remembers" or "God takes note" (*Paw-kod A-donai Et*), Exodus 4:31. In this section of Exodus, God remembers His promise to redeem the Israelites from slavery. The ultimate reason for redemption is that Israel has agreed to accept the Torah. This may suggest that, if we embrace the Torah, God will remember to redeem us.

The next three messages refer to events in the Persian Empire from the same time period (the sixth century B.C.E.).

Message 59: "King Darius" (*Dar-ya-vesh Malkah*), Ezra 6:1. The Persian king Darius rebuilt the Holy Temple in Jerusalem in approximately 500

B.C.E. King Darius is an example of someone that had awe of Torah and God.

Message 60: "King Cyrus" (*Koresh Malkah*), Ezra 6:3. King Cyrus was the predecessor of King Darius, who had previously ordered the Holy Temple rebuilt. King Cyrus is an example of a person who, although not Jewish, had awe of God and of the Torah. (Note: As a further honor to King Cyrus, the Hebrew letters of Cyrus [*Koresh*] can be rearranged to spell the Hebrew word *Kosher*.)

Message 61: "And Mordechai would not bow" (*Oo-Mordechai Lo Yichrah*), Esther 3:2. This phrase refers to the Purim story (approximately 516 B.C.E.), as recounted in the Scroll of Esther. Mordechai, the uncle of Esther, refused to bow down to Haman, who was second to the king of Persia. Mordechai would not bow to a human being because Mordechai had awe of the Torah and of God. From this we learn that it is not appropriate to compromise the laws of the Torah in order to placate or appease those in power.

MESSAGES OF WARNING

If we do not show respect for the Torah or if we mistreat its followers, these warnings or rebukes apply.

Message 62: "Misled My [God's] people" (*Hit-oo Et Ami*), Ezekiel 13:10. This appears to tell us that when we discard the teachings of the Bible we are misled.

Message 63: "Anti-Israel" (*Anti-Yisrael*), found in many Israeli newspaper articles on the topic of anti-Israel sentiment. The numerical equivalence of this term to the Hebrew word "Torah" suggests that those who are anti-Torah are actually anti-Israel, and those who are anti-Israel are against the Torah. To go further, we cannot be for the Bible and at the same time hate any minority, race, or religion. The Torah emphasizes this principle by repeatedly directing us to love our neighbor and the stranger.

Message 64: "Did not hear the voice of God" (*Lo Shimoo B'kol A-donai*), from 2 Kings 18:12. As this verse states: "They did not hear the voice of God their Lord, and they transgressed His covenant." This message seems clear: When we do not read and honor the Torah, we do not hear God.

Message 65: "Iniquity and transgression and sin" (*Ah-von Vah-pesha V'chatahah*), Exodus 34:7. This tells us that if we choose not to follow or honor the Torah, the consequences may be a life of iniquity and sin.

Message 66: "Took to complaining" (*K'mit-onninim*), Numbers 11:1. This suggests that when we do not honor the Torah, what may follow is a life of complaining.

Message 67: "Naked and bare" (*A-rome V'air-yah*), Ezekiel 16:39. This suggests that "Naked and bare" is a consequence of not following the Torah.

It may also refer to the shame and humiliation that always befalls those who hate the Torah, its teachings, or its followers.

Message 68: "Worth a penny" (*Shaveh Perutah*), from Mishnah Kiddushin 2:1 and *The Complete English Hebrew Dictionary,* by Reuben Alcalay. We have the free will to revere the Torah or to behave as if it has low value. But if we choose not to honor it, the consequences may be that the quality of our lives will be of low value.

Message 69: "They shed the blood of the innocent" (*Shaf-choo Dahm Nah-key*), Joel 4:19. This verse refers to the enemies of Israel who shed innocent blood, suggesting that violence against the Jewish people is actually an attack on the Torah.

Message 70: "Men of deceit" (*An-shay Ha-ree-mah*), an alternative reading and translation of Nehemiah 7:30. This may suggest that deceitful people do not embrace the Torah and often attack those who do.

Message 71: "And you shall not find God" (*Et A-donai V'lo Yim-tza-oo*), Hosea 5:6. Because of free will, we have the option not to embrace the Torah, but the result may be that we will not find God.

Message 72: "Running back and forth" (*Rah-tzo Va-shuv*), Ezekiel 1:14. When we do not value Torah, we may feel rootless and without a destination.

FINAL MESSAGES WITH A GEMATRIA OF 611

Message 73: Mark of a mountain (*Tav Har*), the four Hebrew letters of the word "Torah" spell this phrase. This appears to be a reference to Mount Sinai, where the Torah was given and received. In addition, when the age of a mountain is calculated, using the scientific method of carbon dating, the mountain may turn out to be 100 million years old or even a billion years old. This suggests that "Mark of a mountain" refers to the Torah's eternal nature, similar to the age of a mountain.

Message 74: "This is clear" or "This is clarified" (*Zote Ba-air*), Deuteronomy 27:8. This verse states: "You shall inscribe on the stones all the words of this Torah well clarified." The hidden message is that the Torah is clear.

Message 75: "No valley of the shadow of death" or "Valley of the shadow of death no" (*Gay Tzal-mavet Lo*), literal translation of Psalm 23:4. The full verse states: "Though I walk through the valley of the shadow of death I shall fear no evil, for Thou art with me, Thy rod and Thy staff, they comfort me." The hidden message here is that when we embrace the Torah, God is with us, and that the secret to walking through the valley of the shadow of death without fearing evil is to honor and follow the Torah.

Message 76: "Fame in the presence of all the nations" or "Praise in the presence of all nations" (*Tehila Neged Kal HaGoyim*), Isaiah 61:11. The full verse states: "For as the earth sends forth its growth and as a garden sprouts forth its seedlings, so will my Lord God cause righteousness and praise to sprout in the presence of all the nations." This message suggests that Torah is the vehicle to spread and sprout God's message to all the nations.

So far, this chapter has demonstrated how each word or phrase with a numerical value of 611 can be interpreted as referring to an aspect of the Torah. Now, let us analyze the related term, "The Holy Scriptures" that has a numerical value of 841.

THE HOLY SCRIPTURES:
AN ANALYSIS OF ITS NUMERICAL VALUE OF 841

It is worth noting that the Bible can also be referred to as "The Holy Scriptures" (in Hebrew *Kitvay Ha-Kodesh*), with a numerical value of 841. Each Hebrew word or phrase with a value of 841 has been found to refer to an aspect of "The Holy Scriptures." A brief analysis of this phrase appears to answer both the question of truth and authorship of the Holy Scriptures.

ARE THE HOLY SCRIPTURES TRUE?

The four specific and unique Hebrew letters that correspond exactly with 841 are: אמתת. These letters can be used to spell two words, listed here as the first two messages. All other words and phrases here also have 841 Gematrias but consist of a variety of different letters.

A. "Truths" or "Truth of" (*Ami-tote* or *Ami-tot*), slight spelling variation from *The Complete Hebrew English Dictionary,* by Reuben Alcalay. This seems to reinforce the idea that the Holy Scriptures are in fact true.

B. "You will verify," "Shall be verified," or "Shall be authenticated" (*T'amate*), *The Complete Hebrew English Dictionary,* by Reuben Alcalay. This also appears to confirm that the Holy Scriptures are indeed true.

C. "To establish this thing" (*Heh'emid Et Hadavar Al*), *The Complete Hebrew English Dictionary,* by Reuben Alcalay. As the full phrase states: "To establish the truth of this thing."

D. "The truth of Your salvation" (*Emet Yish-echa*), from Psalm 69:14. The verse states: "And may my prayer to You, God, be at an opportune time; O' Lord, in Your abundant kindness, answer me with the Truth of Your Salvation." The simple meaning here is that God answers us by providing truth and salvation through the Holy Scriptures. But there may be a deeper and more powerful interpretation, as if God were saying: "You ask if the Holy Scriptures are true? Not only are they true, but the truth is that your salvation depends on whether or not you honor and embrace them."

WHO WROTE THE HOLY SCRIPTURES?

Here is a brief list of Hebrew phrases with a numerical value of 841. Each of them clearly seems to refer to the Holy Scriptures. The following six messages address the question: Who wrote the Holy Scriptures?

E. "From our Eternal King of the world" (*Malkeinu Tamid Min HaOlam*), from the *Nishmat* prayer. This suggests that God the Eternal King is the author of the Holy Scriptures.

F. "Blessed be the Lord God of Israel" (*Baruch A-donai E-lo-kay Yisrael*), from Book 1 of Chronicles 16:36. Again, this seems to refer to the true author of the Holy Scriptures.

G. "These My [God's] hands made and" (*Eleh Yadai Asatah Va*), Isaiah 66:2. As the full verse states: "My [God's] hands created all these things and thus all these things came into being, the Word of God." This message seems to confirm that God's hands created the Holy Scriptures, and that the Holy Scriptures are the Word of God.

H. "He made and He gave" (*Asah Va-yetain*), Esther 2:18. Verse 2:18 states: "And the King made a great party for all . . . and He made and He gave gifts worthy of the King." In the Scroll of Esther, the word "God" in all its variations is never used. Rabbis and scholars teach that whenever the phrase "the King" (*Ha-melech*) is used, it can be understood to refer to God.

The hidden message here is that God made the Holy Scriptures and gave them, as gifts, to us.

I. "God it is You I seek" (*A-donai Otah Avakesh*), Psalm 27:4. A major reason for reading and studying the Holy Scriptures is to get closer to God. The message here is: If you seek God, read the Holy Scriptures.

J. "And You Shall Seek Out God" (*Oo-Bikshoo Et A-donai*), Hosea 3:5. Note, while this phrase is identical in meaning to, and has the same numerical value as, the previous message, "God it is You I seek," it consists of different letters and words.

K. "And you shall love God" (*V'ahavtah et A-donai*), Deuteronomy 6:5. This phrase, the opening verse of the most famous Hebrew prayer, the *Shema,* is a declaration of commitment to God and to the commandments. "And you shall love God" is the essence of the Holy Scriptures and the key commandment in the entire Torah because true love of God is manifested by treating all of God's creations with love and respect. You cannot have one without the other.

L. "To hear the" (*Lish-mo-ah Et*), Deuteronomy 5:22. As this verse states: "To hear the voice of God." Thus, the hidden message here is that the Holy Scriptures are the way "to hear the voice of God."

The next two phrases with 841 Gematrias refer to the choice of not valuing the Holy Scriptures. Because of free will, we have the choice to embrace them or not. Those who do not believe in them too often put their faith in the "holy dollar" or in business dealings. In biblical times, the currency of the day was the *shekel*. The question for each of us seems to be: Do I have faith in the Holy Scriptures or in the holy dollar? The next two messages appear to answer this question.

M. "In the holy shekel" (*B'shekel Hakodesh*), Exodus 30:13. This message refers to those who revere, and even idolize, the almighty dollar rather than the Holy Scriptures.

N. "In business" (*B'masa Oo-b'matan*), from the confessional prayers (*Al Chet*), recited on Yom Kippur, the Day of Atonement. This repeats the theme of the previous message, "In the holy shekel," that too many of us put our faith in business and not in the Holy Scriptures.

The following example of a Gematria of 841 confirms that the Torah is the same book that Moses placed before the Children of Israel at the foot of Mount Sinai over 3,000 years ago.

O. "That he placed" (*Asher Som*), Deuteronomy 4:44. The full sentence states: "And this is the Torah that he Moses placed before the Children of Israel." This verse is part of a song that is sung whenever the Torah is read. It continues: "According to the word of God and by the hand of Moses." Thus "That he placed," both in the literal text and as a hidden gematrial message, confirms that the Torah, the most important book of the Holy Scriptures, was given to Moses by God, and then from Moses to the Children of Israel.

P: "He gave to man" or "He gave to the human being" (*Natan La-eesh*), Genesis 45:22. This section of Genesis describes Joseph supplying his brothers with clothing and food for their journey home. In the context of the numerical value of 841, "He gave to man" can be interpreted as how God provides each of us with the supplies we need to survive and thrive in the journey of life: "the Holy Scriptures."

Therefore, a gematrial analysis of "the Holy Scriptures" (numerical value of 841) seems to verify the results of the analysis of "Torah," a 611 numerical value: the Bible and the Holy Scriptures were written by God and are true.

Chapter Five

Was Jesus Actually
a Messenger of God?

JESUS OF NAZARETH = 677

Was Jesus actually a messenger of God? Did the miracle of the Resurrection actually occur? What was Jesus' true purpose? Where exactly did the Sermon on the Mount take place? If you are a Christian, you may believe that you have some of these answers already. If you are not a Christian, you may already be dismissing this chapter, but I ask for your patience. While the following pages contain mathematically generated answers to these timeless questions, the answers do not come at the expense of one faith over another. My interpretation is that they confirm that all religions are valid and holy, as long as they promote peace, encourage acts of kindness, and respect the Bible.

In this chapter, the answers to the above questions were found either directly embedded within the Hebrew name for "Jesus of Nazareth" or within messages of wisdom and warning that have the identical numerical value as "Jesus of Nazareth," 677. If you are Christian, while you have the free will to believe in Jesus or not, the consequences of that decision are also disclosed.

Along with many of the messages, I have included brief comments and interpretations for clarity. These comments are just one interpretation, and different ones may be equally, or even more, valid. I can speak to the precise math that generated the messages, but the commentary is mine alone and in no way do I claim to speak for God.

I have chosen to analyze the term "Jesus of Nazareth" (*Yeshu Ha-Notzri* in Hebrew) because it was Jesus' ancient name. The exact spelling was taken from *The Complete Hebrew English Dictionary,* by Reuben Alcalay. The term "Jesus of Nazareth" was also used in the original Talmud, including

Sanhedrin 43a. In both sources, the spelling has a Gematria of 677. There-fore, all known Hebrew words and phrases with a numerical value of 677 were studied and analyzed, and, as you will see, each one seems to refer directly to some aspect of Jesus' life and philosophy. This chapter lists multi-ple examples of such text.

There are four specific and unique Hebrew letters that correspond exactly to 677. They are: זתרע. These letters can be rearranged to spell the first three messages. The other messages in this chapter also have Gematrias of 677 but consist of a variety of different letters that add up to 677.

MESSAGES DIRECTLY EMBEDDED
WITHIN THE NAME "JESUS OF NAZARETH"

Message 1: "The helper of" or "Helps" (*O-zeret* or *Ezrat*), from *The Com-plete Hebrew English Dictionary,* by Reuben Alcalay. This appears to sug-gest that Jesus helped to spread monotheism, the Old Testament, the Ten Commandments, and God's message of peace to the world.

Message 2: "Arms," "Strength," "Power," or "Force" (*Z'row-ote*), Deute-ronomy 33:27. This indicates that Jesus' teachings shall have reach through-out, and a powerful impact on, the world.

Message 3: "Shall scatter," "Shall sow," or "Shall seed" (*Tiz-row-ah*), Exodus 23:10. Jesus has been very successful at sowing and scattering the seeds of God's message to the world.

MESSAGES OF WISDOM

The following messages all have the identical numerical value of 677, the same as "Jesus of Nazareth," but consist of a variety of different letters.

Message 4: "Spread," "To be mixed," or "To be intermingled" (*Hit-ah-reve*), from *The Complete Hebrew English Dictionary,* by Reuben Alcalay. This suggests that the seeds of the Bible will be intermingled throughout the world through the work of Jesus. It is worth noting that although the Hebrew words for "Spread" and the previous message "Shall scatter" consist of dif-ferent letters, they have the identical numerical value of 677.

WHAT WAS THE EXACT LOCATION
OF THE SERMON ON THE MOUNT?

Message 5: "Mount of Olives" (*Har Ha-zay-tim*), Zechariah 14:4. For almost 2,000 years, Christian scholars have debated the precise location of Jesus' Sermon on the Mount. But by using Gematria, we see that the phrase "Mount of Olives" has the same numerical value as "Jesus of Nazareth." This strongly suggests that the Mount of Olives was the actual location where the sermon took place.

A REFERENCE TO JESUS ON THE CROSS

Message 6: "Him upon the wood" (*Alav Et Etz*), a literal translation of Ezekiel 37:19. Out of context, this appears to be a reference to Jesus upon the wooden cross.

WAS JESUS ACTUALLY A MESSENGER FROM GOD?

Message 7: "From the God of Israel" (*Elokay Yisrael Min*), 1 Chronicles 16:36. This is a clear acknowledgment that Jesus of Nazareth was indeed a messenger sent from the God of Israel. This is consistent with the earlier messages—"Helps," "Shall scatter," and "Spread"—that point to Jesus' role in disseminating the Bible and the Ten Commandments throughout the world.

Message 8: "Work done on a contractual basis" (*Avodah B'kablanoot*), from *The Complete Hebrew English Dictionary,* by Reuben Alcalay. This may imply that Jesus agreed in a binding way to take on the work to help spread God's message.

DOES CHRISTIANITY PROVIDE CHRISTIANS WITH A VALID PATH TO GOD?

Rabbi Moses Ben Maimon, known as Maimonides or *Rambam* in Hebrew (1135-1204 C.E.), was a physician to the sultan of Egypt, writer of a commentary on the entirety of Jewish law and the foremost Jewish philosopher of all time. In his Laws of Kings 11:4, he acknowledged and validated both Christianity and Islam, writing that they "are all for the purpose of paving the way for the true King Messiah, and preparing the entire world to worship God together, as is written (Tzefaniah 3:9): 'For then I will change the nations to a pure language, that they may all call in the name of God and serve Him together.'" By using Gematria, we find messages that support Maimonides' belief that Christianity is a valid spiritual path for Christians to follow.

Message 9: "This is none other than an abode of God, and this" (*Ha-zeh Ain Zeh Ki Im Bet Elokim V'zeh*), Genesis 28:17. This verse continues: "And this is a gate to Heaven." This seems to confirm that, for Christians, Jesus is indeed a valid path to God and a gateway to Heaven.

ARE CHRISTIANS OBLIGATED TO OBSERVE
ALL 613 COMMANDMENTS OF THE BIBLE?

In the New Testament, the Sermon on the Mount contains Jesus' core teachings, including a reference to the Torah (the Five Books of Moses). In Matthew 5:18, in regard to the Torah, Jesus states: "Don't change a jot." The literal interpretation is that Jesus preached to his followers to not change an iota of the Torah, and to follow it completely. The following message lists a phrase from the Old Testament that uses slightly different words than "Don't change a jot," but, while agreeing with it, also appears to clarify the issue of whether Christians are obligated to follow all the laws of the Torah. This phrase has the numerical value of 677, identical to "Jesus of Nazareth."

Message 10: "You shall not add onto" (*Lo Tosefoo Al*), Deuteronomy 4:2. In Chapter 4 of the Book of Deuteronomy, Moses reminds the Children of Israel: "Now, Israel, listen to the decrees and ordinances that I teach you to perform, so that you may live, and you will come and possess the Land that God of your forefathers gives you. You shall not add onto the word that I command you, nor subtract from it, to observe the commandments of God your Lord." According to the Talmud, non-Jews are required to observe only the seven commandments known as "the Seven Noahide Laws." The hidden wisdom of "you shall not add onto" seems to be that Christians may subtract from the 613 commandments in the Torah but not add to them.

WHAT IS JESUS' PURPOSE? THE CONNECTION
BETWEEN GOD, ISRAEL, JESUS AND THE WORLD

The purpose of the Bible and the entire Jewish tradition is to teach and encourage us to repair the world. The Bible explains that the specific path of perfecting and healing the world entails honoring and observing God's commandments and performing acts of kindness. According to Jewish tradition, every Jewish soul was present at Mount Sinai when God gave the Torah and the Ten Commandments to Moses. But the rest of the world was not present. The question is: How did God plan on spreading the message of the Bible and its commandments?

It seems that part of God's plan was to have the Jewish people exiled from Israel in 586 B.C.E. and again in 70 C.E., in order to sprinkle them throughout the world, thus exposing people everywhere to the Bible and its laws.

Message 11: "Destruction of the Temple" (*Churbon Ha-bayit*), a 2,500 year-old term used to refer to the destruction of the First or Second Temple. The destruction of the Second Temple in Jerusalem marked the beginning of 1,900 years of exile and persecution for the Jews. As the Jews were dispersed, they established communities throughout the world. This served to further expose other nations to the Bible and its traditions. The term "Destruction of the Temple," having the same numerical value as "Jesus of Nazareth," reveals a relationship between them: both were major events that ultimately led to the Bible and the Ten Commandments being spread throughout the world.

A mathematical analysis of 677, the Gematria of "Jesus of Nazareth," seems to have helped uncover and clarify a divine plan that Jesus was chosen as the specific agent to help spread God's message. The following two messages strongly suggest that Jesus served as a representative of Israel in helping to circulate the Bible to all.

Message 12: "Israel who is like you" (*Yisrael Me Ka-mocha*), Deuteronomy 33:29. The literal biblical text recounts Moses' final prophetic words to the Israelites before his death. The verse states: "Fortunate are you Israel, who is like you, a nation saved by God." The hidden message here may be that Jesus is an answer to the question: "Israel, who is like you?" This seems to support the idea that the purpose of Jesus and Israel are, by example, to teach the world to promote peace, perform acts of kindness, and respect the Ten Commandments and Bible.

Message 13: "Voice of Israel" (*Yisrael Kol*), Deuteronomy 27:14. Out of context, this appears to be a metaphor for Jesus: that he is a voice of Israel, for the non-Jewish world, in order to help spread the Bible and Commandments. This emphasizes the concept that God uses Jesus as part of His plan to publicize the Bible to the world.

AN EARLIER AGENT THAN JESUS
THAT HELPED SPREAD THE BIBLE TO THE WORLD

Message 14: "Greece" [and] "Torah" (*Yavan Torah*), terms found separately in *The Complete Hebrew English Dictionary,* by Reuben Alcalay, but together add up to 677 (66 + 611). The Greek presence in Israel, from approximately 330 B.C.E. until 50 B.C.E., led to the translation of the Old Testament into Greek. From Greek, the Bible was translated into Latin and, eventually, into most current languages. This directly led to the Bible becoming the most read book of all time. Greece, like Jesus, helped to serve God's plan to spread the Bible its laws throughout the world.

GOD, ISRAEL, AND JESUS
HAVE THE SAME ULTIMATE PURPOSE

To act as God's agents and bring the Bible and its commandments to the world summarizes the purpose of Judaism, the Jewish people, and Jesus.

Mathematical support for this idea is found in Isaiah 5:12 which states: "And the plan of God," also translated as "And the work of God" (*V'ate Po-al A-donai*). The Gematria of "And the plan of God" is 613, which is interpreted as referring to the 613 commandments of the Torah.

It is also worth noting that the numerical value of the Hebrew word for "Jesus," *Yeshu,* is 316, and that 316 is the mirror image of 613. In Gematria, I have found that the mirror images of numbers seem to reveal additional information. 316 may suggest that the purpose of Jesus is to serve as a mirror to reflect and spread the 613 commandments throughout the world, or, at the very least, to spread the Ten Commandments.

Message 15: "The nations" "613" (*Ha-Goyim* 613), this phrase was generated by choosing a Hebrew word with the numerical value of 64 to add to 613, because: 613 + 64 = 677. The term "the nations" has a numerical value of 64 and was found in Genesis 10:5. "The nations" "613" may describe the work of Jesus in spreading the commandments to the nations of the world. But as discussed earlier in message 10, the Talmud clarifies that non-Jews are only obligated to follow the Seven Laws of Noah.

JESUS AND HIS WORK

The following series of messages describe Jesus or Jesus' purpose and like all of the messages in this chapter, each one has Gematrias of 677, the same as Jesus of Nazareth.

Message 16: "Removes sleep" (*Ma-avir Shay-na*), from the daily morning blessings. Once sleep is removed, one is awakened. The appearance of Jesus on the world scene did result in many people taking note of his teachings and waking up to his messages.

To underline the connection between Jesus and his message of peace, each of the next two messages contains the word "peace." Even though the other words in these two phrases are different, the total numerical value of each phrase is 677.

Message 17: "And pursue peace" (*Shalom V'rod-fay-who*), Psalm 34:15. This encapsulates the true essence of Jesus' teachings.

Message 18: "Saying peace shall be" (*Lay-more Shalom Ye-he-yeh*), Deuteronomy 29:18. This phrase emphasizes the element of peace in the teachings of Jesus.

Message 19: "Before God with glory" (*La-A-donai B'hah-drot*), 1 Chronicles 16:29. This appears to validate the idea that one of the purposes of Jesus was to bring glory to God.

Message 20: "Praised and glorified" (*M'shoo-bach Oo-m'fow-are*), from the daily morning prayers. Out of context, "Praised and glorified" can be interpreted to mean that Jesus shall be praised and glorified for helping to spread God's messages.

Message 21: "Shall be remembered" (*Tee-zah-kar-nah*), from Ezekiel 3:20. Out of context from the Book of Ezekiel, this may be interpreted to mean that Jesus and his messages will be remembered for a long time to come.

Message 22: "Bestow a blessing" (*Tane Beracha*), from the daily *Shemoneh Esrei* prayer. The full phrase states: "Bestow a blessing upon the face of the earth." This is Jesus' mission: to convey God's gifts of Bible, the Ten Commandments, and peace upon the world.

Message 23: "I said honor" (*Amarti Kabade*), Numbers 24:11. This phrase, taken out of context, can be interpreted to mean that Jesus is worthy of honor.

JESUS AND THE GIVING OF CHARITY

The following two phrases are found in Psalm 49 and refer to the importance of giving charity and of performing acts of kindness, emphasized by both the Old and New Testament.

Message 24: "Together rich and poor" (*Yachad Ah-sheer V'ev-yone*), Psalm 49:3. Psalm 49 is directed to all of humanity as it speaks about the distinction between those who put their faith in material wealth and those who give of themselves to help the poor. Jesus plays a key role in teaching the world, both the rich and the poor, that charity and acts of kindness are essential to living a holy life.

Message 25: "For all of eternity they shall not see the light" (*Ad Netzach Lo Yiroo Ohr*), Psalm 49:20. The literal and hidden messages of this psalm all refer to those who consider themselves and their wealth to be more important than charity and acts of kindness—they do not see the light.

WHAT DETERMINES WHETHER JEWS AND GENTILES ARE CONSIDERED AMONG THE PEOPLE OF GOD?

Message 26: "God gave to His people" (*Natan L'ah-mo E-l*), from the *Yigdal* prayer. The full phrase in this prayer states: "God gave to His people a Torah of truth." Because this message has the identical value as "Jesus of Nazareth," it seems to indicate that anyone who accepts or honors the Torah, both Jews and Gentiles, are His people, God's people.

Chapter 5

WHEN CHRISTIANS EMBRACE JESUS

Message 27: "As lights" (*Lim-o-rote*), Genesis 1:15. This suggests that Jesus and his followers serve to help illuminate and enlighten the world.

Message 28: "Many islands shall be happy" (*Yis-ma-choo Ee-yim Ra-bim*), Psalm 97:1. This is consistent with Jesus' intention to bring joy to humanity.

Message 29: "Whose strength and paths are in you" (*Oz Lo B'cha Misee-lot*), Psalm 84:6. Out of context of this psalm, the message to Christians seems to be that the strength and paths of Jesus are within you.

REBUKE OF THOSE WHO DISTORT JESUS' TEACHINGS TO JUSTIFY VIOLENCE OR HARASSMENT

Message 30: "They were with you for the sake of bloodshed" (*Ha-yu Bach L'ma-an Sh'fach Dam*), Ezekiel 22:6. How often in the name of Jesus has blood been shed? A few historical examples include the Crusades, the Inquisition, and countless blood libels and pogroms.

MESSAGES OF WARNING AND DOUBT

The following five messages seem to address the issue of having the free will to believe in Jesus or not.

Message 31: "According to the will of a human being" (*K'ratzon Eesh*), Esther 1:8. Out of context, this seems to be a statement that each of us has the free will to embrace Jesus as a messenger of God or to dismiss him as just an everyday, mortal human being.

Message 32: "Self-delusion" (*Ho-na-ah Atzmeet*), from *The Complete Hebrew English Dictionary,* by Reuben Alcalay. Because we all have free will, we all have the choice to believe that Jesus suffered from self-delusion or that he did not.

Message 33: "A fool's paradise" (*Gan Eden Shel Ksilim*), from *The Complete Hebrew English Dictionary,* by Reuben Alcalay. This seems to acknowledge that some people consider that believing in Jesus and Christianity, or in any religion, to be a fool's paradise.

Message 34: "Prison" (*Beit Sohar*), from *The Complete Hebrew English Dictionary,* by Reuben Alcalay. Some people feel that believing in Jesus, or in any religion, is like being imprisoned. In addition, this suggests that if you are a Christian and discard the value of Jesus, you may end up in prison, metaphorically or literally.

Message 35: "Bet" or "wager" (*Hit-ah-reve*), from *The Complete Hebrew English Dictionary,* by Reuben Alcalay. This suggests that we are free to make whatever wager we wish regarding Christianity, or any religion.

The next message seems to be directed at the distinction between Jesus and God. It must be repeated that, while the mathematics of these messages are accurate, other, different interpretations may be entirely valid.

Message 36: "I have awe of God" (*Lee Yirot A-donai*), Psalm 34:12. Out of context of Psalm 34, this seems to be a statement that Jesus, too, has awe of God, thereby indicating that Jesus is an entity separate from God.

A REFERENCE TO THE APOSTLE PAUL

Approximately 30 years after Jesus' death, Paul the Apostle liberalized early Christianity, making the religion more accessible. Paul did this by steering early Christians away from focusing exclusively on the Torah and its 613 commandments. The following message can be interpreted as a reference to the Apostle Paul, whose Hebrew birth name was Saul.

Message 37: "Saul as expediter" (*Bisha-lach Shaul*), an alternative reading and translation of Psalm 59:1. Out of context, "Saul as expediter" seems to be an acknowledgement of the huge success that the Apostle Paul had in popularizing Christianity.

POSSIBLE REFERENCES TO THE
MIRACLE OF THE RESURRECTION OF JESUS

Message 38: "From the confines of the grave" (*M'tza-ray Sh'ole*), Psalm 116:3. Taken out of context, this appears to validate the miracle of the Resurrection.

Message 39: "He shall not be put to death according to" or "He shall not die in the way of" (*Lo Yu-mot Ahl Pee*), Deuteronomy 17:6. In context, this verse refers to the biblical law that a condemned person "shall not be put to death according to the testimony of one witness," but only on the testimony of two or three witnesses. Out of context, "He shall not be put to death according to" and "He shall not die in the way of" possibly refer to Jesus' death and Resurrection.

Chapter Six

What Is God's True Religion?

YOU SHALL LOVE = 414

What is God's religion? Many of us have wondered whether God has or even needs a religion. This chapter addresses this question and discloses a mathematically generated answer that may serve to awaken all religions by reminding them of their ultimate purpose. Incredibly, it seems that God's true religion does not conflict with any other one. The messages in this chapter emphasize the importance of God's religion and direct us to embrace it.

The idea that God has a true religion emerged from a gematrial inquiry into three commandments in the Bible containing the phrase "You shall love." Leviticus 19:18 states: "You shall love your neighbor as yourself." Leviticus 19:34 states: "The stranger that dwells with you, you shall love them as yourself." And Deuteronomy 6:5 states: "You shall love God your Lord, with all your heart, with all your soul, and with all your might."

If we actually followed just these three commandments, life would likely seem like heaven on earth. But why must God command us to love? Would it not have been sufficient to command us to obey Him and to treat our neighbors and all strangers well? The Bible repeatedly explains why Jews must be compassionate and show kindness to those who do not exactly fit in: "Because you were strangers in Egypt." But what was the point of adding "You shall love" to these commandments? The phrase "You shall love" was mathematically analyzed to find the answer.

THE HIDDEN MEANING OF THE PHRASE "YOU SHALL LOVE"

The numerical value of the Hebrew term for "You shall love" (*V'ahavtah*) is 414. When all known words and phrases with this numerical value were analyzed, it was determined that all text with a value of 414 referred to some aspect of "You shall love." This included the importance of love, what actions demonstrate love, where the most important place to show love is, and the most common block that gets in the way of expressing love.

There are three specific and unique Hebrew letters that correspond exactly to 414: תיד. These three letters can be used to spell seven Hebrew words, listed as the first seven messages. All the other messages in this chapter also have 414 Gematrias but consist of a variety of different letters.

MESSAGES DIRECTLY EMBEDDED
WITHIN "YOU SHALL LOVE" 414

The following message has multiple possible translations, each one appearing to refer to an aspect of God's true religion. (The multiple translations depend on what vowels are used. In Hebrew, vowels are created by putting dots below, above, to the side of, or inside the letters. In the original form of the Bible, no dots were used, but later on, the Rabbis and scholars added them for clarity.)

The accepted translation of a phrase in Ezra 7:25 states: "Know the Law of your God and teach those who do not know." The four possible translations of the Hebrew term "Law of " (*Dah-tay*), spelled with the three letters that correspond exactly to 414, are listed as the first four messages.

Message 1: "My religion" (*Dah-tee*), alternative reading and translation of Ezra 7:25. Using this translation, this phrase states: "Know My religion, your God's." Because "My religion" is numerically equivalent to the phrase "You shall love," it suggests that God's religion is "You shall love." To ensure that there be no confusion, God clarified in the text of the Bible whom we should love by commanding us to love our neighbor, the stranger, and God Himself.

Message 2: "Religions of" (*Dah-tay)*, alternative reading and translation of Ezra 7:25. Using this translation, the verse states: "Religions of your God." Thus, the hidden meaning here appears to be that, any religion that makes "You shall love" a priority is a religion of God.

Message 3: "Law of" (*Dah-tay*), Ezra 7:25. The phrase "Know the Law of your God" is referring to the Torah or Bible, suggesting that the indicator as to whether or not someone knows or follows the law of God is that they practice "You shall love." This implies that knowing or following the laws of the Bible must be accompanied by acts of loving kindness.

Message 4: "Religious" (*Dah-tee*), also found in *The Complete Hebrew English Dictionary,* by Reuben Alcalay. This appears to reveal the deeper definition of the word "religious," that the ultimate measure of whether or not we are following the commandments is if we love. On Yom Kippur, the

Day of Atonement, the holiest day of the Jewish year, we read in the Book of Isaiah (57:14–58:14) that God is not impressed with just the rigid observance of the commandments. Rather, if we are not performing acts of charity and showing compassion for the poor, the stranger, and the orphan, then God rejects our piety. This seems to clarify that, for God, the designation "religious" is associated with someone who not just honors the commandments but performs acts of kindness and compassion as an expression of love.

Message 5: "Hands" (*Yah-dote*), Exodus 36:22. "Hands" explains that love is a verb, hands-on work, and that by giving charity and performing acts of kindness we express love.

Message 6: "[Tent] pin" (*Ye-tad*), Judges 4:21. Rabbi Aron Mathless, of Brooklyn, New York, said that the significance of a "[Tent] pin" is that: "Without the tent pin, the tent collapses." The metaphor "tent pin" suggests that, without love, charity, and acts of kindness, the Law of God and perhaps the entire world, would collapse.

Message 7: "Vulture" (*Da-yot*), from *The Complete Hebrew English Dictionary,* by Reuben Alcalay. Metaphorically, this suggests that if we lead our lives without making love essential, then we are like vultures that just consume dead and decaying flesh.

MESSAGES OF WISDOM

Message 8: "How shall I repay God?" (*Mah A-shiv LA-donai*), Psalm 116:12. The full verse states: "How shall I repay God for the kindnesses that He has shown me?" The hidden message here is clear: To repay God, accept His true religion of love, and love all His creatures—human and animal—and all His creations. When you do that, you show God that you are truly grateful.

The following two messages were both found in Psalm 36:10 and are from the same sentence: "For with You [God] is the fountain of life, in Your light we see light."

Message 9: "Fountain of life" or "Source of life" (*Ma-kore Chaim*), Psalm 36:10. The hidden message here is clearly that love is the fountain and source of all life. But this message also suggests that, if we do not embrace and express love and kindness, then we will be cut off from the true source of life: God's and our own love.

Message 10: "Light" and "light" (*Ohr Ohr*), words are not consecutive but are found in the same sentence in Psalm 36:10 and together are valued at 414. This appears to reveal that love is the secret to be being in God's light. When we love God, by showing kindness to neighbors and strangers, we bring a kind of dual light into the world: one that illuminates it but that also shines back on us. In addition, rabbinical commentary on the Bible has interpreted repetition of words within the same verse as possibly alluding to both this world and the world to come, possibly suggesting that one who brings light to this world merits light in the next.

Message 11: "The one" or "The primary" (*Ha-achot*), Genesis 4:19. Out of context, this message emphasizes that love should be our primary directive.

While the Bible directly commands us to love God, our neighbors, and the stranger, the following, somewhat more subtle message reminds us of another essential place to show love.

Message 12: "In the home" (*Ba-ba-yit*), Genesis 27:15. Out of context, this is a reminder to love not just our friends, colleagues and strangers but to bring love into our home. It seems that love is the primary legacy that we pass down, or do not pass down, to our children. This one factor alone may determine the quality of life for our future generations.

BENEFITS OF EMBRACING GOD'S TRUE RELIGION OF LOVE

Message 13: "Generation of the righteous" (*Dor Tzadik*), Psalm 14:5. As this verse states: "For God is with the generation of the righteous." Because "Generation of the righteous" has a value of 414, we can understand that the secret to being among the righteous, and for having God be with us, is to love God, our neighbors, and strangers. This will come about when we all embrace God's true religion of love.

Message 14: "God is close to all" (*Karov A-donai L'kol*), Psalm 145:18. As the psalm states: "God is close to all that call upon Him sincerely. The will of those that fear Him He will do, and their cry He will hear, and save them." Therefore, when we treat all people, even the stranger who may be different from or alien to us, with love and respect, God becomes closer to us.

Message 15: "Have compassion upon us" or "Compassion is our duty" (*Rah-chem Aleinu*), from the blessings before the *Shema*. This phrase reveals that, in response to our making love a priority, God will have compassion on us. In addition, it tells us that the way to express love is to adopt the attitude that showing compassion is our duty.

Message 16: "In the Name of God my Lord" (*B'Shem A-donai Elokay*), recited after the bedtime *Shema* prayer. This tells us that, when we act with love, our actions represent the Name of God.

In the next two messages, two different Hebrew words for "dwell" are used, each one referring to the dwelling of God's Holy Presence, but the total value of each phrase is still 414.

Message 17: "Shaddai His [God's] Holy Presence shall dwell" (*Shaddai Yah-lin*), Song of Songs 1:13. This reinforces the idea that, when we religiously practice "You shall love," God's Holy Presence will dwell with us.

Message 18: "For His dwelling place" (*L'Moshav Lo*), Psalm 132:13. This repeats the theme that the secret to accessing God's dwelling place is love.

LOVE GOD AND OTHERS
EVEN IN THE MOST CHALLENGING TIMES

The following two messages emphasize the importance of loving others, even while mourning or in times of personal danger.

Message 19: "Prayer for the dead" (*Kaddish*). After the death of a close relative, the Kaddish, an ancient Aramaic prayer, is recited by the closest family members for either 30 days or 11 months, depending on which relative has died. It is also repeated every year in commemoration of the date of the death (*Yahrzeit*). However, this prayer does not mention death at all—it only praises and acknowledges God. The reason the name of this prayer has the same numerical value as "You shall love" is because the prayer is both a declaration of love for the lost family member and a declaration of love for God.

Message 20: "When come upon me" (*B'krov Alai*), Psalm 27:2. This verse states: "When come upon me evildoers to consume my flesh, my adversaries and foes, it will be they that stumble and fall." Since the numerical value of "When come upon me" is the same as "You shall love," we know that there is a hidden relationship between the phrases. This relationship suggests that a consequence of loving others is that, when we are attacked, God will see to it that our enemies fall. (According to the Old Testament commandments, we are directed to love our neighbors, our strangers, and God; however, we are not commanded to love evildoers and enemies.)

The following two messages are spelled with exactly the same Hebrew letters in the same order (but with different pronunciations), and they describe both the holy and what we normally consider the profane.

Message 21: "The prostitute" (*Ha-kidday-shah*), Genesis 38:21. The prostitute is an example of a "stranger," or someone whom we ordinarily shun. But from this we learn that prostitutes, like all strangers, merit love, kindness, and respect. There are multiple stories in the Bible in which a prostitute behaves bravely and saves the day.

Message 21A: "The holy" (*Ha-Kiddoshah*), alternative reading and translation of Genesis 38:21.

This suggests that from the holy to the prostitute, we should focus on love, treat everyone with love, kindness, and respect, and leave the judging to God.

MESSAGES OF WARNING

The following series of messages reveal the consequences for refusing to practice God's true religion of love. The first is proven true almost daily. Just look at the news headlines and see how those who hate or hurt others ultimately end up shamed and humiliated.

Message 22: "Shame and humiliation" (*Boo-shaw Oo-klee-mah*), from the Blessings of the New Month. This tells us that, when we resist love and choose to promote hate or behave corruptly, we will ultimately face shame and humiliation. Whether we are the president of a great country, head of a large organization, a veteran journalist, or a famous and wealthy Hollywood director or actor: if we act hatefully, we have sealed our own fate.

Message 23: "Spoil and to take booty" (*Sh'lall V'la-voze Baz*), Isaiah 10:6. This suggests that if we do not follow God's directive to love, then we are like a criminal who steals and plunders.

Message 24: "And malignant diseases" (*V'chalim Ra-im*), Deuteronomy 28:59. This message warns that if we do not embrace love, the quality of our life will be like a malignant disease.

Message 25: "Humanity becomes profaned" (*Enosh Ahz Hu-chal*), a literal interpretation of Genesis 4:26. This suggests that humanity becomes profaned when it does not embrace the directive to love.

Message 26: "I am a stranger with You" (*Gare Anochi Imach*), Psalm 39:13. In this psalm, we pray for God to listen to our prayers. But it appears that what truly determines if God will listen is whether or not we embrace His religion of love.

THE CHOICE BETWEEN THE MATERIAL WORLD AND LOVE: A DIVINE TEST

Message 27: "The material world" (*Ha-olam Ha-chomri*), from *The Complete Hebrew English Dictionary,* by Reuben Alcalay. Of course, material needs and possessions are important, but problems arise when our primary concern is their accumulation, particularly to the exclusion of caring about others. Those who have been seduced by the material world too often focus on making money or achieving power or fame and refuse to make love a priority.

It is a recurring theme in this book that God has measuring lines for determining whether we are His allies or His enemies: our choice between love or focusing on material wealth appears to be one of them. When we are committed to the material world, love and kind acts are displaced and hateful behaviors find justification.

Message 28: "With this He [God] divides the human beings" (*B'haf-ree-doe Benay Adam*), Deuteronomy 32:8. This seems to imply that God uses love as His indicator of whether someone is good or evil, deserving of reward or punishment, and whether or not to honor them or have them face shame and humiliation.

A MESSAGE FOR HUMANITY: LOVE OR BE CURSED

The next message, a phrase from Psalm 49, has two possible translations: the first reveals for whom the directive "You shall love" is intended, and the second reveals a divine curse or insult to those who choose to hate. Rabbi Samson Raphael Hirsch has written in his book of commentary, *The Psalms,* that Psalm 49 "has equal significance for all of mankind. Its theme is the relationship of man's material possessions to his moral and spiritual task in life."

Message 29A: "All the inhabitants of earth" (*Kol Yosh-vay Chah-led*), Psalm 49:2. This tells us that embracing God's religion of love is a collective responsibility.

Message 29B: "All those who dwell with rats" (*Kol Yosh-vay Cho-led*), Psalm 49:2. This alternative reading and translation of Psalm 49:2 reveals a divine insult and curse to all those who choose to hate. This vivid image may suggest that if we do not accept God's religion of love as the most important principle in our lives, it is as if we dwell with rats, lowly creatures who scavenge in filth to survive.

Chapter Seven

Do We Really Have Free Will?

FREE WILL = 744

As we walk through our lives, we do so under the assumption that we have free will, that no one is acting as puppeteer pulling our strings to get us to behave in a certain way—we are, we believe, the masters of our own destiny. But in religious systems of belief, this concept is often paired with a seemingly contradictory concept: that God knows our choices before we make them, and even that God knows who will do good and who evil.

This chapter examines the concept of free will through a gematrial lens, and reveals answers to many ancient questions on the subject, such as: Do human beings truly have free will? What was the first incident in human history where it was exercised? What are the usual consequences of free will?

Among other things, mathematically generated messages show that free will is intricately related to the creation of the world. After all, what would be the point of God creating a planet where people could only do, and be, good? That would be very boring and make the earth into what many imagine Heaven to be, a place of pure, unwavering goodness. But our world is more interesting than that—it is one of duality and polarity: up and down, positive and negative, good and bad. Perhaps free will is like a game between two teams, good and evil. When a person chooses to do a good deed, the good team scores a point; if they do a bad thing, the evil team scores. No free will, no game.

This chapter shows that not only do we have free will but that humans are the only species to have received it. However, this difference is also the reason that human beings do not live in balance with the world: While other species must follow their instincts, humans can choose another path, even if it leads to self-destruction.

In Hebrew, the numerical value of "free will" (*Ratzon Chof-shi*), found in *The Complete English Hebrew Dictionary,* by Reuben Alcalay, is 744. After studying all known Hebrew words and phrases with a Gematria of 744, it has been determined that all text with that specific numerical value refers to an aspect of free will. Text with the numerical value of 744 can be divided into two categories: using free will to perform acts of kindness or compassion, and using free will to stray from God's commandments.

Four unique and specific Hebrew letters correspond exactly with 744: תשמד. These letters rearranged spell the first three messages. All other messages in this chapter also have 744 Gematrias but consist of a variety of different letters.

DIRECTLY EMBEDDED MESSAGES

Message 1: "You shall be destroyed" (*T'shah-made*), from *The Complete Hebrew English Dictionary,* by Reuben Alcalay. This warns us that the very choices we make by exercising our free will often end in self-destruction. In other words, while free will is nice in theory, in practice it often leads to bad decisions.

Message 2: "The fields of" (*Shad-mote*), Deuteronomy 32:32. Here, Moses speaks metaphorically about the other nations' wicked ways: "For their vine is of the vine of Sodom, and of the fields of Gomorrah, their grapes are grapes of gall, and their clusters are bitter." "The fields of" Sodom and Gomorrah symbolize sin and self-destruction. Moses warns Israel that in the future they will be seduced by the other nations and choose to stray from God's ways, and he invokes the names of the famously destroyed towns to highlight the results of choosing a path of wickedness. This is a warning that free will can lead to sin.

Message 3: "That the attribute of," "That the measurement of," or "That the characteristic of" (*Sheh-me-dot*), Eruvin 60b. The Hebrew word "*medah*" can mean both a literal measurement as well as a quality or attribute that a person possesses. This message clarifies that free will entails the expression of a particular attribute of oneself; for example, kindness or cruelty. Thus, it suggests that whichever attribute or character trait we choose to manifest is the measure by which God will judge or measure us.

MESSAGES OF WISDOM: TWO BASIC CHOICES

Message 4: "With the attribute of mercy" (*B'medot Rachamim*), from the All Will Thank You prayer (*Hakol Yo-do-cha*). This tells us that we all have the free will to show kindness and mercy.

Message 5: "That you shall stray" (*Key Tis-teh*), Numbers 5:12. This reminds us that, too often free will leads to our straying from God's commandments. This verse concludes: "And commit treachery against him." The phrase "Against him" could also be interpreted as "Against God," meaning that whatever we do when we stray from the commandments is treachery against God.

Message 6: "The head the leg" (*Ha-rosh Ha-regel*), Talmud, Tractate *Yoma*, Chapter 1 Mishna 2. Metaphorically and literally, these are the two basic ways that free will is expressed: either with thought or with actions.

Message 7: "But the work of human hands, wood and stone" (*Im Ma-aseh Y'day Adam Etz Va-even*), 2 Kings 19:18. This refers to the making of wood and stone idols of false gods. The message here is that idolatry, literal or metaphoric, often seems to be a consequence of free will.

Message 8: "Since the world was created" (*Me-sheh-nivrah Ha-olam*), from the morning prayer *Atah Who* (It was You before the world was created). This message suggests that free will has existed since the beginning of earthly time, and that it was an essential element of creation.

Message 9: "In Our image, after Our likeness" (*B'tzal-may-nu Kid-moo-tay-nu*), Genesis 1:26. This verse states: "And God said: 'Let us make man in Our image, after Our likeness." According to the ancient commentary of the Midrash, God here is speaking to the ministering angels, who were created on the second day of creation. Therefore, "In Our image, after Our likeness" reveals that free will is a divine ability that God has given only to divine beings and to humans. Our ability to choose different behaviors is distinct from all other animals, which can follow only their instincts, and separates human from beast.

Message 10: "God the Lord Has made and said" (*Asah A-donai Elokim Va-yomar*), Genesis 3:1. This phrase is from the story of Adam and Eve, when they are seduced by the serpent to eat from the forbidden fruits of the Tree of Knowledge despite God's admonition against it. This is the first recorded instance of a human being exercising free will.

Message 11: "The humans on earth" (*Et Ha-adam Ba-ah-retz*), Genesis 6:6. This section of Genesis introduces the story of Noah and the flood, wherein God is disgusted with the wickedness of human beings and has decided to wipe out all of mankind. The full verse states: "And God reconsidered having made the humans on earth, and He was profoundly sad." The hidden and literal meanings of the text are the same: God recognizes that giving humans free will has led to this moment of massive destruction.

A DIVINE FOCUS ON WOMEN AND FREE WILL

The following four messages emphasize that it is essential that women, specifically, possess free will.

Message 12: "Cohabitating," "Sleeping together," or "Sexual relations" (*He-shag-lut*), from *The Complete Hebrew English Dictionary,* by Reuben Alcalay. That the numerical value of this term equals that of "free will" seems to suggest a clear directive that sexual relations must be the result of a conscious choice or, in other words, free will.

Message 13: "And he slept with her" (*Va-yishkav Otah*), 2 Samuel 13:14. The biblical term in this phrase for "with her" actually connotes an action being done to someone rather than with someone. "And he slept with her," from the story of Amnon raping Tamar, biblically establishes the definition of rape: having sex with a woman whose free will has been denied.

Message 14: "Engagement [and] marriage" (*Ay-roos-in N'su-in*), from Talmud *Yebamot,* page 51b–52a. Clearly, this tells us that a woman's free will must be respected throughout both steps of the marital process.

Message 15: "Conversation with a woman" (*See-cha Im Ha-ee-shah*), Avot 1:5. Out of context, this suggests that even when engaging in a simple conversation, women must have the freedom to participate or not.

MESSAGES OF WARNING

While human beings have the free will to take both negative and positive actions, there are consequences. The following messages, each with the numerical value of 744, reveal the possible negative outcomes of exercising our free will, including death, murder, violence, sickness, shame, and humiliation.

Message 16: "The dead bodies of man" (*Et Pigray Ha-adam*), Jeremiah 33:5. This points out a common end result of choosing a path of violence.

Message 17: "Murder [and] death" (*Chatzar-Mavet*), Genesis 10:26. "Murder [and] death" is an anagram of the name of a descendant of Noah. The Hebrew word "murder" (*Ra-tzach*) was formed by rearranging the Hebrew letters of *Chatzar*. This is interpreted as a clear warning that free will often leads to murder and death.

Message 18: "He destroyed and did not pity and [your enemies] will rejoice" (*Haras V'lo Chamal Va-y'sa-mach*), Lamentations 2:17. This verse refers to God and His unhappiness with the iniquity of Israel. It can be understood as referring to those who use free will to sin: they will be destroyed, will not be pitied, and their enemies will rejoice over them.

Message 19: "In their graves" (*Bik-voo-rah-tam*), Genesis 47:30. Out of context, this tells us that, when free will is exercised in a sinful manner, sinners shall metaphorically or literally be buried.

Message 20: "That sickness of" (*Sheh-cho-lot*), Song of Songs 5:8. This suggests that sickness of mind, body, or soul may be a result of the choices we make when exercising free will. In addition, bad choices can exacerbate an existing sickness.

Message 21: "Our disgrace" (*Char-pa-tay-new*), Isaiah 4:1. The equal value between this phrase and "free will" discloses a warning that our own choices can often lead to our disgrace. In general, when we feel ashamed, we respond with anger and violence at those we believe have shamed us. However, "Our disgrace" reveals that it is our own free-will choices that have led to our shame and humiliation.

Message 22: "To Dathan and Abiram" (*El Datan V'avi-ram*), Numbers 16:25. When the Israelites were wandering in the desert, Moses tried in vain to convince Dathan and Abiram not to participate in a rebellion against him. They chose not to listen, and the rebellion ended with Dathan and Abiram's own destruction. This message reminds us of where free will can lead.

Message 23: "In the strength of the horse" (*Bigvoo-raht Ha-soos*), Psalm 147:10. This may refer metaphorically to the arrogant belief that a strong horse is more important than fear and awe in God. The verse states: "Not in the strength of the horse does He [God] desire." Thus, this message warns us of using our free will to follow a path of arrogantly seeking power.

MESSAGES OF WISDOM

The following five messages refer to the path that God desires for us to follow.

Message 24: "God instructs us in His chosen path" (*A-donai Yo-ranu B'derech Yivchar*), Psalm 25:12. This tells us that the path for us to follow is not a mystery: it is repeated throughout the Holy Scriptures. Earlier in this Psalm, verse 6 stated that God's path is one of "mercy and compassion."

Message 25: "The just path" or "The righteous path" (*Derech Ha-ye-sharah*), from Rambam's *Hilchot Daot* Chapter 1:6. This suggests that we use free will to choose the righteous path of following the commandments and performing acts of kindness.

Message 26: "I [God] desire kindness and not sacrifice" (*Key Ches-sed Cha-phatz-tee V'lo Zevach*), Hosea 6:6. This phrase explains that our kindness fulfills God's desires and reinforces the importance of the earlier message "With the attribute of mercy," because kindness is an aspect of mercy.

Message 27: "A righteous person observes [the commandments]" (*Tzadik Shomer*), Isaiah 26:2. This seems to suggest that we should use our free will to observe the commandments.

Message 28: "I command you today" (*Ah-nochi Mi-tzaveh Etchem Ha-yom*), Deuteronomy 11:13 (part of the daily Shema prayer). The full verse states: "And it will come to pass that if you obey My commandments that I command you today, to love God your Lord, and to serve Him with all your heart and with all your soul." The hidden message here is that, if we use our free will to follow the commandments, then, as the Shema prayer promises us, we will be rewarded with sustenance.

TO MAKE BETTER CHOICES

Message 29: "And He sent books" (*Va-yish-lach Sefarim*), literal translation of Esther 1:22. In context, this phrase concerns a new edict that stated that women no longer had free will and had to obey their husbands. The hidden meaning of "And He sent books" may refer to God having sent the books of Torah, Prophets, Scriptures, and the Talmud to teach us the correct way to exercise our free will.

Message 30: "To be a God to you for I am God" (*L'he-yot La-chem Lay-lo-kim Ani A-donai*), Leviticus 22:33 and Numbers 15:41. In both Leviticus and Numbers, this phrase comes at the end of a paragraph commanding us to remember and perform the commandments. This suggests that, while we have free will regarding the commandments, we should remember that our choices impact our relationship with God.

THE KEY INSIGHT TO MANAGING FREE WILL

Message 31: "That You [God] are God" (*Sheh-atah Who A-donai*), from the daily *Shemoneh Esreh* prayer. At the source of most sins is the conscious or unconscious belief that we ourselves are God. We must all remember, however, that, while we have been given the gift of free will, we are only human and only God is God. In moments of anger or temptation, the only thing that may stand between us and sin is the knowledge that there is a God. Thus, this message encourages us to keep God in mind as we exercise our free will.

GRATITUDE AND FREE WILL

The following two messages refer to the ancient form of showing gratitude to God: the tradition of bringing offerings of food. The Bible is filled with detailed instructions on these offerings, but the hidden message here may be that the offerings must be given with free will, not just because they were commanded. This seems paradoxical: if something is commanded, how can there also be free will? It appears that sometimes it is not enough to merely follow the instructions; what is in our hearts is also critical.

Message 32: "They shall not appear before Me [God] empty-handed" (*V'lo Yay-Rah-oo Pah-nai Ray-kom*), Exodus 34:20. God commands the Israelites to bring an offering on the Three Pilgrimage Festivals: Passover, *Shavuot,* and *Succot.* This tells us that these sacrifices should be brought with free will and not because they are obligated by law.

Message 33: "The Children of Israel brought a free-will offering to God" (*Hay-vee-oo Bnai Yisrael N'davah La-donai*), Exodus 35:29. Most offerings were required, but this particular one was a free-will offering that the Israelites could bring according to their hearts. It is worth noting, that, even though this phrase uses a different Hebrew word for "free will" (*N'davah*), one with a numerical value of 61, the total numerical value of the entire phrase equals 744. This is because the concept of free will remains at the phrase's core.

ADDITIONAL DIVINE INSIGHTS INTO FREE WILL

Free will is the freedom to make our own choices in life. Each day, we have new opportunities to choose actions that lead to kindness and mercy, to death and destruction, or to somewhere in between.

Message 34: "They are renewed each morning" (*Cha-dashim La-b'karim*), Lamentations 3:23. Lamentations 3:22–23 state: "The kindness of the Lord does not end, and His mercies do not finish, they are renewed each morning." The hidden message here is that, because human beings were created with a spark of the divine, we are expected to exercise our free will based on holiness and, like God, to be kind and merciful every day.

Message 35: "Frequency" or "frequent" (*Shi-chee-chut*), from *The Complete Hebrew English Dictionary,* by Reuben Alcalay. This emphasizes that we all have frequent opportunities to exercise our free will.

Message 36: "Flames of fire" (*La-ha-vote Aish*), Psalm 29:7. This may be a metaphor for the passion that too often determines our choices. As a result, we do not think clearly, and act instead in response to strong feelings.

Message 37: "I was asleep, but [the God in] my heart was awake" (*Ah-nee Ye-shay-nah V'lee-bee Air*), Song of Songs 5:2. Song of Songs is often translated as a metaphor for the connection between God and the Jewish people. In this context, we can understand this verse to mean that, when Israel feels secure, its devotion to God slumbers, but in Israel's heart there remains a dormant connection to God. In the context of free will, we could understand that, despite our usual bad choices, there remains within our hearts a dormant spark of using our free will for the divine attributes of mercy and kindness.

BLESSINGS MAY BE A CONSEQUENCE OF FREE WILL

Message 38: "God shall increase you and your children" (*Yo-safe A-donai Alei-chem Alei-chem V'ahl B'nay-chem*), Psalm 115:14. This suggests that, as a consequence of our wise exercise of free will, a blessing of prosperity, either literal or metaphoric, will result.

Message 39: "All the children of Your covenant" (*Kal Bnay Britecha*), recited between Rosh Hashanah and Yom Kippur. The full verse states: "And inscribe all the children of your covenant for a good life." The numerical equivalence of "All the children of Your covenant" and "free will" seems to reveal that the secret to being inscribed for a good life is how we use our free will.

BIBLICAL EXAMPLE OF EXERCISING FREE WILL FOR THE GOOD

Message 40: "The prophetess sister of Aaron" (*Ha-nivea Achote Aharon*), Exodus 15:20. Miriam, the sister of Aaron and Moses, used her free will to make a difference: she made sure that Moses, her infant brother, would not drown, arranged for their mother to raise him, and led, encouraged, and nurtured the Jewish people in Egypt during their difficult time of slavery and then freedom.

TWO ANCIENT DEBATES RESOLVED

Scholars and rabbis have long debated whether Pharaoh had free will in regard to the freeing of the enslaved Israelites. That the Gematria of the following phrase from the Book of Exodus is identical to the numerical value of "free will" seems to answer this question.

Message 41: "When the cavalry and chariots of Pharaoh came" (*Key Baw Soos Pharaoh B'rich-vo*), Exodus 15:19. When Pharaoh's horses, chariots, and horsemen chased the Israelites into the Reed Sea, the Israelites safely crossed but the Egyptians drowned. Because this phrase has a Gematria of 744, it seems to reveal that Pharaoh acted with free will when he gave the order to pursue.

Did the Children of Israel accept the Bible and commandments out of free will or because they were coerced by God? Rabbis and biblical scholars have long argued this question, but the following message may reveal the answer.

Message 42: "To him at Mount Sinai" or "With him at Mount Sinai" (*E-tow B'har See-nai*), Exodus 31:18. According to Jewish tradition, the entire

Jewish people were present at Mount Sinai to accept the Ten Commandments and the Torah (the Five Books of Moses). The Talmud (Avodah Zarah 1:2b) discusses the question of whether God coerced them to accept it or they did of their own free will. "With him at Mount Sinai," with its numerical value of 744, clearly seems to suggest that Moses and the Jewish people accepted the yoke of the commandments and the Torah out of free will. Earlier, Exodus 24:7 stated that the Jewish people accepted God's offer at Mount Sinai by saying: "Everything that God says, we shall do and then we shall understand," a declaration of free will.

Chapter Eight

What Are the Minimum Requirements for Entry into Heaven? And What Happens after Death?

AFTER DEATH = 665

As humans, we are all bound to face one final experience, one that generates timeless questions and mysteries: death. This chapter lists mathematically generated messages that seem to answer some of the timeless questions regarding death, including: What happens to us physically and spiritually after we die? What are the minimum requirements for entering Heaven? What major question will greet us when we arrive at the Gates of Heaven? Why are some people refused entrance? What eternal secrets will be answered after death?

While the math in this chapter is accurate, the interpretations and comments presented are, as always, mine alone, and different ones may be equally or even more valid.

The Hebrew phrase "After death" (*Ah-cha-ray Mote* or *Ah-cha-ray Mavet*), from Leviticus 16:1, has a Gematria of 665. Because the numerical values of Hebrew letters only go up to 400, there are two possible sets of letters that correspond exactly to 665, and they can be used to spell five words, listed here as the first five messages. The first set of Hebrew letters (תרסה) can be used to spell four words, listed as the first four messages; the second set of Hebrew letters (ששסה) can spell one word, listed as the fifth. All other messages in this chapter have Gematrias of 665 but consist of a variety of different letters.

DIRECTLY EMBEDDED MESSAGES

It seems that after we die, at our first interview at the Gates of Heaven, God asks us a question the answer to which may determine whether or not we gain entry into Heaven: "Did you work to repair the world or destroy it?" The first message, below, appears to be God's usual conclusion about our lives. The first set of Hebrew letters that correspond exactly with 665 spell the following four messages.

Message 1: "You have destroyed" (*Ha-rastah*), Judges 6:25. Out of context, "destroyed" may refer to how easily we responded with hatred and how we have allowed others to suffer due to our tolerance of corruption, war, and hunger, or our mistreatment of the environment. In context, "You have destroyed" refers to the destruction of idolatry. As a metaphor, idolatry can also refer to the worship of money, power, and fame, which often leads to destruction. This message appears to be an indictment of our behavior as human beings and is a sad epitaph for us. The question "Did you work to repair the world or destroy it?" makes complete sense because the purpose of the Torah and of the entire Jewish tradition, as well as of virtually all other religious traditions, is to repair the world through acts of kindness and charity.

Message 2: "Secret," "hidden," or "concealed" (*Has-tare*), Deuteronomy 31:18. In context, "concealed" refers to God concealing His face from us when we are evil. This may also imply that when we are evil, God conceals His face from us both while we are alive and after death.

Message 3: "Removal of" or "Dismissal of "(*Ha-saw-rot*), from *The Complete Hebrew English Dictionary,* by Reuben Alcalay. This may warn that the cost of continuing to destroy may be to remove ourselves from this world and disqualify ourselves from meriting the World to Come.

Message 4: "You [God] shall destroy" (*Ta-ha-ros*), Exodus 15:7. As the full phrase states: "You [God] shall destroy Your enemies." In the context of "After death," this seems to be a warning to the enemies of God that they will be destroyed. (It is worth pointing out that the enemies of God include those who hate any other human being.)

THE SECOND SET OF LETTERS
THAT CORRESPOND EXACTLY WITH 665

The second set of letters (שסשה) that correspond exactly to 665 can be used to spell one word that exactly repeats the first message: "You have destroyed." This seems to support the idea that a conversation takes place with God when we arrive in Heaven; the topic being: During our lives, did we repair the world or destroy it?

Message 5: "That you plundered" (*Sheh-sha-sah*), from the *Milog Hebrew Hebrew Online Dictionary.* "Plundered" seems to refer to our relationship with and behavior towards the natural world. How we treated the air, water, fish, bees, the earth itself, and countless species of animals can be summed up with one word: "Plundered."

WHERE DO WE GO IMMEDIATELY AFTER DEATH?

The following two messages, when looked at together, seem to explain that, after death, our souls are brought to the Gates of Heaven.

Message 6: "In order to bring us" (*L'ma-ahn Havee O-tanu*), from the Passover Haggadah. The Passover Haggadah is recited on the first two nights of Passover at the festive *Seder* dinner. The Haggadah commemorates the Exodus from Egypt by recounting the story of the Children of Israel escaping slavery and becoming a free people. The hidden meaning of "In order to bring us" may suggest that, after death, our souls become free and are brought to Heaven.

Message 7: "Gates of the King" (*Sha-ar Ha-Melech*), Esther 4:2. In the Book of Esther, according to the rabbis, the Hebrew word for "The King" (*Ha-Melech*) refers to God. Therefore "Gates of the King" can be interpreted as the Gates of God, verifying that after death our souls go to the Gates of Heaven to face judgment.

WHO DETERMINES ENTRY INTO HEAVEN?

The following five messages seem to refer to the ultimate arbiter of entry into Heaven, God.

Message 8: "God of the spirits" (*El-okay Ha-ru-chote*), Numbers 16:22. This may imply that, after death, all spirits return to God to be judged. In addition, "God of the spirits" may tell us that the Bible and the mystics were right: within each of us is a divine spirit or soul.

Message 9: "The knowledge of God the Omnipresent" (*Da-aht Hamakom*), from the introduction to the *Kol Nidre* prayer recited on Yom Kippur, the Day of Atonement. According to Jewish tradition, on Yom Kippur our fate for the following year is determined. So, too, this message tells us our fate after we die is determined and known only by God.

Message 10: "The judgments of God are righteous" (*Mishpatai A-donai Tzadko*), nonconsecutive words found in Psalm 19:10. The hidden message here seems to be that, after death, God judges the wicked and the good, and that His judgments are always fair.

Message 11: "He creates all" (*Bo-ray Et Ha-kol*), from the daily prayers before the *Shema*. This suggests that God created both this world for the living and the World to Come for after death.

Message 12: "That God shall divide" or "That God shall distinguish" (*Asher Chalak A-donai*), literal translation of Deuteronomy 4:19. An alternative translation of this verse is: "That God your Lord shall divide all of the peoples under the entire Heaven." This seems to suggest that God will distinguish between souls, possibly distinguishing between those who merit punishment and those who merit blessings.

THE MINIMUM REQUIREMENTS FOR ENTRY INTO HEAVEN

Message 13: "True path" (*Derech Emet*), Genesis 24:48. This tells us that, after death, our lives may be evaluated and judged by whether or not we stayed on the right path. The "true path," according to the Bible, is a life spent honoring God, observing the commandments, performing acts of kindness, and repairing the world (in Hebrew *Tikkun Olam*).

Message 14: "Orphan and stranger" (*V'y'tome Gare*), Zechariah 7:10. The commandment to "treat the stranger well" is mentioned in the Bible over 30 times. A "stranger" is a member of a minority or an outsider (sometimes a convert to Judaism), and "orphan" may have a literal or metaphoric meaning. The key indicator as to whether or not we were on the true path in life is how we treated the orphan and stranger. Therefore, if we treated them with kindness, then we have a greater chance of being granted entry into Heaven.

Message 15: "[Depends] upon our thanking Him" (*Al Sheh-anachnu Modim Lach*), from the thanksgiving section of the *Amidah* prayer, or "Prayer of the 18" (*Shemoneh Esreh*). This message suggests that a minimum requirement for entry into Heaven is that, while we were alive, we thanked God and we taught our children to be grateful to Him.

WHAT IS THE MOST BASIC REQUIREMENT FOR ENTRY INTO HEAVEN?

Message 16: "Walk humbly" (*Hatz-naya Lechet*), Micah 6:8. In this verse, the prophet Micah tells us exactly what God wants from us while we are alive, but these requests are also exactly what determine our entry into Heaven after we die: "God has told you mankind what is good and what the Lord demands of you: to do justice, to love kindness, and to walk humbly with your God." While this sentence can be viewed as a summary of the entire Bible, the prescription "to walk humbly with your God" by itself seems to be sufficient to guarantee entry into Heaven. The opposite of "walk humbly" is arrogance, the belief that you can take the law into your own hands, and that you determine right from wrong based on your personal feelings and beliefs. Arrogance is at the source of most wrongdoing.

When you have gratitude towards God and are kind to the orphan and stranger, then you are considered righteous and can be confident of gaining entry to Heaven. The following seems to confirm this notion.

Message 17: "The righteous with Me" (*Tzadikim Ee-tee*), nonconsecutive words found in Talmud Ketuvot 105a. Out of context, this may be interpreted that, after death, the righteous shall be with God.

EXAMPLES OF RIGHTEOUS PEOPLE

Message 18: "Priests Your holy people" (*Kohanim Ahm Kiddu-shecha*), from the *Shemoneh Esreh* priestly benediction prayer. A priest seems to be an example of someone who is on the true path and who merits a good after-death reward. Priests (*Kohanim*) are considered to be God's holy people because they have dedicated their lives to serving God and to blessing Israel.

Message 19: "To them [with] tzitzit" (*La-hem Tzitzit*), Numbers 15:38. Tzitzit are the ritually knotted fringes worn by religious Jews. Like the previous message, this seems to provide an example of someone who is righteous.

TWO ADDITIONAL REQUIREMENTS JUST FOR JEWS?

According to the Talmud, all Jewish souls were present on Mount Sinai when God gave them the Bible and the Ten Commandments. Because the Jews were eyewitnesses, it seems that there may be additional requirements for them to gain entry into Heaven.

Message 20: "The *Shema* twice with love" (*Pa-amah-yim B'ahava Shema*), from the *Kedushah* prayer of the Sabbath *Mussaf Shemoneh Esrei*. The *Shema* is the most famous Jewish prayer and begins, "Hear O' Israel the Lord is our God, God is One" (Deuteronomy 6:4). Religious Jews recite this prayer at least twice a day. But in the context of "after death," "The *Shema* twice with love" may suggest that to recite this prayer twice with love during the course of your entire life may be a minimum requirement for entering Heaven—but the recitation must be done with genuine love.

Message 21: "The people of the exile Passover" (*Bnai Hagolah Et Ha-Pesach*), Ezrah 6:19. After the destruction of the First Holy Temple in Jerusalem in 586 B.C.E., the Jews were exiled to Babylonia. The Book of Ezra speaks of life in exile and of the Jews' eventual return to Israel. The verse states: "The people of the exile brought the Passover offering on the fourteenth of the month." Because the numerical value of the phrase "The people of the exile Passover" (665) is the same as "after death," it may reveal that a minimum requirement for entering Heaven is for Jews who live outside of Israel to celebrate and remember Passover.

A TASTE OF HEAVEN FOR THOSE WHO MERIT IT

Message 22: "The kindness of God that will not end" (*Chas-day A-donnai Ki Lo Tamnoo*), Lamentations 3:22. If you are kind, especially to the orphan and stranger, then you may merit the kindness of God, even after death. "That will not end" may refer to both this world and the next.

Message 23: "Your [God's] kindness is bigger than the Heavens" (*Gadol May-ol Shamaim Chas-de-chah*), Psalm 108:5. This teaches us that, after death, we will realize that God's kindness is infinite.

Message 24: "The voice of God our Lord" (*Et Kol A-donai Elokenu*), Deuteronomy 5:22. In the text, Moses reminds the Children of Israel that, at Mount Sinai, when they heard God speaking the Ten Commandments, they were afraid they would die. Since the phrase "The voice of God our Lord" has a numerical value of 665, it suggests that after we die it may be possible to hear the voice of God without fear.

Message 25: "The house of God shall be a pillar [a monument]" (*Ma-tzay-vah Y'he-yeh Bait Elokim*), Genesis 28:22. Out of context, "the house of God" may refer to Heaven, and the phrase "shall be a pillar" may be a metaphor for God's strength and constant presence, suggesting that after death God will be a constant strength and presence for the righteous.

WHAT IS HEAVEN LIKE?

Message 26: "Flies by day" (*Yashud Tzsa-ha-raim*), Psalm 91:6. Out of context, this seems like a lovely description of our souls.

Message 27: "On your entry and blessed you shall be" (*Be-vo-echa Oo-Baruch Atah*), Deuteronomy 28:6. The full sentence states: "Blessed you shall be on your entry, and blessed you shall be when you go out." Rashi interprets this phrase as referring to birth and death. Therefore, we can interpret this as referring to being blessed that you are entering Heaven.

Message 28: "[God] Master of Legions shall be with us" (*Tziva-ote Ima-nu*), Psalm 46:8. This may suggest that after death we can see God as Master of Legions.

THE OLD WAY TO THINK ABOUT DEATH

The following three messages refer to what happens to our physical bodies after death.

Message 29: "Decayed" (*Hit-kal-kale*), *The Complete Hebrew English Dictionary*, by Reuben Alcalay. This confirms what we all know, that after death our bodies decay.

Message 30: "Shall be dried up" (*Yay-vo-shoo Key Ho-vish*), Joel 1:12. This is similar to the previous message, that after death our physical bodies dry up.

Message 31: "To skin [an animal]" (*Paw-shot Ohr*), *The Complete Hebrew English Dictionary*, by Reuben Alcalay. Some believe that, after death, there is nothing and our existence will be analogous to that of a skinned animal.

A NEW WAY TO THINK ABOUT DEATH

For the most part, as human beings we fear death as a dark and horrifying condition but through the use of Gematria we can uncover messages that paint quite a different picture.

Message 32: "Unit of measure" (*Me-dot Erech*), from *The Complete Hebrew English Dictionary*, by Reuben Alcalay. This phrase may imply that physical death is just a measurement of heart and brain activity but is not necessarily the end.

Message 33: "Latency" (*T'me-root*), from *The Complete Hebrew English Dictionary*, by Reuben Alcalay. After death, it is possible that a period of latency occurs, perhaps for self-evaluation or for preparation for the next life.

Message 34: "At that which is within" (*B'mah Shey-yesh Bo*), Avot 4:27. This phrase is part of the aphorism: "Don't look at the jar but at that which is within." This may be a metaphor for how we view our souls, that during our lifetime we can see only the jar, but after death we can finally see what was hidden within us our entire lives: our divine souls.

WHAT MYSTERIES ARE ANSWERED AFTER DEATH?

Message 35: "General support" or "General leaning," an Aramaic term whose literal translation is "Eternal support" (*Ahs-machta B'almah*), Talmud Brachos 41b. When the rabbinic authorities of the Talmudic period (200–500 C.E.) and later were unable to find a clear precedent in Scripture for a legal ruling, they would find some related general principle that hinted at a basis for their ruling. Since the term "General support" has a numerical value of 665, it suggests that after death the rabbis will find out if their interpretations were correct. In addition, the literal interpretation, "Eternal support," may imply that those who merit entry into Heaven will receive ongoing support from the Eternal One, God.

Message 36: "Reasons for the commandments" (*Tah-ah-may Mitzvote*), from *Reasons for the Commandments,* by Rabbi Menahem Habavli. No one knows the reasons for all of the 613 commandments in the Torah, but this message seems to suggest that after death we may finally learn them.

WILL WE HAVE GENDERS AFTER WE DIE?

The following two messages seem to conflict. Could it be that both are possible?

Message 37: "And no males" (*V'et Zachor Lo*), Leviticus 18:22. Out of context, this suggests that in Heaven there may not be a distinction between male and female. This is consistent with the belief that the soul has no physicality but is instead comprised of pure energy.

Message 38: "Behold and they took for themselves wives" (*He-nay Va-yikchoo Lahem Nashim*), Genesis 6:2. Out of context, this may suggest that after death there will be husbands and wives.

AFTER DEATH WE FIND OUT A SECRET ABOUT GOD

The following two messages are located in the same verse of Exodus 9:1. In this verse, God tells Moses to speak to Pharaoh and say: "Thus spoke God the Lord of the Hebrews: Send out My people that they may serve Me." Within this sentence, there are two phrases with a value of 665. They follow consecutively one after the other, intersecting on the word "the Hebrews" (*Ha-ivrim*), possibly suggesting that after death we learn more about the connection between God and the Jews (biblically called "Hebrews").

Message 39: "Thus spoke God the Lord of the Hebrews" (*Ko Amar A-donai Elokay Ha-Ivrim*), Exodus 9:1. This seems to reveal that, after death, we fully learn that it is accurate to describe God as "the Lord of the Hebrews." While the Bible is respected by most, too often Jews are not treated as if they were actually the people described in the Bible and as having a special relationship with God. It appears that, after death, we find out that the same God who today is worshipped by all faiths is actually the biblical God of the Hebrews.

Message 40: "The Hebrews He [God] sent" (*Ha-Ivrim Shalach*), literal translation of Exodus 9:1. In this verse, God tells Pharaoh that the Jews serve Him and not Pharaoh. The hidden message here seems to be that, after death, we learn that Jews serve God as agents to spread the Bible and Commandments to the world.

AFTER THE DEATH OF ABRAHAM AND MOSES

Message 41: "Isaac and Ishmael" (*Yitzchak V'Yishmael*), Genesis 25:9. In full, Genesis 25:8–9 state that, after the death of Abraham, "his sons Isaac and Ishmael buried him in the cave of Machpelah." This is a case of the hidden meaning of the verse being identical with its literal meaning: a description of what happened "after the death" of Abraham.

Message 42: "God to Moses on the very day" (*A-donai el Moshe Bih-etz-em Ha-yom*), Deuteronomy 32:48. This section of Deuteronomy describes the last conversation God has with Moses just before Moses' death. It may be that, normally, God would explain the reason for someone's death after the person dies, but Moses seems to merit an explanation beforehand. The verse states: "And God spoke to Moses on the very day of his death." Again, the hidden message here seems to refer to the literal story of Moses' death.

WHAT HAPPENS TO THE WICKED?

The following eight messages refer to people who were evil. Included in these messages are references to the most evil characters in the Bible. It seems beyond coincidence that each of these phrases has the identical numerical value of 665.

Message 43: "From the evil inclination" (*Yetzer Ha-ra Min*), from the prayer some recite before the Torah reading. Central to Judaism is the belief that, while all human beings possess both good and evil inclinations, each of us has the free will to choose which to follow. This message reveals the cause of most sinful behavior, that when we succumb to our evil inclination, we commit transgressions against God and people.

Message 44: "They are wicked" (*Resha-im Hame*), from the Rashi commentary of Genesis 5:32. In discussing the sons of Noah, Rashi comments that if the sons of Noah are wicked then they will drown in the flood. The phrase "They are wicked" suggests that the wicked, after death, will be similarly punished, and certainly not merit entry into Heaven.

THREE INFAMOUS EXAMPLES OF WICKEDNESS IN THE BIBLE

When it comes to wickedness, three biblical characters stand out: Amalek, Korach, and Haman. In each case, key phrases in the Bible relating to these three characters were found to have a numerical value of 665. These individuals may also serve as warnings to the evildoers of today, that their fate will be the same as that of Amalek, Korach, and Haman: they will be totally defeated, shamed, and their names will not be remembered. At the very least, that these messages have the same numerical value as "After death" should warn all the haters and evildoers that they face punishment whether in this world or in the next.

Message 45: "What Amalek did to you" (*Ah-saw Le-cha Amalek*), Deuteronomy 25:17. Amalek is singled out in the Bible as the most wicked of nations. It murdered the weak, the elderly, and the young of the Israelites. In addition, Amalek had the intention to prove that the God of Israel was not all-powerful. This same intention seems to be repeated throughout Jewish and world history and may explain why Jews have been targets of anti-Semitic attacks for over 3,000 years.

Message 46: "Korach son of Izhar" (*Korach Ben Yitzhar*), Numbers 16:1. Korach was the leader of a revolt against Moses. He enlisted and ensnared other followers, but they were all destroyed by a divine miracle when the earth swallowed them up. This may suggest a similar fate for all evildoers.

Message 47: "Haman enemy of the Jews" (*Haman Tzo-rare Ha-Ye-hoo-dim*), from Esther 8:1 (one of two possible spellings). The Book of Esther relates the story of Haman's attempt to wipe out all the Jews in the Persian Empire in approximately 516 B.C.E. Haman plotted against the Jews, but he himself ended up shamed and humiliated. This pattern of the hateful being brought down in shame and humiliation has been repeated throughout all of history, and continues to occur today.

OTHER FORMS OF WICKED BEHAVIOR

Message 48: "Amassed much silver and gold" (*Harbay Kesef V'zahav Hir-bee-nu*), Avodah Zarah 1:2b. This message is found in the Talmud in the tractate of Avodah Zarah, which translates in English to "idol worship." This suggests that anyone whose main purpose in life is to amass silver and gold seems to be considered wicked or evil by God, and that after death they may be judged accordingly. What makes the amassing of silver and gold into a sin is that the "worship" of wealth is a form of idol worship or idolatry.

Message 49: "You shall have other gods before Me [God]" (*Ye-he-yeh Lecha Elohim Achay-rim Ahl Pah-nai*), Exodus 20:2. In full, this Commandments states: "You shall not have other gods before Me." But here, in this message, the first word in the biblical text "Not" (*Lo*) is left out. So, when we do worship other gods instead of the real God, it is a serious sin by which we will be judged after death. To worship "other gods" or "strange gods" is both a literal and metaphoric prohibition. We often "worship" other gods, such as fame, money, and power, and when we put these other gods before the one true God, we are considered wicked and, after death, may be held accountable.

Message 50: "Who ensnares" or, literally, "Who sells" (*Ha-mo-cherit*), Nahum 3:4. The evil person who ensnares others in evil activities shall be punished, whether in this world, the World to Come, or in both.

Message 51: "To be cut off" (*L'hach-reet*), Exodus 8:5. Out of context, this suggests that the wicked may be cut off from God during their lives, and that after death they will be cut off from Heaven.

WHAT PUNISHMENTS AWAIT THE WICKED?

Message 52: "And God shall not listen to your voice" (*V'lo Shamah A-donai B'kol-chem*), Deuteronomy 1:45. The biblical text refers to those who do not listen to God's commandments and in return are denied God's attention. This may imply that if we are wicked we will not be able to talk God into allowing us to enter heaven. In addition, this may also be a warning that, if we are evil, God will not listen to our voice even while we are alive.

Message 53: "Double [the punishment] for all your sins" (*Kif-lah-yim B'chal Cha-toe-teh-cha*), Isaiah 40:2. In context, this message literally discloses that those who are evil will receive double the punishment for their sins.

FOR THE WICKED:
FOUR POSSIBLE BIBLICAL REFERENCES TO HELL

The following four messages are all biblical phrases that seem to be haunting warnings to evildoers of what shall befall them after death. The messages seem to describe hell or some similar terrible punishment.

Message 54: "And shall descend" or "And shall go down"(*V'tay-rod-nah*), Jeremiah 9:17. Out of context, this message may be interpreted literally or metaphorically. If taken literally, it may indicate that evil people will be sent down, possibly to somewhere like hell. And if taken metaphorically, it may suggest that, even before they die, evil people shall go down.

The following two phrases are located in successive verses in the Book of Amos.

Message 55: "If they dig down" (*Im Yach-t'roo*), Amos 9:2. The full phrase states: "If they dig down to the grave," which can also be translated: "If they dig down to hell." In the context of "after death," these two translations appear to describe, both literally and metaphorically, where the wicked are headed.

Message 56: "And the last of them" (*V'acha-ree-tam*), Amos 9:1. The phrase states: "And the last of them I [God] shall slay by the sword; no fugitive among them will flee and no refugee among them will escape." This seems to be a clear warning to the wicked of their fate after death.

Message 57: "Shall befall them" (*Tea-pole Alay-hem*), Exodus 15:16. This phrase is found in the "Song by the Sea," sung by the Israelites after the Splitting of the Sea and the drowning of Pharaoh's army. The full phrase states: "Fear and terror shall befall them." The meaning seems clear, that after death fear and terror shall befall the wicked.

Chapter Nine

Suffering

Is It Divine Punishment?

Most people believe that suffering is either divine or karmic punishment that comes as a consequence of a wrongdoing or sin. There is an ancient debate found in the Talmud (Tractate *Berachot* 5a), transcribed close to 2,000 years ago, which reveals that suffering is not a punishment at all but actually a blessing. While this chapter discloses some mathematical support for this concept, for the most part the logic and explanation have been derived from the ancient Talmudic text.

The debate begins with the statement: "If a person sees that afflictions are befalling him, he should investigate his deeds to determine which sin he committed that would cause such suffering." But another rabbi brings up the concept of "afflictions of love" and quotes Proverbs 3:12 which states: "God rebukes those He loves." A third rabbi quotes from Isaiah 53:10 which, when translated literally, states: "God was pleased with him [Israel] so He crushed him with pain." Why would God crush someone who had pleased Him? How are we to understand this? We all know that good people and beautiful innocent children sometimes get sick, have accidents, or are victims of horrific attacks. So, suffering itself cannot be a punishment. The question is: Why is suffering necessary?

My explanation of the divine mind is completely consistent with the text in *Berachot* (a tractate whose very title means "blessings"). Heaven is a place of complete goodness and no suffering, but when God created the Earth, distinct from Heaven, there needed to also be the potential for evil and suffering. The idea of creating a world with the dualities of good and bad, positive and negative, and healthy and sick can be explained through Gematria. In the second chapter of this book, a discussion of the creation of the world analyzed the phrase "In the beginning" (*Bereishis*), which has a numerical value of 913. The mirror image of 913 is 319. In Gematria, mirror images have been found to reflect and reveal additional information about the original number. When all known words and phrases with a value of 319 were studied, each was found to refer to an aspect of cancer (*Sarton*), a 319 numerical value. Cancer, in one word, reminds us that this world is not perfect. Cancer symbolizes the difference between being on Earth and being in Heaven.

If the reason why our world has both health and disease is because dichotomy itself is essential, this would explain the function and existence of suffering. But how much suffering is necessary? What percentage of it does God create and how much do we? Reading the headlines of any newspaper, it seems clear that the vast majority of suffering is man-made.

Regarding the page of Talmud that we are discussing, *Artscroll's The Schottenstein Daf Yomi Edition* explains that when average people are subjected to afflictions, they usually respond with anger and sin. However, when the righteous suffer, they have more capacity to continue to be kind and compassionate. To me, it is as if before we are born we are given the opportunity to volunteer for some of the afflictions, thereby decreasing the suffering of everyone else. The more truly devout people volunteer to take on a greater share of the suffering.

Suffering, in effect, is a gift of charity to others. This idea is supported by analyzing the numerical value of the Hebrew word for "charity," *Tzedakah,* which has a Gematria of 199. All words and phrases with a numerical value of 199 can be interpreted as referring to "charity." Following are eight examples of Hebrew text with a value of 199, the same as the Hebrew word for "charity": the first five relate to charity in general while the other three reveal that mourning is actually a form of both charity and suffering.

MESSAGES RELATING TO CHARITY (*TZEDAKAH*):
A NUMERICAL VALUE OF 199

Message A. "The poor [and] needy" (*Ani Evyone*), from Deuteronomy 24:14. This discloses who should be receiving charity.

Message B. "God and human beings" (*Elokim Oo-bnay Adam*), Psalm 36:8. When we give charity we become partners with, or agents of, God.

Message C. "Click here" (*Lachatz Kan*), a modern Israeli phrase. The purpose of a "Click here" icon is to facilitate your experience at the particular Internet site. In regard to charity, "Click here" is metaphoric and appears to be a divine suggestion: "To facilitate your life, click here on the charity icon and give."

Message D. "Success now" (*Hatzlecha Na*), Psalm 118:25. This suggests a relationship between giving charity and being successful.

Message E. "First place" (*Makom Echad*), literal translation of Genesis 1:9. Out of context, this implies that giving charity is equivalent to being in first place.

Message F. "You will mourn" (*S'fodna*), Jeremiah 49:3. The hidden message here is that mourning is a form of charity.

Message G. "There was great mourning" (*Ma-ge-ah Avel Gadol*), Esther 4:3. Another example that shows how mourning or suffering is actually a charitable offering.

Message H. "Mourners of Zion" (*Avalay Tzion*), recited at the home of a Jewish mourner during *Shiva,* the initial seven-day period of mourning. Over the last 3,000 years, Jews have probably mourned more than most others.

But even if some people volunteered for their suffering, the rest of us are still required to help them. Actually, because they volunteered out of a desire to decrease our suffering, we should be even more grateful to them, and, whenever possible, offer charity and every kindness to thank them.

III

Divine Wisdom and Warning Regarding Science

Chapter Ten

Do Science and the Bible Conflict?

SCIENCE AND TORAH = 731

In a 1930 *New York Times* article, Albert Einstein wrote: "Science without religion is lame, religion without science is blind." This chapter completely validates Albert Einstein's view.

The historic conflict between science and the Bible is addressed here through an analysis of the numerical value of the phrase "Science and To-rah": 731. This particular phrase was chosen because "Torah" is the Hebrew word used in the Old Testament to refer to itself, and the phrase "Science and Torah" (*Torah U'Madda*) has been used for over 100 years to refer to the relationship between secular knowledge and the Bible. Since 1946, Yeshiva University has used this exact phrase as their motto. The mathematically generated messages in this chapter, revealed through a gematrial analysis of the Hebrew phrase for "Science and Torah," seem to answer age-old questions, including: Is it acceptable to question the Bible? What will happen if we discard either science or the Bible? What is the secret to having our prayers answered? Can science and education help overturn wickedness in the world?

In addition, a numerical analysis of the first sentence of the Bible appears to thoroughly reconcile Darwin's theory of evolution with the biblical account of creation.

THE MAJOR CONFLICT:
DID CREATION TAKE SIX DAYS OR FOUR BILLION YEARS?

Scientific data clearly proves that the world evolved over billions of years, but the Old Testament states that the world was created in six days. While that sounds like a conflict, there is actually none. If you are religious and certain that God created the world, you can therefore also be certain that God created evolution. And if you believe only in science, then a mathematical explanation of the first verse of the Bible will illustrate how to reconcile the difference between six days and more than four billion years, thus showing that the issue here is not science versus the Old Testament but science in concert with the Old Testament. In this chapter, the terms Bible, Old Testament, and Torah are used interchangeably.

THE FIRST VERSE OF THE BIBLE RECONCILES THE CONFLICT BETWEEN CREATIONISM AND EVOLUTION

Genesis 1:1 states: "In the beginning God created the heavens and the earth." The Hebrew word for "created" (*Barah*) has a numerical value of 203. Notice the Bible does not use the word "formed" (*Yatzar*), which has a value of 300. Using a gematrial lens, we find that the numerical difference between the Hebrew words "formed" and "created" resolves the discrepancy between six days and four billion years. What distinguishes creation from form is time: for example, it takes an instant to create the idea to build a house, but the actual process of building, or forming, the house takes time. For those who are interested, the following paragraph explains the mathematics of the numerical difference between "formed" and "created."

The numerical value of "formed" (300) minus the numerical value of the word for "created" (203) equals 97 (300 - 203 = 97). After studying all known words and phrases with the value of 97, I found each to relate in some manner to time (*Z'man*), a 97 Gematria. Thus we can generate the gematrial equation: Creation (203) + Time (97) = Form (300). Therefore, the act of creation plus time (or the process of evolution) equals form. This could mean that in six days God created the idea of each element in the world, then time passed (billions of years), over the course of which the diversity of species, organisms, and molecules took form. "Time passing" is the key to evolution and evolutionary changes. Therefore the Bible's literal truth does not conflict with modern science or Darwin's theory of evolution.

DIRECTLY EMBEDDED MESSAGES WITHIN "SCIENCE AND TORAH" — A NUMERICAL VALUE OF 731

The numerical value of the Hebrew phrase "Science and Torah" (731) generates four specific and unique Hebrew letters that correspond exactly to 731: תשלא. These letters can be used to spell six words, listed as the first six messages. All other messages in this chapter also have 731 Gematrias but consist of a variety of different letters.

Message 1: "You shall ask" (*Tish-al*), Genesis 32:30. This message is from the story of Jacob wrestling the angel. When Jacob asks the angel his name, the angel responds by blessing Jacob. In the context of science and the Torah, this suggests that asking questions about both science and Torah is to be encouraged, and that asking those questions may even lead to blessings.

Message 2: "You asked" (*Shaw-al-tah*), Deuteronomy 18:16. The full phrase states: "About all that you asked from God your Lord." This suggests that all answers can be found either in science or Torah or in both.

Message 3: "For elevation," "for dignity," or "for strength" (*L'sate*), from *The Complete Hebrew English Dictionary,* by Reuben Alcalay. This tells us that the embrace of both science and Torah will elevate and strengthen us.

Message 4: "For a tumor" (*L'sh-ate*), from *The Complete Hebrew English Dictionary,* by Reuben Alcalay. If you value the Bible and tend to dismiss science, this offers a reminder that science is the primary modality for the treatment of a tumor.

Message 5: "For suffering" or "For endurance" (*Liss-ate*), from *The Complete Hebrew English Dictionary,* by Reuben Alcalay. This suggests that the combination of science and Torah is the best treatment to alleviate suffering. It may also indicate that discarding either science or Torah leads to suffering.

Message 6: "To calamity," "To disaster," or "To ruin" (*L'shate*), from *The Complete Hebrew English Dictionary,* by Reuben Alcalay. This may be a warning of where we are headed if we do not embrace and honor both science and the Torah.

THE SECRET DIVINE FORMULA FOR A GOOD LIFE

Message 7: "And sealed for a good life all the children" (*Va-chatom L'chaiim Tovim Kal Banay*); the phrase can also be read "And sealed for a good life all My [God's] children" (*Va-chatom L'chaiim Tovim Kal Banai*), from the *Neilah* prayer, recited at the conclusion of Yom Kippur. This is the final plea before the Gates of Heaven are closed at the conclusion of Yom Kippur and God determines our fate for the coming year. However, by converting this phrase into its numerical value (731), it is revealed that embedded within this prayer is the secret divine formula for having a good life: Embrace science and Torah.

MESSAGES OF WISDOM

Message 8: "I have called to You" (*K'ra-tee-cha*), Psalm 130:1. The full phrase states: "Out of the depths I have called to You O' Lord." This suggests that when we call to God for help, we may find His answer in science and Torah.

Message 9: "God shall be close to all those that call upon Him" (*Kah-rove A-donai L'kol Kor-ave*), Psalm 145:18. This tells us that when we call upon God, He shall be close by in the form of science or Torah.

Message 10: "A Psalm by David to the victor, God shall answer you" (*La-m'na-tzay-ach Mizmor L'David Ya-an-cha Ado-nai*), literal translation of Psalm 20:1-2. Psalm 20 is a request that God answer us in our time of need. The hidden message here indicates that science and Torah are the tools through which divine help is rendered.

Message 11: "Seek a blessing" (*Doraish Bracha*), from Talmud Berachot 63a; words not consecutive. This tells us that, when we seek a blessing, we may find it in either science or Torah or both.

Message 12: "For it shall be that your child shall ask you tomorrow" (*Hayah Ki Yish-alcha Bincha Mahar*), Exodus 13:14. As this verse states: "For when your child asks you tomorrow what is this?" This tells us that the study of science and Torah will provide the answers to the questions our children will ask.

SCIENCE AND TORAH: POWERFUL GIFTS FOR GOOD

Message 13: "Offerings of peace" or, literally, "Fire offerings of wholeness" (*Ha-shalamim E-sheh*), Leviticus 3:3. According to *The Stone Edition* of the Bible, the commentators Rashi and Ramban explained that "Offerings of peace," unlike guilt offerings, were brought purely as a gift for God, "motivated out of a sense of wholeness and perfection." The hidden message here, then, seems to be that Torah and science are divine gifts that will contribute to a state of profound well-being.

Message 14: "To repair the world" (*L'Ta-kain Ha-olam*), from Rashi's commentary on 1 Chronicles 16:29. This tells us that, by granting us access to science and Torah, God has provided the spiritual and physical tools to repair the world.

Message 15: "Overturn the wicked" (*Ha-phoch Resha-im*), Proverbs 12:7. In this context, Torah may not be a literal prescription but rather a metaphor for the power of a good education. By providing better medicine, hospitals, and nutrition, by building and establishing good schools to provide for a decent education, we may be able to change the hearts and minds of our enemies, transforming those who have been or might have become wicked into good citizens of the world.

THE CONNECTION BETWEEN
GOD AND SCIENCE AND THE BIBLE

The following four messages all refer to God yet possess the same numerical value as "Science and Torah," thus connecting God with science and Torah.

Message 16: "And from Your wisdom O' Supreme God" (*Oo-may-chach-mot-cha E-l El-yone*), from the prayer of putting on the *Tefillin*. This message reminds us that both science and Torah reflect and represent God's wisdom.

Message 17: "You have found favor in My [God's] eyes" (*Mah-tzah-tah Chane B'ay-nigh*), repeated in both Exodus 33:12 and 33:17. This seems to be a clear declaration of divine approval of both science and Torah.

Message 18: "For His Name shall be exalted" (*Key Nis-gahv Sh'mo*), Psalm 148:13. This tells us that whenever we reap the rewards and gifts of science or Torah, we should be praising and thanking God.

Message 19: "The Name of the Master of the universe" (*Shmay D'mah-ray Alma*), from the Aramaic prayer *Brich Shmay* (Blessed Is the Name). This ancient prayer asks that God make us receptive to His wisdom. Because this phrase has the numerical value of 731, it suggests that God's wisdom is manifested by the combination of Torah and science.

BENEFITS TO EMBRACING BOTH SCIENCE AND TORAH:
DIVINE ANSWERS TO OUR PRAYERS

Message 20: "And they shall say only a wise people" (*V'om-roo Rock Ahm Chah-cham*), Deuteronomy 4:6. This promises that a nation that embraces both science and Bible will be viewed as possessing wisdom.

Message 21: "I [God] healed them" (*R'fa-tim*), Hosea 11:3. This seems to reveal that science and Torah are the instruments of God's healing.

Message 22: "You will prolong your days" (*Ta-ariche Ya-mim*), Deuteronomy 4:40. The extension of life is a promise made elsewhere in the Bible, including Deuteronomy 11:21, as a reward for following the commandments and may apply to both spiritual longevity and good health. Science, in a more literal manner, can be a mode through which life may be improved or extended.

Message 23: "A life with much strength and peace" (*Chaim B'rav Oz V'Shalom*), from the prayer for the well-being of Israeli soldiers. This is a clear message that embracing science and Torah may lead to a life of strength and peace, the ultimate goal of battle.

AN ANTIDOTE TO DEPRESSION

The following four messages appear to refer to either a benefit of embracing science and the Bible or a consequence for not.

Message 24: "Worry in a person's heart shall depress" (*De-ah-gah B'Lev Eesh Yash-cheh-nah*), Proverbs 12:25. This could be interpreted that science and Torah can decrease worry and alleviate depression if we accept them, but if we shun either one, worry and depression may result.

Message 25: "Those that are on the way down" (*Ha-holchim La-redet*), Isaiah 30:2. This message has a similar meaning as the previous one, that without both science and Torah we may become depressed.

Message 26: "Humans shall be brought low" (*Yish-pahl Eesh*), Isaiah 2:9. While in its original context, the bringing "low" of humans was God's assessment of what idolatry did to the Hebrews—both literally, as they bowed before idols that they themselves had made, and figuratively, sinking to a new level of betrayal—it can also be read as a description of anxiety and depression. However, it seems that the embrace of science and the Bible will serve to elevate us.

Message 27: "For you shall elevate" (*Key Tisa*), literal translation of Exodus 30:12. The verse states: "You shall elevate the head." This suggests that, literally, science and Torah may raise our mental health.

THE FINAL THREE WORDS IN THE TORAH

Message 28: "Eyes of all Israel" (*Ay-nay Kal Yisrael*), Deuteronomy 34:12. This refers to all of the great miracles and events that Moses performed before the "eyes of all Israel." Looking at this last phrase mathematically may reveal that the Bible, which began with the creation of the world and established the Sabbath to commemorate creation, ends with the hidden message of "science and Torah" the tools to help sustain us. The phrase "Eyes of all Israel" may also refer to Israel's leading the world in both Torah and science. Certainly Israel has been responsible for introducing Torah to the world, and, in regard to science, the contributions from Jews residing both in and out of Israel have been remarkable. Pick any scientific field—medicine, physics, economics, even chess—and you find many examples.

TWO METAPHORS FOR SCIENCE AND TORAH

Message 29: "The fountainhead" (*Beit Ha-sho-ay-vah*), Tractate of Sabbath 21:a. The fountainhead is the origin or principle source of a body of water—a metaphor for science and the Bible. This suggests that every field of human interest contains contributions from either science or Bible or both.

Message 30: "The sun will not harm you" (*Ha-shemesh Lo Ya-kehkah*), Psalm 121:6. The sun here is a metaphor for the brilliance and warmth of science and Torah.

MESSAGES OF WARNING:
IF SCIENCE OR TORAH IS DISCARDED

There are, of course, people who are either strongly anti-Bible or anti-science. The following messages seem to be directed at those who reject one or even both of these tools.

Message 31: "Such shall not be seen again" (*Ha-zote Lo Ar-eh Ode*), Deuteronomy 18:16. This suggests that if we squander the wisdom of science and Torah that God has given to us, it will not be found anywhere else.

Message 32: "There is no wisdom no understanding nothing" (*Ain Chach-mah V'ain Tevunah V'ain*), Proverbs 21:30. This tells us that without both science and Torah there is nothing of value.

Message 33: "Nonsense" (*Shtu-yote*), Rashi on *Eruvin* 53:b. This warns us that if we ignore either science or Torah, then all we are left with is nonsense.

Message 34: "Decorations" (*M'oo-tah-rote*), Mishna *Avodah Zarah* Chapter 1:4. This tells us that, if we fail to embrace both science and Torah, our lives will be filled with only superficial and frivolous decorations.

A WARNING TO
BOTH RELIGIOUS AND ANTI-RELIGIOUS FANATICS

Message 35: "Without the crazies" (*Cha-sar M'shoo-ga-im*), 1 Samuel 21:16. This message seems to refer both to the extreme religious fanatics who are against science and to the crazed anti-religious fanatics who are against the Bible. It is as if God were saying: "It is not about being a fanatic for either science or Bible but about embracing the two together."

Message 36: "You shall sin through error [or ignorance]" (*Teh-che-tah Bish-gah-gah*), Leviticus 4:2. This suggests that by learning from both science and Torah, we can obtain the tools to keep from making serious mistakes and help prevent us from sinning.

Message 37: "Shall not know how to speak" (*Lo Yadah-tee Dah-bare*), Jeremiah 1:6. This tells us that literacy in and the embrace of both science and Torah enable intelligent speech: without knowledge of both, it is as if we cannot speak at all.

Message 38: "Pork and abominable creatures" (*Ha-chazeer V'ha-she-ketz*), Isaiah 66:17. In this section of Isaiah, God warns those who worship false idols that it is as if they are eating forbidden foods. (The practice of idolatry is not just about the literal worship of idols; it also includes the metaphoric worshipping of honor, wealth, and fame.) Thus, this message suggests that if we do not embrace both Torah and science, it is as if we are idolaters.

However, if the religious and the non-religious accept the value of both science and the Bible, then the following message applies.

Message 39: "This thing is kosher," or, as commonly translated, "The proposal seems proper" (*Kosher Ha-davar*), Esther 8:5. In the Book of Esther, there is no mention of God's Name, but the commentators say that every time the text uses the phrase "the King" it can be understood to refer to God. This verse states: "If it pleases the King, and I have found favor before Him, and this is kosher before the King." In the context of science and the Bible, this suggests that God finds it pleasing and kosher when we embrace both science and the Bible.

SCIENCE ALONE IS NOT THE ANSWER

Message 40: "Atomic bomb" (*P'tzah-tzah Ah-toe-mitt*), from *The Complete Hebrew English Dictionary,* by Reuben Alcalay. In terms of military history, the atomic bomb is the ultimate symbol of scientific achievement and effectiveness, but it also is an example of pure science and no Torah. This may imply that our choice as humans is to either embrace Torah and science together or to discard one or both of them and face the consequences, a world filled with nuclear destruction.

Message 41: "The horse is vanity" (*Sheker Ha-soos*), Psalm 33:17. The horse is a biblical symbol of arrogance and power. This suggests that the extremists on both sides of science and the Bible are arrogant and power seeking.

BIBLICAL MIRACLES WHERE SCIENCE AND TORAH COMBINE

Message 42: "And you shall bow down to" (*V'hish-tachavoo*), Exodus 11:8. In this verse, Moses warns Pharaoh that Egypt will be brought to its knees because God is about to deliver the final plague upon it. This implies that the final plague was a combination of science and the divine power of Torah.

Message 43: "Like the very day the sea was split" (*K'ha-yome Hazeh Vih-ha-yom Bah-katah*), Nehemiah 9:10,11. This refers to the biblical miracle of the Splitting of the Reed Sea, as described in the Book of Exodus. Several years ago, the History channel aired a documentary called *The Exodus Decoded,* by Simcha Jacobovici and James Cameron. The film showed the possible sequence of natural scientific events that could explain the Ten Plagues and the Splitting of the Sea. The film did not invalidate the biblical miracles but instead revealed the science behind the miraculous timing of the events. The power of science and Torah were never better on display to the world than on that day.

Message 44: "And the ten at the Sea" (*V'eser Al Ha-yam*), Ethics of the Fathers 5:5. This verse states: "Ten miracles were performed for our ancestors in Egypt, and ten at the Sea." "And the Ten at the Sea" refers not to the Ten Plagues, but to the additional miracles at the sea, the most famous of which was the "Splitting of the Sea." Therefore, this verse seems to definitively distinguish the miracles at the sea as a combination of science and the divine power of the Torah.

Message 45: "The Jordan River shall be turned around" (*Ha-Yarden Tee-sov*), Psalm 114:5. This refers to another divine miracle in the Bible, described in Chapter 3 of the Book of Joshua, and appears to be yet another instance of science and Torah working together.

Chapter Eleven

The Environment

Heal It or Ignore It?

SKY + EARTH = 681

Everyone has an opinion regarding the condition of the environment. Some say that all environmental change is natural, and therefore nothing needs to be done, while many others claim that environmental and climate changes are due to our carelessness, and demand that we take decisive action. Still others are undecided and call for "more studies."

By applying my gematrial techniques to this issue, we reveal clear messages regarding the environment and uncover answers to major questions, including: How important is it to take care of the environment? Are we required to clean it up? What are the consequences for ignoring our environmental challenges?

This chapter presents us with a choice: fulfill our responsibilities in an ethical way or ignore our obligations to the physical world. This chapter provides mathematically generated messages of wisdom about the appropriate actions to be taken and attitude to have toward the environment, and discloses warnings for failing to show basic courtesy and respect for it.

Scientists agree that almost all of our environmental problems result from human behavior. For example, it is clearly incorrect to blame God for our air and water pollution. However, through the use of Gematria, we can view our environmental problems through a different lens and interpret these issues as divine retribution for our disregard.

The information disclosed here is based on a gematrial analysis of the first sentence of the Bible. Genesis 1:1 states: "In the beginning God created the Heavens and the Earth." The Hebrew word for "heaven" can also be interpreted as "sky" (*Sha-ma-im*) and has a numerical value of 390. The numerical value of the Hebrew word for "earth" (*Eretz*) is 291. When 291 is added to 390 the sum is 681. The equation is: "Earth" (291) + "Sky" (390) = 681.

After extensive research, I have found that every known Hebrew word or phrase with the numerical value of 681 can be interpreted as referring in some way to the environment. This holds true whether the origin of the Hebrew text is the Bible, the prayers, or modern Hebrew dictionaries. There-fore, the number 681 represents and symbolizes the environment and its care.

Because the range of values of the Hebrew letters goes only from 1 to 400, there are two ways to represent the number 681 with Hebrew letters. Both of the following sets of letters will be analyzed.

A. (תרפא) 400 + 200 + 80 + 1 = 681

B. (ששפא) 300 + 300 + 80 + 1 = 681

The first set of four Hebrew letters that correspond exactly with 681 is תרפא. These letters can be used to spell five words, listed here as the first five messages. The second set of specific letters that correspond to 681 can be used to spell the sixth and seventh messages. All other messages in this chapter also have 681 Gematrias but consist of a variety of different letters.

DIRECTLY EMBEDDED MESSAGES WITHIN "SKY [AND] EARTH"

Message 1: "You shall heal" (*T'ra-peh* or *Tay-rah-pay*), Jeremiah 51:8. In addition to providing a clear numerical connection between the environment and the term for "You shall heal," this may also imply that by healing the environment we may heal ourselves.

Message 2: "Healing of" (*R'foo-ot*), *The Complete Hebrew English Dictionary*, by Reuben Alcalay. This term is used in many prayers, including a prayer for the healing of our bodies and souls. This may be interpreted as a suggestion that we make healing the environment an imperative.

Message 3: "You shall beautify," "You shall glorify," or "You shall praise" (*T'pha-air*), *The Complete Hebrew English Dictionary*, by Reuben Alcalay. Instead of approaching the environment with a sense of entitlement, where we pollute in the name of profits and expedience and systematically destroy ourselves and other species, we should extol and respect it.

Message 4: "Grey" or "gloomy" (*Ah-pho-rote*), an alternative spelling from *The Complete Hebrew English Dictionary*, by Reuben Alcalay. This is both a literal and metaphorical warning of what will occur if we do not heal the sky.

Message 5: "Savagery" or "barbarism" (*Pir-oot*), an alternative spelling from *The Complete Hebrew English Dictionary*, by Reuben Alcalay. This accurately describes the way we viciously consume the resources of the earth and treat the sea, sky, and land.

The second set of four letters that corresponds exactly with 681 (שׁשׁפא) spells two words that form the next two messages.

Message 6: "That breathes" or "That inhales" (*Sheh-sha-af*), from the *Milog Hebrew Hebrew Online Dictionary*. Breathing is essential to life, but we too often do not seem to care about the air quality. Even those of us with children seem indifferent.

Message 7: "That a magician" (*Sheh-a-shaf*), from the *Milog Hebrew Hebrew Online Dictionary*. In regard to the loss of species due to pollution and global climate change, and to the dreadful quality of our water and air, it is as if God is saying, "Only a magician need not be concerned." This may be interpreted as divine sarcasm.

ENDING THE DEBATE ON WHETHER THE ENVIRONMENT SHOULD CONCERN US?

Message 8: "The task that" or "That this task is" (*In-yan Asher*), Ecclesiastes 3:10. This verse states: "The task that God has given to humanity to be concerned with." In addition, Verse 3:13 reminds us why we should be concerned when it states: "Indeed, every person who eats, and drinks, and sees the good in all their labor—it is a gift from God." This encourages us to appreciate the planet for providing us with divine gifts, and implies that we should treat the earth accordingly.

Today, many ask: What kind of a world are we leaving for our children? Everyone is aware that the quality of the air and water on earth has declined dramatically. There are multiple reports on the skyrocketing rates of cancer, autism, and asthma in children. And yet, very little is being done to reverse this trend. If we truly love our children, if not ourselves, the following messages should serve to awaken us to the need for real action regarding the environment.

Message 9: "Your child shall ask you tomorrow" (*Yish-al-cha Bincha Machar*), Exodus 13:14. This is a literal reminder that we will be held accountable to our children. In the context of the Book of Exodus, this phrase is part of the biblical injunction to celebrate the festival of Passover, commemorating and recounting the Exodus from Egypt. There is no world event of greater import than the Exodus, because it led to the Children of Israel receiving the Bible, and subsequently to their sharing it with the world. The phrase "Your child shall ask you tomorrow" connects the importance of Passover with the importance of healing the environment by encouraging us to teach our children about both, and implies that as essential as the Bible is for our spiritual existence, so too is the care of our environment critical for our physical life.

MESSAGES OF WARNING

Message 10: "It is a time of vengeance" (*Et Nkamah He*), Jeremiah 51:6. The verse states: "For it is a time of vengeance of God He is paying her due." Because most of our environmental problems are a consequence of human actions, ultimately these problems can be interpreted as a result of God's anger at our negligence.

Message 11: "And you disregard the work of God" (*V'et Poe-al A-donai Low Ya-be-too*), Isaiah 5:12. The earth and sky are, literally, God's first recorded works. The message here is that, if we disregard them, it is an especially arrogant and wicked thing.

Message 12: "Difficult and evil" (*Kaw-sheh V'rah*), from 1 Samuel 25:3. In regard to the topic of how we treat the earth, "difficult and evil" describes the behavior of many of us.

Message 13: "And I shall destroy" (*V'harasti*), Ezekiel 13:14. The Book of Ezekiel recounts God's anger at the people of Israel for forsaking Him and His commandments. Ezekiel warns that destruction will be the consequence. The previous verse, Ezekiel 13:13, states: "Therefore, thus said God the Lord, I will cause a stormy wind to break out in My wrath, and there will be pouring rain in My anger, with huge hailstones in My fury, to cause annihilation." This clearly warns of natural catastrophes if we forsake God, and implies that neglecting the environment is equivalent to turning away from God. Furthermore, this seems to indicate that forsaking the environment will, in turn, cause the environment to forsake us.

Message 14: "Sackcloth [and] ashes" (*Sok Ay-fair*), Esther 4:1. Sackcloth and ashes are biblical signs of mourning and repentance, invoked as preemptive measures to admit wrongs and avert serious punishment. This suggests that we too need to admit our sins regarding the environment and, metaphorically, don sackcloth and ashes.

Message 15: "Nations have heard your shame" (*Shah-moo Goyim Kilonech*), Jeremiah 46:12. This reminds us that healing the planet is our responsibility, but if we do not fulfill it, we will be shamed.

Message 16: "The outcry of Sodom" (*Za-ah-kot Sodom*), Genesis 18:20. According to the Bible, the city of Sodom was destroyed because of its wickedness and corruption. *The Stone Edition* of the Bible quotes Ibn Ezra (1089–1164), a commentator on the Bible, as claiming that the outcry was "caused by the violence against the innocent." Here, metaphorically, the innocent party is the environment.

Message 17: "The bad" or "The evil" (*Hara-ote*), Deuteronomy 31:17. In this section of the Book of Deuteronomy, God expresses His anger at those who stray after other gods. Metaphorically, this tells us that the worship of profits and expediency, a form of idolatry, leads us to disregard the environment.

Message 18: "The land will be desolate" (*Ha-ah-retz Sh'mama*), Exodus 23:29. This is a divine warning of what will happen if we do not change our ways.

Message 19: "That I'm a fool" or "That I'm stupid" (*Sheh-ani Shoteh*), Talmud Yoma, page 84a, words are not consecutive. Out of context, this phrase clearly describes most of mankind because we, as a species, have not made healing the environment a priority.

Message 20: "Still continue to be arrogant" (*Tosifi L'gav-ah Ode*), Zephaniah 3:11. This chapter in Zephaniah begins: "Woe to the filthy and polluted one." This reminds us we have spewed filth and pollution into the environment, arrogantly behaving as if we can do exactly what we please without there being any negative consequences.

Message 21: "And the day will come when you shall cry out" (*Ooz-ock-tem Ba-yom*), Book 1 of Samuel 8:18. This is a consequence of what lies ahead if we do not mend our stewardship of the earth. The verse continues with a warning: "God will not answer on that day."

Message 22: "Only evil all the time" (*Rock Rah Kol Ha-yom*), Genesis 6:5. The full verse of Genesis 6:5 summarizes human history. It states: "And God saw that the wickedness of man was great upon the earth, and that every plan devised by his mind was only evil all the time." Genesis verses 6:6–7 provide an introduction to the story of Noah and the flood, the first and worst natural disaster in human history. They state: "And God regretted that He had made humans on earth, and His heart was saddened. God said: 'I shall blot out from the earth the humans I have created; humans along with beasts, creeping things, and birds of the sky; for I regret that I made them." It is interesting that these verses from Genesis also accurately describe the global loss of species today.

Message 23: "And deceit shall be" (*Oo-rih-me-yah Tih-he-yeh*), Proverbs 12:24. Chapter 12 of the Proverbs discusses the distinctions between wisdom and foolishness. The hidden wisdom in the phrase "And deceit shall be" may refer to both the deceit associated with polluting the environment and the deceit associated with false gestures to clean it up. The next word in this verse from Proverbs 12:24 is "melt." It is well known that the deceit in our treatment of the earth and sky has lead to the melting of our glaciers, ice caps, and permafrost. (Note: The Gematria of the Hebrew term for "And deceit" (*Oo-rih-me-yah*) is 261. It is interesting that 261 generates three specific and unique Hebrew letters that can be used to form two key words: "forbidden" (*Aw-soor*) and "poison" (*Eress*). Does this not precisely describe our deceitful treatment of the environment? In addition, the term "The commandments" (*Hadevarim*), from Exodus 34:28, also has a Gematria of 261. This is a reminder that we can choose to follow either the commandments or a path of deceit, but not both.)

Message 24: "Malignant" (*Mom-eret*) from *The Complete Hebrew English Dictionary*, by Reuben Alcalay. As we continue to pollute our earth and sky, "malignant" describes ever more aspects of our behavior and the consequences.

Message 25: Anti-Torah (*Ante Torah*), a phrase generated by taking the Hebrew word for "anti" (a 70 numerical value) and adding it to Torah (611), because 70 + 611 = 681. The message here seems clear, that those who claim to be religious should take note: If you ignore environmental problems, you are absolutely against the teachings of the Bible.

Message 26: "Temporary" or "haphazard" (*Ah-rah-eet*), from *The Complete Hebrew English Dictionary*, by Reuben Alcalay. This warns us that most actions taken to help the environment provide only a temporary fix. This is because more decisive and permanent action would be more expensive and difficult. Therefore, we merely pretend to address the problem.

Message 27: "Pretend" (*Mit-a-mere*), from *The Complete Hebrew English Dictionary*, by Reuben Alcalay. Sadly, most any action we take, or legislation we pass, to help the environment only pretends to address the problem.

Message 28: "The rats themselves shall be prey" (*Ha-ach-barim Hame Tereph*), from *The Complete Hebrew English Dictionary*, by Reuben Alcalay. This metaphor refers to us, the human beings, as rats! This is because "rat" as a slang term refers to a liar, an evildoer, or a contemptible person. In addition, "rat" refers to a consuming, filthy, and aggressive animal. This message implies that we humans, who have preyed upon and polluted so much of the planet, now find ourselves falling prey to the toxicity and climate changes that we ourselves caused.

Message 29: "In the sea none remain of them" (*Bayam Lo Nishar Bahem*), Exodus 14:28. Out of context of the Book of Exodus, we can interpret this message as referring to the dramatic collapse of most species of fish and marine life due to pollution and overfishing. We are well on the way to manifesting this message. How prescient is the Bible?

Note: In the above phrase, if we substitute the Hebrew word for "land" (*Adamah*) for the word for "sea" (*Yam*), the numerical value of the resulting phrase remains 681. This is because the Hebrew words for "land" and "sea" have the same numerical value. Therefore the phrase "On [land] none remain of them" (*Ba-adamah Lo Nishar Bahem*) also has a numerical value of 681. Because the populations of tigers, lions, most birds, bees, and other species have decreased so dramatically, this message is also quite appropriate.

Written Hebrew has no letters for vowels; the vowel sounds are indicated by dots below, above, or to the side of the letters. (The original Bible had no dots; the rabbis added them later, for clarity.) Therefore it is possible, by changing only the dots, for one word to have two or more different meanings and still retain its numerical value. There is a phrase from the Book of Genesis that has three possible meanings. Each one has a numerical value of 681 and appears to refer to the environment.

Message 30A: "People are shepherds of" (*Anashim Ro-ay*), Genesis 46:32. Out of context, this encourages people to be shepherds or stewards of the earth.

Message 30B: "People are friends of" or "People are My friends" (*Anashim Ray-ee*), Genesis 46:32. This tells us that when we are shepherds, we are God's partners and friends.

Message 30C: "People are excrement" (*Anashim R'ee*), Genesis 46:32. This tells us that when we just consume and digest the earth's bounty, we are considered like dung.

The next two messages have the identical spelling but different translations and appear to refer to the choice between being stewards of the earth or just consuming its resources.

Message 31: Steward of the earth (*So-chenet Ha-olam*); this phrase was found by translating the English phrase "Steward of the earth" into the Hebrew equivalent. It suggests that we have the choice to be caretakers of the world or to face the consequences. It is up to us.

Message 32: Endangered of the world (*Sa-ka-note Ha-olam*). This seems to refer to the endangered species of the world, which may soon include the human species.

MESSAGES OF WISDOM

How is the care of the environment connected to God and the commandments? The following messages all directly or indirectly refer to God or the commandments.

Message 33: "I rejoice" (*Sass Anochi*), Psalm 119:162. The verse states: "I rejoice at Your [God's] word." The hidden message seems to suggest a causation: that listening to the word of God and saving the environment will cause us to rejoice.

Message 34: "And I shall remove" (*V'Ha-see-ro-tee*), Exodus 23:25. The full phrase states: "And I [God] shall remove sickness from your midst." Because this phrase has a value of 681, the same value as "healing of," it suggests that worldwide healing may happen if all nations work together in repairing the environment.

DOES GOD THINK THAT
CARING FOR THE ENVIRONMENT IS IMPORTANT?

Whatever your religion, the following seven messages are reminders that the care of the environment is actually part of one's religious and spiritual practice. A repeating theme in the Bible is that the observance of a law or tradition is not considered sufficient on its own but must be accompanied with acts of kindness. The following messages reveal that the care of the environment is as much a priority as acts of kindness or even the Ten Commandments.

Message 35: "Keep the commandment" or "Observe the commandment" (*Shomer Mitzvah*), Proverbs 19:16. The full verse states: "He that keeps the commandment shall keep his soul; but he that despises [God's] ways shall die." This message makes care for the environment equivalent to a commandment that we all must keep.

Message 36: "Observes the faith" or "Keeps the faith" (*Shomer Eh-moo-nim*), Isaiah 26:2. This goes beyond the previous message, "Keep the commandment," and makes the care of the environment equivalent to observing one's faith or religion.

Message 37: "For behold the Lord God of Hosts" (*Key He-nay Ha-Adon A-donai Tz'va-ote*), Isaiah 3:1. This verse continues with a warning, that if we do not alter our ways, we will endure the "removal of all support of bread and all support of water." The message may also hint that, regardless of how we treat the environment in the future, we are on a path of beholding God. If we unite to heal the planet, we may behold a beneficent God, but if we continue our selfish ways, we may witness divine wrath.

There are some religions where individuals do not worship God but do believe that the earth itself is holy. The following message reveals that God as creator of the earth and the Bible also considers the earth holy.

Message 38: "The earth that you stand upon" (*O-made Aw-lawv Ahd-mot*), Exodus 3:5. In this section of the Book of Exodus, God introduces Himself to Moses and instructs him that he must remove his shoes because the ground upon which Moses is standing is holy. For Moses, being made aware that the earth is holy is fundamental and the first step in his relationship with God. Perhaps this message is pointing us toward a similar path: honoring the earth's holiness and treating it with respect will build our relationship with God.

Message 39: "For my eyes are always toward God" (*Ainai Tamid El A-donai Ki*), from Psalm 25:15. Again, this message connects our relationship to God with our relationship to the environment.

Message 40: "What God asks from you" or "What God demands from you" (*Mah A-donai Doe-resh Mim-cha*), Micah 6:8. The Torah and the entire Bible are filled with laws, statutes, and directives from God. How could anyone know where to start? That the message "What God asks from you" has the numerical value of 681, the same as "earth + sky," may imply that the minimum requirement of any decent person is to show respect for the environment. Otherwise we will face the consequences.

Message 41: "Person of Integrity" (*Ish Shalem*), taken from Menachot 73b (words not consecutive). This describes someone who works to heal the world.

We can summarize our environmental situation quite simply: either we will be intelligent and take appropriate actions or we will continue our indifferent and deceptive policies. The final two messages reflect this choice.

Message 42: "Surely that great nation is a wise and intelligent people" (*Rok Ahm Cha-cham V'navone Ha-goy Ha-gadol Ha-zeh*), Deuteronomy 4:6. In this section of the Book of Deuteronomy, Moses tells the Israelites that if they observe God's commandments the nations will consider them intelligent. Because the numerical value of the above phrase is equal to "Sky [and] Earth" it connects the environment with the commandments. In addition, it implies that only nations that take positive action regarding the environment are to be considered wise and discerning.

Message 43: "Shall eat well or the soul of the treacherous [shall eat] violence" (*Yochal Tov V'Nefesh Bogdim Chamas*), Proverbs 13:2. This tells us that, as a consequence of our actions concerning the environment, the world will either eat well and thrive or eat violence and destroy itself.

Chapter Twelve

The Mystery of
Quantum Theory Revealed

QUANTUM = 217

According to quantum mechanics, at any particular moment either the velocity of a subatomic particle or its location can be determined. But not both at the same time. The very act of observing the particle affects it. This is known as the Heisenberg Uncertainty Principle. Quantum mechanics also postulates that once two particles interact and are measured, they stay connected even if they are then separated by a large distance. In other words, if a force is exerted on one, the other responds accordingly. This phenomenon is known as "spooky action at a distance," and even Albert Einstein was confounded by it. Another fundamental principle of quantum theory is that light has a dual nature, behaving both as a particle and as a wave. The incredible phenomena of quantum mechanics are difficult to believe, much less understand.

Quantum effects may also provide answers to the seemingly unrelated topics of free will and divine providence. How is it possible for God to be in charge and, at the same time, for humans to have free will? The holiest name of God in Hebrew is the unpronounceable four-letter word called the tetragrammaton (*Y-H-W-H*). It is translated as: "He was, He is, and He will be." This name implies that all time and space already exist. But if that is the case, how can human beings have free will since everything would already be according to God's will? It seems impossible that the principles of free will and divine providence could coexist. Philosophers and scholars have addressed this paradox, and as of yet no satisfactory answer has been offered. This chapter will introduce what seems to be an answer to this paradox.

This chapter discloses mathematically generated messages that seem to explain and clarify why quantum effects are strange and seem beyond our comprehension. According to *Merriam-Webster's Collegiate Dictionary: Tenth Edition,* the word "quantum" can also be defined as "significant" or "large." Some messages here will refer to this definition, including a list of the secrets to a successful and satisfying life.

The Hebrew spelling of the word "quantum" (*Kvan-toom*) used here was found in *The New Dictionary English-Hebrew,* by Yisrael Lazar. Its Gematria is 217, and the three Hebrew letters that correspond exactly to 217 are: ריד. These three letters can be used to spell four Hebrew words, listed as the first four messages. All the other messages in this chapter also have 217 Gematrias but consist of a variety of different letters.

DIRECTLY EMBEDDED MESSAGES

Message 1: "My secret" or "My mystery" (*Ra-zee*), an alternative translation of Isaiah 24:16, and also found in *The Complete Hebrew English Dictionary,* by Reuben Alcalay. This suggests that quantum is specifically God's secret and mystery and, therefore, not possible for humans to understand completely.

Message 2: "Strange" or "strangers" (*Za-ree*), from *The Complete Hebrew English Dictionary,* by Reuben Alcalay. This seems to be a simple acknowledgment that the principles of quantum mechanics are strange. In addition, it may refer to the concept of "strangeness" in particle physics, or to the concept of "strange matter."

Message 3: "Laurels" or "Wreaths of flowers" *(Zay-ray),* from *The Complete Hebrew English Dictionary,* by Reuben Alcalay. Laurels and wreaths of flowers seem to be metaphors for something that is special. In addition, they may be an allusion to the shape of the atomic and subatomic pathways. Scientists have described the pathways as having a horseshoe shape, similar to that of a wreath or laurel.

Message 4: "Woe to me" or "A secret to me" (*Rah-zee*), Isaiah 24:16. Isaiah has a vision of terrible things to come. Out of context from the Book of Isaiah, this could be taken as a warning against using quantum theory as a destructive force.

MESSAGES OF WISDOM

As we have seen in the other chapters, the messages that emerge from our analysis fall into the category of either wisdom or warning. The following eight messages of wisdom seem to suggest that quantum is beyond human comprehension and can only be fully understood by God.

Message 5: "Infinite" or, literally, "There is no end to Me" (*Ain Sofee*), from *The Complete Hebrew English Dictionary,* by Reuben Alcalay. The phrase "There is no end to Me" refers to God Himself. Quantum too is infinite, but because human beings are limited, it is impossible for us to truly understand it.

Message 6: "Beyond calculation" (*Ain Nivdak*), from the *Y-ah E-li* prayer. The full phrase states: "Beyond calculation, for His [God's] intelligence there is no limit." This seems to be an appropriate description of both quantum and its creator.

Message 7: "God effects" or "God performs" (*E-l Po-ale*), from the Ahavah Rabah prayer. "God effects" is a most resonant description of quantum phenomena. Much of quantum seems explainable only by including the concept of God.

Message 8: "Place of God" (*E-L Makom*), alternative translation of Leviticus 6:4. The hidden message here is that quantum is the realm of God, and therefore, although beyond our comprehension, it gives us a glimpse of the presence of God.

Message 9: "That He [God] created" (*Dee V'rah*), from the Mourner's Kaddish prayer. The hidden message here is that God created the quantum effects.

Message 10: "My light" (*O-ree*), Psalm 27:1. This can be understood as referring to the light of God, that quantum can be considered God's light. (Note: The complete phrase states, "God is my light and my salvation." The numerical value of "My light and my salvation" is 613, the total number of commandments in the Torah. This suggests that the 613 commandments are of quantum, or great, significance.)

Message 11: "The whole world" (*Olam Maleh*), from the Talmud Sanhedrin 4:5. This may imply that the whole world is affected and controlled by quantum mechanics. These mysterious and secret quantum forces may also relate to the earlier question: How can the principles of free will and divine providence coexist in the world?

Message 12: "ABC children's book" (*Al-pho-nim*), from *The Complete Hebrew English Dictionary,* by Reuben Alcalay. This appears to be a divine comment regarding quantum: that although it is mysterious and impossible for humans to fully understand, to God it is like child's play.

When will we understand quantum phenomena? The following message seems to reveal the answer.

Message 13: "In the life of the world to come" (*L'chayay Ha-olam Habah*), from the *U'va L'Tzion* prayer. When confronted with questions that seem unresolvable in this world, we often choose to believe that answers will be revealed in the world to come. This implies that, after we die, we will more fully understand quantum and other secrets of God.

Inherent to quantum theory is the dual nature of light. What follows seems to suggest that light has another dual nature: it possesses both physical and spiritual components.

Message 14: "And Saw" (*Va-yarr*), Genesis 1:4. The full verse states: "And God saw the light, that it was good, and God separated between the light and the darkness." This verse contains two different phrases that have the numerical value of 613, the total number of commandments in the Old Testament. The commandments are the spiritual core of the Torah. This suggests that when God creates light in Genesis 1:3–4, it is both the physical light described by quantum theory and the spiritual light of the 613 commandments.

The full sentence from Genesis 1:4 contains two hidden references to the 613 commandments: "The light" (*Et Ha-ore*), from Genesis 1:4, has a numerical value of 613. This reveals the hidden wisdom of this verse, which can now be read: "And God saw the light of the 613 commandments, and that it was good."

The second phrase with a numerical value of 613 from Genesis 1:4 is: "Between the light and the darkness" (*Ha-ore Oo-ben Ha- cho-shech*). The hidden message here is that God tells us that "between the light and the darkness" are the 613 commandments. The 613 commandments are the bridge between the darkness and the light.

When we look at a more contemporary source, *The Complete Hebrew English Dictionary,* by Reuben Alcalay, we find that the Hebrew word for "lights" (*O-rote*) also has a 613 Gematria.

The following three messages refer to other characteristics of quantum theory.

Message 15: "Irregular" (*Cho-reg*), from *The Complete Hebrew English Dictionary,* by Reuben Alcalay. This acknowledges that quantum theory is irregular and strange.

Message 16: "Unexpected" (*Lo Tzah-foo-ee*), from *The Complete Hebrew English Dictionary,* by Reuben Alcalay. This acknowledges that quantum theory is unexpected.

Message 17: "Worthy" (*Ra-oo-ee*), from *The Complete Hebrew English Dictionary,* by Reuben Alcalay. This instructs that, even with all their strangeness, quantum phenomena and theories are worthy of study and thought.

The next two messages seem to be common terms used in association with atoms or atomic reactors.

Message 18: "To split" or "To break" (*L'hav-kee-ah*), 2 Kings 3:26. Split is a key word in the quantum sciences, as in "to split the atom" and "the split nature of light."

Message 19: "Rod" (*Chotare*), Proverbs 14:3. Out of the context of the Book of Proverbs, fuel rods are used in nuclear reactors.

The word "quantum" can also used to describe something of great significance. The following four messages disclose four major principles of life, all with Gematrias of 217. These principles, if honored and followed, seem to guarantee a satisfying and successful life. In addition, these doctrines form the core of the Old Testament.

Message 20: "And appeared" (*Va-Yay-ra*), Genesis 17:1. This verse introduces the concept of monotheism to the world when God appears to Abraham. Monotheism is the core of the entire Bible and is of such importance that both the first and second of the Ten Commandments relate to the belief in one God. However, monotheism also has a metaphoric component. Today, while not many people actually practice idolatry, most of us do worship other gods, such as the gods of wealth, fame, and power.

Message 21: "And the commandment" (*V'ha-dee-bare*), alternative reading and translation of Deuteronomy 1:17. This tells us that each of the 613 commandments in the Bible has quantum importance. The honoring and observance of them may be the secret to our spiritual and physical satisfaction.

Message 22: "And love the stranger" (*V'o-hayv Gare*), Deuteronomy 10:18. Of the 613 commandments in the Old Testament, to love the stranger, or to not mistreat the stranger, is mentioned more times than any other. The repetition reveals that it has quantum significance, and the results of observing this law cannot be calculated. Imagine: what would the world look like if we all followed this command?

Message 23: "Feared" or "revered" (*Yor-oo*), Exodus 1:21. This section of the Book of Exodus describes the Jewish midwives who "feared God" and resisted the command of Pharaoh to kill all the Jewish male children in ancient Egypt. This led to the birth of Moses, the Exodus from Egypt, and the receiving of the Ten Commandments and the Torah. Eventually, Israel shared the Bible with the entire world. As the verse explains: "It was because the midwives feared God" that they ignored Pharaoh and thus altered both Jewish and world history. From this we learn that fearing God is of quantum importance.

Message 24: "The Zohar" (*Ha-Zohar*), an alternative reading and translation of Ecclesiastes 12:12, and from the Book of the Zohar (transcribed in either the 13th century C.E. or, possibly, as early as the 2nd century C.E.). The Zohar, the most important work of the *Kabbalah,* contains mystical interpretations of the Old Testament. It also discusses the origin and structure of the universe. This appears to teach us that the Zohar has quantum significance.

MESSAGES OF WARNING

Following are eight messages of warning associated with quantum. Read them with a contemporary lens, as each one seems, either literally or metaphorically, to caution against the misuse of quantum for the purpose of conflict.

Message 25: "Great fear," "worry," or "alarm" (*Charah-dah*), Genesis 27:33. Although this is a different word for fear than the earlier "feared," it has the identical numerical value of 217. This may tell us that quantum misused can cause great fear.

Message 26: "With trembling" (*B'rahg-zah*), Ezekiel 12:18. This suggests that the power of quantum can cause us, or the earth, to tremble.

Message 27: "Trouble" or "burden" (*Toh-rach*), Isaiah 1:14. This tells us that, if the power of quantum is used for conflict, it could cause trouble.

Message 28: "Regret" (*Charat*), from *The Complete Hebrew English Dictionary,* by Reuben Alcalay. This warns us that we could come to regret quantum science.

Message 29: "Cursed" (*Yoo-are*), Numbers 22:6. Out of context, this suggests that, if we misuse quantum science, we may be cursed.

Message 30: "Dried up" (*V'ach-riv*), 2 Kings 19:24. This verse warns of a river becoming dried up, possibly suggesting that a consequence of quantum science could be water sources disappearing.

Message 31: "And the plague" (*V'ha-deh-vair*), an alternative reading and translation of Deuteronomy 1:17. Again, this may refer to the consequences of using quantum science inappropriately, that we may be visited metaphorically by a plague.

Message 32: "Fight" (*Re-vah*), Psalm 35:1. Out of context, this may refer to the verbal arguments over quantum theory between Albert Einstein on one side and Neils Bohr and Werner Heisenberg on the other.

The next message and its surrounding text in the Bible are very revealing. The biblical text summarizes the messages of warning and lists principles of quantum importance. This section of the Bible also seems to suggest the ideal way to exercise free will.

Message 33: "Be warned" (*He-za-hare*), Ecclesiastes 12:12. Ecclesiastes 12:13 states: "The sum of the matter, when all has been considered: Fear God and keep His commandments, for that is a person's entire purpose." This is consistent with the earlier messages about the quantum importance of fearing God and obeying the commandments.

Ecclesiastes 12:14 also seems to refer to human beings' having free will to do good or evil. It states: "For God will judge every deed, even everything hidden, whether good or evil." Thus, these verses reveal that the purpose of life is to give us free will so God may see whether we use it to do good or evil. A divine test, so to speak.

To summarize this chapter, it could be said that quantum is a combination of science and some kind of God power. Writing this in the form of an equation would look like this: Quantum = Science + God Power. When this equation is translated into Hebrew, we can then convert the words into numbers by calculating their numerical values.

The word for "science" (*Ma-dah*), from *The Complete Hebrew English Dictionary,* by Reuben Alcalay, has a numerical value of 114. The phrase "God Power" (*A-donai Oz*) is found in Psalm 29:11 and it has a numerical value of 103. Now we check the math of the equation: Quantum (217) = Science (114) + God Power (103). The numerical values confirm the equation because: 217 = 114 + 103.

Message 34: "Science" + "God Power" (*Ma-dah + A-donai Oz*), "Science" is from *The Complete Hebrew English Dictionary,* by Reuben Alcalay, and "God Power" is from Psalm 29:11. That the numerical values of the Hebrew terms "Science" and "God power" add up to 217, the same as the value of "quantum," appears to confirm that quantum is part science and part divine—a perfect summary to this chapter.

FINAL NOTE ABOUT QUANTUM

Albert Einstein's theories led directly to the development of quantum theory. In Hebrew, the name Albert Einstein has a numerical value of 692. Here are some other phrases that have a numerical value of 692. Each one seems to refer to Einstein's achievements.

1. "By Your light we shall see the light" (*B'orcha Nir-eh Ohr*), Psalm 36:9.

2. "Bring forth a new thing" (*Oseh Chada-sha*), Isaiah 43:19.

3. "Heard the sayings of God" (*Sho-may-a Imray E-L*), Numbers 24:4.

4. The era of quantum or The time of quantum (*Hah-Ate Quantum or Ate Ha-Quantum*), this phrase was generated by adding the Hebrew word for "quantum" (numerical value 217) as one of the words, and then adding the Hebrew word for "the era of" (numerical value 475). This yields the phrase "The era of quantum," which has a total numerical value of 692, because 217 + 475 = 692, the same value as the name Albert Einstein when written with Hebrew letters. The phrase "The era of" was chosen because it consists of the letters that correspond exactly with 475.

Chapter Thirteen

Did the Biblical Miracle of the "Parting of the Sea" Actually Occur?

EXODUS FROM EGYPT = 891

The Exodus of the Jewish people from Egypt is the central event of the entire Bible. The second book of the Five Books of Moses, the Book of Exodus, recounts a story filled with incredible divine miracles, plagues, and drama. The Exodus occurred 3,250 years ago and is invoked annually in the Passover Haggadah, referred to throughout Jewish holy texts, and mentioned in many of the daily prayers. The story has inspired both Hollywood and famous artists including Leonardo da Vinci.

But did the Red Sea (biblically "Reed Sea") actually split to allow the Jewish people to escape from Pharaoh? What was the real purpose of the Exodus? Were the Ten Plagues the result of a vengeful God or the just consequences of Pharaoh's actions? The messages disclosed in this chapter appear to reveal answers to these questions and others.

Before analyzing the numerical value of the phrase "Exodus from Egypt," let us first look at the question: Did the miracle of the "Parting of the Sea" actually occur?

A DIVINE MESSAGE TO THE ARAB REPUBLIC OF EGYPT AND THE KINGDOM OF SAUDI ARABIA?

What follows appears to be an archeological suggestion or insight, possibly from God, directed to Egypt and Saudi Arabia. A phrase from the Bible mathematically generates a message that could prove whether or not the biblical account of the Exodus from Egypt was true, including the miracle of the "Parting of the Sea."

Exodus Chapter 15 (verses 4–5 examined here) recounts the miracle of the "Parting of the Sea" and how the Israelites crossed but Pharaoh's army drowned. The verses state: "Pharaoh's chariots and army He [God] threw in the sea. Deep waters covered them, they descended in the depths like stone." The numerical value of the Hebrew phrase "They descended in the depths" (*Yardoo Bim-tzo-lote*) is 788. The four specific and unique Hebrew letters that correspond exactly to 788 (תשפח) spell the word for "You shall search" (*T'cha-pace*). This can be interpreted as a divine suggestion to those who inhabit the area around the Red Sea, Egypt, and Saudi Arabia: Search for the remains of Pharaoh's chariots and army.

Even after 3,250 years of being under water, the helmets, swords, and metal of the chariots should be intact. With the recent news of a submersible going seven miles deep, and the use of high-tech sonar, it may be possible to actually find the evidence. If Egypt and Saudi Arabia succeed in uncovering proof of the most famous miracle in the Old Testament, most everyone would be interested in witnessing the find.

POSSIBLE PROOF THAT THE EXODUS WAS A MONUMENTAL EVENT

According to the biblical account, the Exodus consisted of a series of incredible, awesome, and miraculous events. While many believe the biblical version in an act of faith, some wish for tangible or scientific proof. And that is where the "Merneptah Stele" comes in, a seeming eyewitness account.

In general, it appears that when a Pharaoh was still alive, he would prepare his tomb and stele (like an inscribed gravestone with hieroglyphics), often embellishing and exaggerating his accomplishments. The Merneptah Stele, the 3,200-year-old stone monument found at the entrance of King Merneptah's pyramid tomb and today residing in the Egyptian Museum in Cairo, is no exception. The inscription on Merneptah's stele describes great victories over the superpowers of his day: among the triumphs listed is a victory over Israel. Inscribed on the stele is the phrase: "The seed of Israel is laid waste." The stele was written in approximately 1,200 B.C.E., about 50 years after the Exodus occurred. At that time, Israel was an insignificant nomadic nation. Why would a Pharaoh include Israel among the superpowers? We may infer from this inscription that Israel must have had great renown, probably from its earlier amazing victory over Pharaoh, as described in the Book of Exodus, and thus deserving of inclusion with the other powerful countries.

AN ANALYSIS OF 891:
THE NUMERICAL VALUE OF "EXODUS FROM EGYPT"

The Hebrew phrase for "Exodus from Egypt" (*Yitziat Mitz-raim*) has a Gematria of 891. After studying all known Hebrew texts with this numerical value, every word or phrase was found to refer to an aspect of the Exodus. The four letters that correspond exactly to 891 (תתצא) can be arranged to spell the Hebrew word that is listed as the first message. All other messages in this chapter also have Gematrias of 891 but consist of a variety of different letters.

MESSAGE DIRECTLY EMBEDDED
WITHIN THE PHRASE "EXODUS FROM EGYPT"

Message 1: "Consequence of" or "Consequences" (*Toe-tzah-ot* or *Toe-tzah-ote*), taken from Joshua 18:12. This suggests that the Ten Plagues, and the other punishments that Egypt suffered during the Exodus, can be explained as divine consequences for Pharaoh's actions against the Hebrews, including enslaving the Children of Israel, killing their male newborn children, and refusing to let the Israelites go. In addition, the consequences of the Exodus itself had a profound effect on shaping the history of the world, including the Ten Commandments, the Bible, monotheism, Judaism, Jesus, and Christianity.

MESSAGES OF WISDOM

Many have questioned whether all the miracles, signs, and wonders of the Exodus from Egypt actually occurred. The following message seems to reveal the answer.

Message 2: "And all these My hands made" (*Kal Ay-leh Yadai Astah Va*), Isaiah 66:2. As the full phrase says: "And all these My hands made, and all these have come into being, says the Lord."

This seems to teach us that all the events of the Exodus were performed by the hand of God.

The following three messages refer to the four major characters of the Exodus: Moses, Miriam, Aaron, and Pharaoh.

Message 3: "Moses" + "Miriam" + "Aaron" (*Moshe + Miryam + Aharon*), from the Book of Exodus. Moses, his sister, and his brother were the three leaders of the Israelites during and after the Exodus from Egypt, and the sum of their individual numerical values is 891, the same as "Exodus from Egypt."

Message 4: "These three" (*Ti-lah-tay-hone*), Daniel 3:23. In the context of the Book of Daniel, the phrase "These three" refers to three divinely protected people. So, too, in the Book of Exodus, Moses, Miriam, and Aaron were three divinely protected people.

Message 5: "And he would not let the people go" (*V'-lo She-lach Et Ha-ahm*), Exodus 9:7. This refers to Pharaoh's refusal to free the Israelites from slavery, a decision that led to the Ten Plagues, which eventually forced Pharaoh to relent.

THE JEWISH PEOPLE AGREE TO BE GOD'S PARTNERS

Message 6: "We shall do and then we shall understand" (*Na-aseh V'-nish-ma*), from Exodus 24:7. After the Exodus from Egypt, Israel agreed to follow the commandments and then later to understand them. The commentary from *The Stone Edition* of the Bible states: "This declaration has remained for all time the anthem of Israel's faith in God and devotion to His word." According to the Bible, the consequence to this declaration was a promise of eternal divine protection, which may explain why out of all the ancient cultures and civilizations, virtually only the Jewish culture has survived with its traditions intact.

PHARAOH'S CRIMES AND PUNISHMENTS

Message 7: "For the judgments against Egypt" or "For the crimes within Egypt" (*L'mishpatim B'Mitzraim*), from the High Holy Day service. God punished Egypt with the Ten Plagues because of Pharaoh's crimes. The Talmud teaches that God's punishment fits the crime.

Message 8: "And the judgments," (*V'et Ha-mishpatim*), Deuteronomy 7:11. It is worth noting that although this phrase has a similar meaning and the same numerical value as Message 7, it consists of different words.

Message 9: "The human being shall be judged" (*Ben Adahm Ha-tish-pote*), Ezekiel 22:2. Out of context, Pharaoh the King of Egypt considered himself a God, but this message points out that he was only a human being, and that only God is God. To make this point crystal clear, this message refers to Pharaoh as "the human being."

Message 10: "A man for the judgment is God's" (*Eesh Key Hamishpat L'Elokim*), Deuteronomy 1:17. Out of context, this message can be interpreted that Pharaoh is being referred to as "a man." This is similar to the previous message, which refers to Pharaoh as a "human being." When Pharaoh enslaved the Israelites and decided to drown all the Jewish male infants, he acted like a god, but the final plague, the "slaying of the first born," reminds us that judgment is God's realm alone.

Message 11: "And His [God's] hand came upon him there" (*Va-t'hee Ah-lav Shahm Yad)*, Ezekiel 1:3. With a hero or an enemy of the Jewish people, God's hand will come upon them in the appropriate way: God's hand came upon Pharaoh in rebuke and upon Moses with miracles and blessings.

Message 12: "The evil of the decree" (*Et Ro-ah Ha-gezay-ra h*), from the *Unisaneh Tokef* prayer, recited during the High Holy Day service. This prayer states: "But repentance, prayer, and charity remove the evil of the decree." Because Pharaoh refused to repent, God did not avert the evil decree.

Message 13: "Death of the dead" (*Mote Ha-mate*), Ezekiel 18:32; Rashi on Tractate Sabbath 157:b, and from the High Holy Day service. The word "death" refers here to the actual death of an evildoer. The phrase "of the dead" refers to the evil person who has already been divinely sentenced to death but whom God, for His own reasons, has chosen to keep alive. The full phrase from the High Holy Days prayer book states: "God does not wish for the death of the dead but for his repentance and that he shall live." This teaches us that God gave Pharaoh opportunities for repentance, but Pharaoh refused each one.

THE FIRST ENEMY OF THE NATION OF ISRAEL

Message 14: "Amalek did to you on the way" (*Asah Lecha Amalek Ba-derech*), Deuteronomy 25:17. As the verse states: "Remember what Amalek did to you on the way, when you were leaving Egypt." After the Exodus, as the Israelites traveled through the desert, the nation of Amalek attacked the young and elderly that walked the slowest. The consequence of Amalek's wickedness is that God commands the Jewish people to wipe out all of Amalek.

THE ESSENTIAL LESSON OF THE EXODUS

The Exodus story describes the conflict between the arrogant Pharaoh and the lowly enslaved Israelites. Because the Israelites endured 200 years of slavery in Egypt, they viscerally learned the horrors of slavery and the pain of being strangers. Throughout the remainder of the Bible, the Jewish people are repeatedly reminded that they were once slaves and strangers. These constant reminders serve to instill an eternal Jewish commitment to compassion and awareness of the suffering of others. Because of that awareness, Jews have been in the forefront of civil rights, workers' rights, women's rights, and have led the world in the giving of charity. The following message emphasizes this important lesson of humility.

Message 15: "The human being is from dust" (*Et Ha-adam Min Ha-aphar*), Genesis 2:7. On Passover, Jews eat matzah as a symbol of the bread of poverty and affliction that the Israelites ate during the Exodus from Egypt. As the Children of Israel left Egypt, they could not wait for their dough to rise, so they cooked and ate it unleavened. According to the rabbis and the Talmud, leavened bread, or *chametz,* symbolizes arrogance and is strictly forbidden during the holiday. Only matzah, the unleavened bread that represents humility, is permitted. Out of context, "the human being is from dust" serves to remind us to be humble and not arrogant like Pharaoh, who behaved as if he were God.

MOTHER AS A METAPHOR FOR GOD

Message 16: "That I arose as a mother" (*Sheh-kamtee Aim*), Judges 5:7. The metaphor of "mother" connotes a caring and loving entity. According to the Book of Exodus 2:24, after the Children of Israel were enslaved and suffering, God heard their cries. God as "mother" took His children out of harm's way, protected them, housed them in huts (*Succot*), fed them with manna, and made sure they would receive the best education possible: by giving them the Torah.

THE GIFTS AND BLESSINGS OF THE EXODUS

Message 17: "Unto His treasured people" (*El Anshei S'gulato*), from the *Yigdal* prayer. This prayer describes the greatness of God and His gifts: Moses and the Torah. This tells us that God granted the Exodus unto His treasured people because they agreed to accept the Torah and all the responsibilities inherent in being God's partner in repairing the world.

Message 18: "The King of the Universe shall release" (*Melech Ha-olam Mateer*), from the morning blessings. As the verse states: "God, the King of the Universe, releases the imprisoned." This is consistent with the Israelites being freed from slavery in Egypt.

Message 19: "Escape of the imprisoned" (*B'richot Asir*), from *The Complete Hebrew English Dictionary,* by Reuben Alcalay. This phrase is an appropriate description of the Exodus from Egypt.

THE EXODUS: GIFTS FOR ISRAEL AND THE WORLD

The next two messages identify the scriptures (both written and oral) that the Children of Israel received after the Exodus from Egypt and eventually shared with the world.

Message 20: "All the Holy Scriptures" (*Kal Kit-vay Ha-Kodesh*), Mishnah Shabbat 16:1. This refers to the written Holy Scriptures. The actual purpose of the Exodus was for Israel to receive the Holy Scriptures and to eventually share them with the world. The term Holy Scriptures refers to the Torah, the entire Bible, to the Talmud, and the Mishnah.

Message 21: "The Mishnah and the Talmud" (*Ha-Mish-nah V'ha-Talmud*), a phrase used in countless courses, articles, and Websites. The purpose of the Exodus was for Israel to receive both the written and the oral tradition, called the Mishnah and the Talmud, which explains and expounds on how to follow the Torah. According to tradition, when God gave the Ten Commandments and the Torah to Moses on Mount Sinai, He also gave him the oral tradition or the oral Torah. Approximately 1,400 years later, beginning in 200 C.E. and ending in 500 C.E., the oral Tradition was written down in the form of the Mishnah and the Talmud.

Message 22: "I shall surely bless and greatly increase you" (*Va-rech Avarech-acha Vih-harbah Arbeh*), Genesis 22:17. In this section of Genesis, the Angel of God calls to Abraham and blesses him. The Exodus from Egypt leads to the manifestation of this blessing.

Message 23: "God your Lord gives you an inheritance and it shall be upon you" (*A-donai Elokecha Natan Lecha Nachalah Vih-hayah Alecha*), Deuteronomy 19:10. At Mount Sinai, God gave the Jewish people an inheritance of Torah, Mishnah, and Talmud. It has since been the Jewish people's responsibility to pass down the tradition to future generations and to share this inheritance with humanity.

Message 24: "God teaches Torah to the people" (*A-donai M'lamade Torah L'Am*), formed by deleting only the word "the" from the morning Blessings of the Torah. This reminds us that the Exodus led directly to the people of Israel, and ultimately the world, receiving and learning the Torah.

Message 25: "Bringing peace to humanity" or "Bringing of peace between humanity" (*Hah-vah-ot Shalom Ben Ah-dahm*), Talmud Shabbat 127:a, and the daily blessings of the Torah. The purpose of the Exodus was for the Jewish people to receive both the written and oral Torah at Mount Sinai, so that the scriptures could achieve their purpose: to bring peace to humanity.

Message 26: "Might of Israel" or "Ray of Israel" (*Keren Yisrael*), Lamentations 2:3. The story of the Exodus demonstrated the might of Israel. In addition, "Might of Israel" and "Ray of Israel" are metaphors for God, who orchestrated the Exodus.

Message 27: "And with the crown of victory" (*Oo-b'ateret Nitza-chone*), from the prayer for the Israeli Defense Forces. As described in the Bible, the Exodus story is the most miraculous victory in the history of the world.

Message 28: "The heights from the depths" (*Ha-ma-ah-lote Me-ma-ah-ma-kim*), Psalm 130:1. This phrase summarizes the story of the Exodus from

Egypt: the nation of Israel went from the depths of slavery to the heights of the Revelation at Mount Sinai—where they received the Ten Commandments and the Torah.

Message 29: "Three principles" (*Shloshah Devarim*), Ethics of the Fathers 1:2. The full phrase states: "Upon three principles the world depends: on Torah, on prayer, and on acts of kindness." The Exodus from Egypt made it possible for these three principles to be shared with the world.

Message 30: "One shall grow rich" (*Ya-ah-sheer Eesh*), Psalm 49:17. This is a metaphor for the wisdom and richness that resulted from the Exodus: the Holy Scriptures, the Mishnah, the Talmud, the Ten Commandments, and the beautiful traditions of Passover.

Message 31: "Intelligence of Israel" or "Wisdom of Israel" (*Say-chel Yisrael*), from 2 Chronicles 2:11 (the words come from the same verse but are not consecutive). The Exodus from Egypt led to the wisdom of Jews and Israel: from the experience of being strangers and slaves in Egypt they learned compassion, and from studying the Torah and observing the commandments they became intelligent. As Deuteronomy 4:6 states regarding the commandments: "And observe them and perform them, for it is your wisdom and your understanding in the eyes of the other peoples, who shall hear of all these laws and who shall say: Surely a wise and insightful people is this great nation!"

Message 32: "Find favor and good wisdom in the eyes of God and humanity" (*Nimtzah Chane V'sechel Tov B'ay-nay Elokim V'ah-dam*), from the Grace After Meals, and similar to Proverbs 3:4. The Bible and the other books of wisdom are perceived as classic moral texts and sources of wisdom, not just by God and the Jewish people but by the rest of humanity. The Exodus led to the receiving of the Bible, and therefore to the receiving of wisdom.

Message 33: "Bonds of love" (*Ah-vo-tote Ahavah*), Hosea 11:4. This verse in Hosea metaphorically describes God drawing in Israel with bonds of love: the commentators explain that this verse alludes to God providing the Israelites with provisions, both before and after the Exodus from Egypt.

GRATITUDE FOR THE EXODUS AND ITS GIFTS

Approximately 3,250 years ago, the Exodus from Egypt led to the Israelites' receiving the Bible and the Ten Commandments, their conquering of the Land of Israel, and eventually to the spread of monotheism, the Bible, and the Ten Commandments everywhere. The purpose of Passover is to remember and thank God for the miracles and gifts that were given to Israel and, eventually, the world. The next two messages list offerings or sacrifices that the Israelites were commanded to give as a thank-you to God. Each phrase has a numerical value of 891.

Message 34: "Therefore I offer to the Lord every firstborn issue of the womb" (*Ahl Kain Ah-nee Zo-vay-ach La-donai Kawl Peh-tare Reh-chem*), Exodus 13:15. This verse states: "When Pharaoh stubbornly refused to let us go, the Lord slew every firstborn in the land of Egypt, the firstborn of both man and beast, therefore I offer to the Lord every firstborn issue of the womb." Thus, this verse literally refers to a sacrifice of gratitude for the Exodus from Egypt.

Message 35: "And when you sacrifice the thanksgiving offering" (*V'kee Tiz-b'choo Zevach Todah*), Leviticus 22:29. This section of Leviticus connects the offering with the Exodus, as stated in Leviticus 22:33: "That [I God] took you out of the land of Egypt to be a God unto you; I Am God."

PRAISE OF AND GRATITUDE FOR GOD

The following six messages all have similar meaning: to give thanks and praise to God for the Exodus. But while the messages are similar and the Gematrias are the same, they consist of different words.

Message 36: "Our praise," "Our adoration," "Our songs of praise," and "Our Psalms" (*Tehila-taynu*), from the daily *Amidah* prayer. This reminds us that, to show our gratitude for the miracles of the Exodus from Egypt, we sing songs of praise to God.

Message 37: "Saying: I shall sing to God for He is exalted above the arrogant" (*Lay-more Ah-shira La-Donai Kee Gah-owe Gah-ah*), Exodus 15:1. This phrase is part of the "Song of the Sea," sung by the Israelites after they witnessed the miracle of the splitting of the sea, and in gratitude for having walked safely across the seabed while the pursuing Egyptian army drowned.

Message 38: "I shall sing praise to God Lord of Israel" (*Ah-za-mare LA-do-nai E-l-o-hay Yisrael*), Judges 5:3. In Judges 5:5, two verses after "I shall sing praise to God Lord of Israel," Mount Sinai is mentioned, thus clearly connecting this phrase with the Exodus.

Message 39: "You shall sing praise to God" (*A-donai Tit-halal*), Psalm 34:3. This is yet another example of biblical text of praise with a numerical value of 891.

Message 40: "My soul shall acknowledge" or "My soul shall thank" (*Nafshee L'ho-dote*), Psalm 142:8. As the verse states: "Out of prison bring my soul to give thanks to [God's] name." With the numerical value of this phrase equaling that of "Exodus of Egypt," we can draw a metaphorical line: the prison in this verse is the slavery in Egypt.

Message 41: "And Miriam chanted for them" (*Vah-tah-on Lah-hem Mir-yam*), Exodus 15:21. God split the Reed Sea, the Children of Israel passed across safely, and Miriam chanted for them. This celebration by Miriam and the Israeli women signified that the Exodus from Egypt was complete.

MOSES FULFILLS A 400-YEAR-OLD PROMISE

Message 42: "Attending or escorting the dead [to the grave]" (*L'-va-yot Ha-mate*), Talmud Shabbat 127a, and from the morning blessings. In approximately 1650 B.C.E., 400 years before the Exodus from Egypt, Joseph made his brothers swear to bury him in the Land of Israel (Genesis 50:25). When Moses led the Israelites out of Egypt, Moses fulfilled that promise and took the bones of Joseph with him. The taking of Joseph's bones completed Israel's experience in Egypt because Joseph had positioned the Jews in Egypt to begin with.

MEETING GOD

Message 43: "And you shall know" (*V'ya-dot Et*), Hosea 2:22. The full verse states: "And you shall know God." This may refer to the Israelites, who were embraced and protected by God during the Exodus, or to the Egyptians, who encountered God through the Ten Plagues.

Message 44: "God your Lord shall walk in the midst" (*A-donai Elokecha Mit-ha-lech B'keh-rev*), Deuteronomy 23:15. From the time of the Exodus from Egypt until the end of the Book of Deuteronomy, the Bible states that God walked in the midst of Israel. However, once the Book of Deuteronomy ends and the Children of Israel enter Israel, God acts in a more hidden way. At times, it may even look like He is no longer present.

PASSING DOWN OF THE TRADITIONS

Message 45: "This day of the new month" (*Yom Rosh Ha-chodesh Ha-zeh*), from the Blessing on the New Month in the *Shemoneh Esreh* prayer. In Exodus 12:2, 15 days before the Exodus, God commands the nation of Israel to sanctify the new month. This is the first commandment given to the entire nation of Israel.

Message 46: "Members of the [Great] Assembly" (*Anshay Knesset*), from Ethics of the Fathers 1:1. From 586 B.C.E. to 70 C.E., the members of the [Great] Assembly continued the traditions and laws that Moses received after the Exodus from Egypt.

WERE ALL JEWISH SOULS
ACTUALLY PRESENT AT MOUNT SINAI?

According to Jewish tradition, after the Exodus from Egypt all Jewish souls were present at Mount Sinai to witness the receiving of the Ten Commandments and the Torah. The following two messages seem to confirm this belief.

Message 47: "All the souls" (*Kol Ha-ni-pha-shote*), Ezekiel 18:4. Out of context, "All the souls" clearly supports the traditional belief that all Jewish souls witnessed the giving and receiving of the Bible at Mount Sinai.

Message 48: "To his closest relative" (*Lish-ay-ro Ha-karov Ay-lav*), Leviticus 21:2. The Rashi commentary on this phrase states that this refers to a Jewish man's wife. Hence, the hidden message here may be that the spouses in every Jewish marriage were present together at the Exodus and at Mount Sinai.

MESSAGES OF WARNING:
IF WE FAIL TO REMEMBER THE EXODUS

Message 49: "You shall cover over" (*Chee-see-tah Et*), Deuteronomy 23:14. This tells us that if we choose to dismiss and ignore the Exodus from Egypt and its gifts, we cover over this great event as if it were garbage.

Message 50: "To cremate" (*Saw-raff La-ay-phair*), from *The Complete Hebrew English Dictionary,* by Reuben Alcalay. This tells us that if we dismiss and ignore The Exodus from Egypt, it is as if we are cremating the Jewish tradition.

Message 51: "Dementia" *(L'kut Ha-sechel*), *The Complete Hebrew English Dictionary,* by Reuben Alcalay. At the very least, this appears to be a rebuke to Jews that dismiss the importance of the Exodus: It is as if they have dementia.

THE ULTIMATE PURPOSE OF THE EXODUS

Message 52: "Wake up" (*Hit-o-riri*), Isaiah 51:17, and the Sabbath eve prayer *Lechah Dodi.* Moses, Miriam, and Aaron's purpose was to inspire the Children of Israel to spiritually wake up. The purpose of the Exodus from Egypt was for the Israelites to receive the Bible and the commandments and share them with all nations, in order to rouse the world to action.

Even when these three leaders made mistakes, their mistakes still served to wake us. For example, over 3,200 years ago, Miriam made a negative comment about Moses' African wife. Immediately, she became afflicted with a skin disease, leprosy or something similar. While there are several interpretations of this story, my interpretation is that God punished Miriam because of her racist remark. The Torah lesson for us is that racism is a serious sin punishable by the likes of leprosy. It could be said that racism today is still punished by an invisible, internal leprosy of the spirit: because if it were visible, no one would have the free will to be a racist because the punishment of leprosy is too frightening.

THE MOST FAMOUS EVENT IN WORLD HISTORY?

Message 53: "For it is the most widely circulated" (*Key Who Ha-nafootz B'yo-tare*), from *The Complete Hebrew English Dictionary,* by Reuben Alcalay. The Exodus consists of well-known events commemorated annually on the festival of Passover, portrayed in famous movies, and priceless paintings. (Da Vinci's *The Last Supper* depicts Jesus celebrating the Passover Seder on the first night of the holiday.) But the major reason that the Exodus is the most famous event in human history is that it led to Israel receiving the Ten Commandments and the Bible, the best-selling book of all time. Had the Exodus not occurred, the Jewish people would have been wiped out in Egypt and the world would not now have the Bible, the Ten Commandments, Judaism, Israel, Jesus, or Christianity. Thus, the impact of the Exodus is felt not just by Jews but across all of human experience.

IV

Divine Wisdom and Warning
for Major Concepts, Issues, and Events

Chapter Fourteen

Was 9/11
a Random Date or Preordained?

911

The attack of 9/11 is a sensitive topic. It was a tragedy for the United States and the world, and made us aware of our vulnerability. The events are still recent enough that conversations on the topic are fraught with emotion. So, it is with a degree of trepidation and excitement that I share the gematrial findings on this subject, which reveal that every Hebrew word or phrase with a total numerical value of 911 can be read as referring either to an aspect of the attack or to its aftermath.

Hebrew text with a value of 911 generates answers to many complex questions regarding the event, including: Did 9/11 have a hidden purpose? What should we learn from the event? What should our response be? What will be the ultimate outcome—will we win or lose? In addition, mathematically generated messages, each with a value of 911, appear to disclose specific details about the attack, including a description of the victims and attackers, allusions to the Twin Towers, the lack of survivors in the fallen buildings, and a reference to the first responders. The date of September 11, 2001, heralded the beginning of a new war, but what was unknown until now is that 3,200 years ago the Bible seems to have warned and counseled us about it.

The terrorists attacked on 9/11, but was the date of the attack random or divinely preordained? As discussed in Chapter One, the numbers 9 and 11 are connected to three other tragic historical events. In 586 B.C.E., the First Holy Temple in Jerusalem was destroyed by the Babylonians on the 9th day of the 11th month of the Hebrew calendar, the Ninth of Av (*Tisha B'Av*). The Second Holy Temple was destroyed by the Romans in 70 C.E., on the exact same date. Metaphorically, just as the Holy Temples in Jerusalem were destroyed on the 9th day of the 11th month, so too the "temples of commerce" the Twin Towers were destroyed on 9/11 (albeit the 11th day of the 9th month). The third event that occurred was in Nazi Germany, on November 9, 1938. On the 9th day of the 11th month of our modern calendar, *Kristall-nacht,* the Night of Broken Glass, occurred. The Nazis destroyed and burned thousands of Jewish stores, hundreds of synagogues, and sent over 20,000 Jews to concentration camps, thus foreshadowing the coming Nazi atrocities. This should have been a wake-up call to the world about Nazism, but it was ignored.

All of the following Hebrew words and phrases have a numerical value of 911 and were found either in the Bible, the Jewish prayers, or the Hebrew dictionary. There are five specific and unique Hebrew letters that correspond exactly to 911: איתשר. These five letters can be used to spell the first two messages and Message 23. All the other messages in this chapter also have Gematrias of 911 but consist of a variety of different letters.

DIRECTLY EMBEDDED MESSAGES

Hebrew text with the numerical value of 911 seems to signify an action or event of primary importance. The five specific letters that correspond exactly with the number 911 spell the first two messages.

Message 1: "Beginning," "first," or "primary" (*Ray-sheet*), Genesis 10:10. In this verse, "beginning" refers to the kingdom of Nimrod, "the mighty hunter." In Artscroll's *The Stone Edition* of the Five Books of Moses, the commentary on this verse states: "Before Nimrod there were neither wars nor reigning monarchs," thus suggesting that one hidden meaning of the numbers 9 and 11 is that they alert us to the beginning of a war.

THE NUMBERS 9 AND 11 SIGNIFY THE BEGINNING OF WISDOM

Message 2: "Beginning" (*Ray-sheet*), from the Book of Psalms 111:10. This verse states: "The beginning of wisdom is fear of God." This is a second biblical occurrence of the Hebrew word for "beginning." From this verse we can learn that the events of 9/11 serve as the beginning of wisdom, revealing that, just as *Kristallnacht* should have prompted the world to action, so too should 9/11. In addition, this message tells us that the numbers 9 and 11 serve to remind us to fear and respect God.

THE PURPOSE AND PRIMARY LESSON OF 9/11

The following series of messages refer to awakening the world from its slumber, or, perhaps, from its complacency. They seem to suggest what we are supposed to learn from 9/11, and appear to also apply to the Holocaust and other genocides, as well.

Message 3: "The beginning of wisdom" (*Tih-chee-lot Chachmah*), Proverbs 9:10. It is worth noting that although this message uses a different Hebrew word for "beginning" (*Tih-chee-lot*) than the previous two messages (*Ray-sheet*), the Gematria of this phrase is still 911.

Message 4: "God the Lord: there is a deep sleep upon mankind" (*A-donai Elokim Tar-day-ma Ahl Ha-Adam*), Genesis 2:21. Out of context, this suggests that before 9/11 and before *Kristallnacht* mankind was unconscious and asleep to a major developing problem. This may imply that the purpose of 9/11 and *Kristallnacht* were to wake up the world.

Message 5: "Slumber upon my eyelids" (*T'numah Al Afapai*), from the bedtime *Shema* prayers. This metaphor emphasizes the previous message, that before these horrific events we were asleep to these threats.

Message 6: "The year 2000" (*Sh-not Alpa-yim*), from numerous Israeli articles. Approximately one year before 9/11, in September of 2000, the second intifada began in Israel, and suicide bombers began to murder innocent civilians, including women, teenagers, and children. This message tells us that these events foreshadowed 9/11. In addition, while the 9/11 attack took place in 2001, it had been planned in the year 2000.

Message 7: "A sign of what's to come" or "An omen of what's to come" (*Mah Hayo Ote L'va-ote*), from *The Complete Hebrew English Dictionary,* by Reuben Alcalay. Just as *Kristallnacht* was an omen of the future, so too 9/11 may be a sign of what is to come.

DIVINE WARNINGS TO THE TERRORISTS

Message 8: "There shall be consequences" (*Hayah Totz-ote*), alternative translation of Joshua 18:2. Out of context, this seems to warn the terrorists of both military and divine repercussions for their actions.

Message 9: "You shall know God" (*Yah-dot Et A-donai*), from Hosea 2:22. Out of context, this appears to offer a warning to all evildoers that they will face divine judgment.

Message 10: "But for this day I shall punish" or "And for this day I shall reprimand" (*Hayom V'To-chach-ti*), Psalm 73:14. This psalm refers to the apparent success and wealth of the wicked, but that in the end the wicked themselves shall fall.

Message 11: "God shall fight against" (*A-donai T'lachamoo Et*), nonconsecutive words from Jeremiah 32:5. Because this verse ends with the words "They shall not succeed" (*Lo tatz-lee-choo*), it seems to confirm which side God is on.

BIBLICAL DESCRIPTION OF THE 9/11 ATTACKERS

The following six messages appear to refer directly to the perpetrators or their actions.

Message 12: "From the men of terror" or "By the men of terror" (*May-ate B'nay Chet*), literal translation of Genesis 23:20. This is a clear reference to the 9/11 perpetrators. For the contextual translation of this phrase, see Message 20: "From the children of Chet."

Message 13: "The men who committed the crime" or "The men who sinned" (*Ha-anashim Ha-poshim*), Isaiah 66:24. This verse states: "See the corpses of the men who sinned against Me [God] . . . and they will lie in disgrace before all mankind." This seems to disclose how the 9/11 terrorists will be viewed by history.

Message 14: "There with only a few in number" (*Shahm Bimtay M'ot*), Deuteronomy 26:5. Out of context, this describes the small number of terrorists that carried out the 9/11 attacks.

Message 15: "That plotted against" (*Asher Chah-shahv Ahl*), Esther 8:3 and 9:25. The Scroll of Esther, read at the Purim holiday, describes Haman, the second to the king, who 2,500 years ago plotted to kill all the Jews in the Persian Empire. The hidden message here may be that, as what befell Haman was shame, humiliation, and utter defeat, so too may this be the fate of the terrorists and those who support them.

Message 16: "Death blow" (*Makat Ha-Mavet*), from the *Tachanun* prayer. This literally describes the horror of the 9/11 attack.

Message 17: "Only the Third Reich" (*Ach Ha-reich Ha-shlishi*), *The Complete Hebrew English Dictionary,* by Reuben Alcalay. The terms "only" and "the Third Reich" were listed separately in the dictionary, but together they add up to 911. This message references the horrors of the Nazi Germany era and tells us that the barbarism of 9/11 can be compared only with that of the Third Reich.

Message 18: "He [the conspirator] sent back: 'No, for here I shall die'" (*Lo Key Po Amut Vayashev*), alternative translation of 1 Kings 2:30. This biblical story recounts a declaration from a rebel and conspirator (Joab) that he will die, thus alluding to the suicidal attackers of 9/11.

Message 19: "Duplicities" (*Tah-phoo-chote*), Proverbs 2:12. This is a valid description of the 9/11 plot.

911 NOTIFIES US OF ISSUES AND EVENTS
OF PRIMARY IMPORTANCE

Below, are two biblical examples of the numbers 9 and 11 alerting us to a critical issue, event, or process. The first phrase describes land purchased 3,800 years ago but which is still under dispute today.

Message 20: "From the children of Chet" (*May-ate B'nay Chet*), Genesis 23:20. In this section of Genesis, Abraham negotiates the purchase of a cave in Hebron, the "Cave of the Patriarchs and Matriarchs," in which his wife, Sarah, and their descendants will be buried. This transaction is discussed for a full 18 sentences. Usually, the Bible is very terse with language, but why here is it so verbose? It is as if the Old Testament (or its Author) knew that, almost 4,000 years later, the issue of ownership of this tract of land would still be a matter of extreme contention. Today, both Jews and Arabs argue and even die over it, but the biblical text clearly states that, although he was offered the cave as a gift, Abraham insisted on legally purchasing it from the descendants of Chet, so that there would be no question about ownership.

Message 21: "King Achashverosh" (*Melech Achashverosh*), Esther 1:2. Achashverosh was the Persian king at the time of the story of Purim and the writing of the Scroll of Esther. King Achashverosh signed an edict sentencing all the Jews in the Persian Empire to death, but the annihilation was averted due to the actions of Esther and her uncle Mordechai. Had it not been prevented, it would have been an event as significant as 9/11 or *Kristallnacht*.

GOD'S OPINION OF WHETHER OR NOT TO RESPOND

Message 22: "A positive commandment" (*Mitzvat Aseh*), Mishnah Kiddushin 29a. This seems to suggest that God has made the response to 9/11 a positive commandment.

The following message consists of the five specific letters that correspond exactly with the number 911: ראשית.

Message 23: "I have endorsed" or "I have approved" (*Ee-shar-tee*), from *The Complete Hebrew English Dictionary,* by Reuben Alcalay. This suggests that God has approved of our response.

GOD'S OPINION OF THE TERRORISTS AND THEIR ACTIONS

Message 24: "For, from the beginning enemies" (*Key may-rosh Tzarim*), alternative translation of Numbers 23:9. Out of context, this seems to refer to the terrorists of the 9/11 attack.

Message 25: "In [God's] sight hatred" (*Ay-necha Sinot*), alternative reading and translation of Psalm 5:6. As verses 5:5–6 state: "For You are not a God that wants wickedness, You will not reside with evil. The boasters shall not stand in Your eyes, You [God] hate all men of violence." This message reminds us that there can be no doubt that God hates those who perpetrate violence and wickedness.

Message 26: "It shall be considered a curse to Him [God]" (*K'lala Taychashev Lo*), Proverbs 27:14. Reading "It" as referring to 9/11, this appears to be a divine comment that God considers the attack not a noble action, but rather a direct curse at Him.

Message 27: "Foundations of Heaven" (*Mos-dote Ha-shama-im*), Book 2 Samuel 22:8. The full verse states: "Then the earth rocked and quaked, the Foundations of Heaven shook—rocked by His [God's] indignation." This may also be read as God's reaction to the 9/11 attack, when the very "Foundations of Heaven" shook because of God's indignation. It serves as a serious warning to the terrorists, and as a physical description of what happened when the towers fell: "The earth rocked and quaked." It was literally recorded as a seismic event.

REFERENCES TO THE TWIN TOWERS

Message 28: "Land of Shinar" (*Eretz Shinar*), Genesis 11:2. Shinar was the location of the Tower of Babel. Genesis 11:4 states: "And they said, Come, let us build us a city, and a tower with its top in the sky." "Land of Shinar," then, appears to be an allusion to the Twin Towers.

Message 29: "That it towered high" (*Asher Gah-vatah*), literal translation of Ezekiel 31:10. This again evokes the image of a skyscraper. The echoes of 9/11 continue in Ezekiel 31:12, which states: "Strangers cut it down."

Message 30: "At the time she gave birth" (*B'ate Lay-dahtah*), Genesis 38:27. This phrase is taken from the story of Rebecca. The full sentence reads: "At the time she gave birth and behold, there were twins in her stomach." These twins were Jacob and Esau, and their conflict has continued through the millennia. Of course, in our contemporary context, when we think of "twins" and 9/11, we think only of the Twin Towers of the World Trade Center.

Message 31: "But the glory remains intact" (*V'Ha-keren Ka-yemet*), an alternative translation of Talmud Shabbos 127a. Out of context, this suggests that, despite the destruction of the Twin Towers, their glory remains intact, and the glory of America and the victims also remain intact.

REFERENCES TO GROUND ZERO

Message 32: "Grave," "hell," or "nethermost pit" (*B'air Sha-chas*), Psalms 55:24. This is an appropriate literal and metaphoric description for Ground Zero in particular, and to the psychological and physical impact of all the events associated with the numerical value of 911.

Message 33: "And the wind upon the face of chaos" (*Al P'nay T'hom V'ru-ach*), an alternative translation of Genesis 1:2. Anyone who was in New York on that day or on the days that followed can relate to the feeling of swirling chaos, dust, and horror after the towers collapsed.

Message 34: "And you shall not see a survivor in the entire borders" (*V'lo Yay-rah-eh Lecha Sh-or B'chal G'vu-laycha*), an alternative reading and translation of Exodus 13:7. This reminds us that sadly, virtually no survivors were found within the entire Ground Zero site.

The following message appears to refer to a medical condition common to many of those who worked cleaning up Ground Zero.

Message 35: "With sclerosis" (*B'taw-reh-shet*), from the Israeli Medical Association Website. Many of the emergency responders who were exposed to the toxic dust at Ground Zero suffer from either atherosclerosis (plaques in the arteries of the heart) or of sclerosis of the lungs, defined as a thickening and hardening of the lung tissue due to prolonged exposure to toxins.

THE VICTIMS

The following three messages all seem to refer to the holiness of the victims.

Message 36: "The flesh of the Holy" (*Bah-sar Ha-kodosh*), Talmud Ethics of the Fathers 5:7. This seems to refer to the victims who perished on 9/11.

Message 37: "Martyrdom" or, literally, "Death of the holy" (*Mote Ha-Kidoshim*), from Google Translate. There are some who support terrorism and consider the suicide bombers martyrs, but to the rest of us "Death of the holy" refers only to the victims.

Message 38: "And sanctify them today" (*Vee-Kee-dash-tem Ha-yome*), Exodus 19:10. This message continues the theme of the holiness of the victims.

POSTMODERN THEORY VERSUS THE TRUTH

Postmodern theorists say that there is no such thing as absolute truth. They believe that truth depends on your point of view, and therefore no clear distinction exists between victim and aggressor, or between good and evil. God and the Bible disagree. Since 9/11, a postmodern lens has often been used to portray the victim and the terrorist as equivalent, even when discussing the terrorists who died flying planes into the buildings. The following two messages refer to the conflict between truth and postmodernism in this context.

Message 39: "Conflicts shall be made equivalent" (*M'doe-nim Nish-tah-vah*), Proverbs 27:15. This phrase seems to refer to a pattern that has occurred many times since 9/11: terrorists target and murder innocent civilians, the victimized country's army retaliates, and innocent civilians are killed along with the terrorists. The terrorists then use the pretext of civilian casualties to claim that they are the victims and that the army that attacked them is the aggressor. Incredibly, many in the West accept this misguided concept of equivalence.

Message 40: "A time for truth" (*Ate Emet*), Ynet Yediot Achronot article. Each of us has the free will to choose to interpret events with the logic of postmodern thinking. This message, however, suggests that there is a just and an unjust side, and that now is a time for truth.

SPECULATION ABOUT 9/11

The following message is pure speculation—not an accusation. It is only a theoretical reference to someone who may have hired the terrorists.

Message 41: "A lying man" or "A liar" (*Eesh Sheh-kare*), nonconsecutive words found in same verse in Micah 2:11. "A lying man" may possibly refer to someone who was considered an ally of America but who may have secretly supported the attack.

OUR RESPONSE: HOW ARE WE DOING?

The following series of messages seem to describe the process of responding.

Message 42: "There shall be difficulties" (*L'he-yote K'sha-yim*), from *The Complete Hebrew English Dictionary,* by Reuben Alcalay. "Difficulties" is an appropriate word to describe each aspect and consequence of 9/11, including the attack, clean-up, rebuilding, and military response: none of it has been easy.

Message 43: "Foe and adversary from upon us" (*Tzar Oo-Mas-tin May-aleinu*), from the "Our Father, our King" prayer (*Avinu Malkeinu*). The full stanza states: "Our Father, our King, destroy every foe and adversary from upon us." While this is an appeal to God, it also may be a directive to us to take action.

Message 44: "And I [God] shall redeem you" (*V'Ga-altee Etchem*), Exodus 6:6. *The Soncino Edition of the Pentateuch and Haftorahs* (The Five Books of Moses) notes that the Hebrew word for "redeem" is associated with the person "whose duty it was to ransom or, if need be, avenge the person or property of his relative." Therefore, this message can also be understood as implying that God, along with us, shall avenge the victims of 9/11.

HOW WILL IT ALL END? THE ULTIMATE OUTCOME OF 9/11

The next series of messages all seem to be prophetic.

Message 45: "The entire earth is for God and shall serve God" (*La-donai Kol Ha-ah-retz Iv-do Et A-donai*), Psalms 100:1–2. This suggests that there are two paths available to humans a peaceful one and a violent one. While human beings have the free will to choose which path to take, the destination of both shall ultimately serve God's will. As the full verse in Psalm 100:2 states: "Serve God with happiness and come before Him with singing." This implies that, whether or not the terrorists continue on their path of violence, the final result will be a world that serves God, not with violence but with happiness and joy.

Message 46: "God: peace and truth in My day" (*A-donai Shalom V'Emet B'yamai*), nonconsecutive words found in same verse in Isaiah 39:8. The verse states: "The word of God that you have spoken is good, for there shall be peace and truth in My day." In the context of 9/11, this seems to suggest that, ultimately, peace and truth will be the results of 9/11.

Message 47: "Justice shall be seen in the country" (*Tzedek Tiryeh Ba-mih-denah*), Ecclesiastes 5:7. Again, this seems to be a prediction that justice will ultimately prevail.

Message 48: "And He [God] shall not allow our feet to falter" (*V'lo Nah-tahn La-mote Rahg-lay-nu*), Psalms 66:9. This seems to predict that God shall not allow us to falter in this war against terrorism.

Message 49: "And I shall bless you and I shall make your name great and you shall be a blessing" (*Va-avarech'cha Va-ah-gadla Sh'mecha V'heyeh Beracha*), Genesis 12:2. Out of context, this seems to suggest that the ultimate outcome of 9/11 is that God shall bless us and make our name great, and that we will be a blessing to the world.

Message 50: "Unto the upright a gracious light" (*Ohr La-Yesharim Cha-nun*), Psalm 112:4. This verse states: "As a shining in the darkness, unto the upright a gracious light, full of compassion and righteousness." This seems to remind and reassure us that, although 9/11 was a dark day, the light of God still shines.

Message 51: "You shall offer a Thanksgiving offering to God" (*Tiz-bih-choo Zeh-vach Todah La-donai*), Leviticus 22:29. This appears to be a directive to express gratitude to God, even if it is in advance of our victory.

Message 52: "I was afraid and to You God I shall call" (*Ha-yeetee Niv-hal Ay-lecha A-donai Ekrah*), Psalms 30:8–9. Prayer was a common response to 9/11, both on the day of the attack and afterwards. In addition, Psalm 30 is known as the "psalm of reversal" because almost each verse contains a reversal. For example, Verse 30:12 states: "You turned my mourning into dancing, you loosened my sackcloth and girded me with joy." This may be prophetic, that the grief of 9/11 shall eventually be turned into joy—a profound reversal that most of us, especially those who lost a loved one on that day or as a result of that day, can barely imagine.

REVEALING THE SECRET TO PREVENTING FUTURE ATTACKS?

Message 53: "He [God] shall save them [by] overturning the wicked" (*Ya-tzee-lame Ha-phoch R'sha-im*), Proverbs 12:6–7. Out of context, this suggests that God will save us by overturning the wicked. But a gematrial analysis of "Overturning the wicked" may reveal the secret for reaching the hearts and minds of those who hate us, thus hopefully preventing future attacks.

THE FORMULA TO REACH THE HEARTS AND MINDS: THE NUMERICAL VALUE 731

The phrase "Overturning the wicked" (*Ha-phoche Reshaim*), from Proverbs 12:7, has a numerical value of 731. The theme of all text with 731 Gematrias has been determined to be "Science and Torah." "Science" might be in the form of medicine, sanitation, clean water, or helping with that community's agricultural or business needs, while "Torah" may be metaphoric, a reference to providing schools, teachers, and supplies for the children. Therefore, this suggests that to overturn evil in a community, even in the community of our enemy, we should provide them with access to both science and education.

APPROPRIATE VENUE FOR NATIONALISM AND AGGRESSION

The final message with the numerical value of 911 refers to the appropriate and healthy way to express nationalism, channel aggression, anger, and even envy.

Message 54: "Football game" or "Soccer game" (*Mischak Kadur Regel*), Israeli newspapers. "Football game" appears to be a divine suggestion that the smarter and more peaceful way to be nationalistic is through athletic competition.

Chapter Fifteen

What Is the Lesson of the Holocaust?

SHOAH = 312

The Holocaust is the most documented event in world history. According to the United States Holocaust Memorial Museum, in Washington, D.C., there have been over 85,000 volumes of books written on the subject. In addition, thousands of hours of visual testimony have been recorded, hundreds of movies made, and millions of pages of historical documents studied. As you will see, through the use of the new gematrial technique introduced in this book, all of this study can, in a way, be summarized with just three Hebrew letters. These three letters are embedded within the Hebrew word for Holocaust (*Shoah*) and will be used to spell the first series of messages.

This chapter will show that all Hebrew words or phrases with a 312 numerical value, whether found in the Bible, the Talmud, or any Hebrew dictionary or prayer, can be interpreted as referring to an aspect of the Holocaust. The Hebrew text may be analyzed out of its original context, but often that context enhances the meaning. Also, you will see how, when multiple messages refer to the same aspect of the Holocaust, even though they consist of different words, the total numerical value still turns out to be 312.

This chapter discloses messages that can be interpreted as referring to multiple aspects of the Holocaust, including the survivors; the Righteous Gentiles, who saved Jewish lives; the governments of much of the world that sat silently by even though they were aware of the atrocities; the villagers who collaborated with the Nazis or stole the property and possessions of their Jewish neighbors; the banks who stole billions of dollars from Jewish bank accounts; the insurance companies who refused to honor hundreds of thousands of victims' life-insurance policies; the murderers themselves; and the Holocaust deniers.

In addition, the end of this chapter provides a mathematical answer to the question: After 1,900 years of exile, how did the Jewish people go from the near decimation of the Holocaust to re-establishing their ancient homeland of Israel?

The messages that are directly embedded within the word *Shoah* summarize and comment on much of the history and repercussions of the Holocaust. There are three specific and unique Hebrew letters that correspond exactly with the numerical value of 312: יבש. These letters can be used to spell nine Hebrew words, listed here as the first nine messages. All the other messages in this chapter also have the numerical value of 312 but consist of a variety of different letters.

DIRECTLY EMBEDDED MESSAGES

Message 1: "Sat" or "sit" (*Yaw-shav, Yo-shave*), *The Complete Hebrew English Dictionary,* by Reuben Alcalay. This is a reminder that, in spite of being aware of the atrocities taking place during the Holocaust, the entire world sat by in silence. Even today, the world continues to ignore atrocities occurring in Darfur and the Congo, just as it did during the Armenian, Bosnian, and Rwandan genocides.

Message 2: "Shame" (*Ba-yesh*), *The Complete Hebrew English Dictionary,* by Reuben Alcalay. Shame on the villagers who collaborated with the Nazis or stole the property or possessions of their Jewish neighbors. Shame on the banks, insurance companies, and museums who still refuse to return Jewish assets. Shame on the world for sitting by in silence. Shame on the countries that, even today, actively or passively, support regimes that are perpetrating genocides. Shame on anyone or on any country that denies any genocide, past or present. While the evildoers may not themselves feel ashamed, eventually they will all be humiliated. Just recently, a notorious guard at the Treblinka extermination camp died, and no country would accept his body for burial.

Message 3: "Bad" (*Beesh*), *The Complete Hebrew English Dictionary,* by Reuben Alcalay. The banks that never returned Jewish bank accounts, the insurance companies who refused to honor life-insurance policies, the museums who are in possession of stolen Holocaust art, and the perpetrators of the Holocaust were or are bad.

Message 4: "Captivity" (*Sh-vee*), *The Complete Hebrew English Dictionary,* by Reuben Alcalay. "Captivity," metaphorically and literally, may refer to the murderers who lived or live in constant fear of exposure, arrest, and imprisonment. They never get to rest because at any moment the Mossad, a Nazi hunter like Beate Klarsfeld, or the next Simon Wiesenthal might hunt them down.

Message 5: "Dry" (*Ya-vaish*), *The Complete Hebrew English Dictionary,* by Reuben Alcalay. This seems to suggest that the Holocaust deniers will have dry lives, as distinct from fruitful, verdant, and fertile ones. Even if the deniers are famous, powerful, or wealthy, the quality of their lives shall be dry and filled with shame.

Message 6: "Repent" (*Shoo-vee*), *The Complete Hebrew English Dictionary,* by Reuben Alcalay. This appears to refer to Germany and other countries (e.g., Poland) that should continue to repent by building monuments, opening museums, honoring the victims, and making certain that the world knows the truth. In addition, all the evildoers should come forward and repent. This includes the museums that continue to withhold stolen Jewish art and the banks and insurance companies described earlier. If they do not, a divine reckoning seems to await them. (See the chapter "What Happens After Death?" for details.)

Message 7: "Shall return" (*Ya-shuv*), *The Complete Hebrew English Dictionary,* by Reuben Alcalay. The Holocaust marked a turning point in Jewish history: after 1,900 years of exile, the Jewish people could return to their homeland, Israel.

Message 8: "Old age" (*Save*), *The Complete Hebrew English Dictionary,* by Reuben Alcalay. This seems to be prophetic: that the Righteous Gentiles and the Holocaust survivors often live to old age. A recent longevity study showed that Holocaust survivors live longer on average than those who did not go through the Holocaust.

Message 9: "Dwell" (*Ya-shav*), *The Complete Hebrew English Dictionary,* by Reuben Alcalay. This suggests that the survivors shall dwell in peace.

MESSAGES OF WISDOM

Message 10: "The Jewish Quarter" (*Rovah Ha-Yehudi*), *The Complete Hebrew English Dictionary,* by Reuben Alcalay. In Europe, the Jewish Quarter of many cities was where Jews often lived before World War II. For example, three million Jews lived in Poland, but by the time the war ended over 90 percent had been murdered and only 1 percent remained in that country. Poland's Jewish Quarter had been decimated.

Message 11: "In the towns of Judah" (*B'aray Yehudah*), Lamentations 5:11. This verse and the entire Book of Lamentations describes the devastation of Israel in 586 B.C.E., when the First Holy Temple in Jerusalem was destroyed. It is interesting that Verse 5:10 states: "Our skin was scorched like ovens," a phrase that evokes the Holocaust.

Message 12: "A large multitude of people" (*Am Rav*), Numbers 21:6. As the full phrase states: "A large multitude of people of Israel died," a reference to the six million Jews who were murdered.

Message 13: "Who has witnessed such events?" (*Me Rah-ah Kah-eleh*), Isaiah 66:8. The hidden message here seems to be that the question "Who has witnessed such events?" is a prophetic comment alluding to the Holocaust. This section of the Book of Isaiah foretells that, after a period of suffering, Israel shall be re-established, and speaks metaphorically of the labor and birth of Zion and Israel.

Message 14: "With casualness" (*B'kerri*), Leviticus 26:21. In November 1938, when *Kristallnacht* occurred, the entire world was alerted to what was happening in Nazi Germany, yet it reacted with casualness, and, as the Holocaust unfolded, little changed. Sadly, today the world too often reacts to news of genocide with the same indifferent attitude.

According to the *Oxford English Dictionary,* Holocaust is defined as: "a destruction or slaughter on a mass scale, especially caused by fire; the mass murder of Jews under the German Nazi regime." The next message refers to the fire and is spelled by rearranging the Hebrew letters that spell *Shoah.*

Message 15: "And the flames" or "And the fire" (*V'ha-aish*), Leviticus 6:5. This refers to the millions of Jewish victims who were burned in the flames of the crematoria.

Message 16: "Who shall stand up for us?" (*Me Ya-amode B'ah-denew*), Rashi on Isaiah 33:14. This is the question that the victims of the Holocaust, indeed those of all genocides, ask. It reminds us that, if we don't take action now to stop such atrocities, there may be no one to stand up for us if we fall victim.

Message 17: "To his neighbor" (*El Ray-ay-hu*), 1 Samuel 10:11. Out of context, this may be interpreted as referring to the neighbors of the victims of the Holocaust. The Nazis and their sympathizers often arrested and murdered their own acquaintances. In addition, the villagers would often steal their murdered neighbors' property and homes. But there were also a few brave souls who tried to save their Jewish friends. They are honored for their courage by being designated as "Righteous Gentiles."

Message 18: "Returning," "restoring," "Giving back," or "reinstating" (*Hashavah*), from *The Complete Hebrew English Dictionary,* by Reuben Alcalay. This seems to be a divine suggestion that returning, restoring, giving back, and reinstating are the appropriate actions in response to the Holocaust. This includes the insurance companies, banks, governments, museums, and art dealers that, even today, refuse to return the stolen property to their rightful owners. Not to be forgotten either are the villages, towns, and cities that have not made restoration for the abandoned property.

Message 19: "Shall approach" or "Shall draw near" (*Yikrov*), Genesis 37:18. Taking this phrase out of context of the Book of Genesis, it may be interpreted as referring to Germany's repentance for the Holocaust. By continuing to honor and teach the true history of the Holocaust, Germany may one day again approach and draw near to God.

THE MURDERED VICTIMS

Message 20: "From starvation" (*May-ra-av*), Job 22:7. This reminds us that, literally, many of the victims of the Holocaust died this way.

The following three messages emphasize God's personal relationship with the victims of the Holocaust.

Message 21: "My cattle" or "My herd" (*Bah-kaw-ree*), *The Complete Hebrew English Dictionary,* by Reuben Alcalay. Many of the six million victims were transported by cattle car, and they have been compared to a herd led to slaughter. God honors them here by declaring that they are His cattle and His herd.

Message 22: The Lord is my shepherd (*A-donai Row-ee*), slightly different Hebrew spelling from Psalm 23:1. The meaning is clear: that God is the shepherd of the victims.

Message 23: "With God your Lord all of you are alive" (*Ba-A-donai Elo-kay-chem Chaim Kool-chem*), Deuteronomy 4:4. This suggests that all the murdered victims are with God and "alive" in the world to come.

WHY DID THE SIX MILLION HAVE TO DIE?

The next two messages seem to hint at an answer to the eternal question of Why? Obviously, no explanation, however erudite, will be satisfactory. Ultimately, though, we can always ask: Was this the only way for God to teach us these lessons? The following two messages seem to provide some insight.

Message 24: "My battle" (*K'rah-vee*), *The Complete Hebrew English Dictionary,* by Reuben Alcalay. This combines several earlier themes and takes them to a conclusion. It is as if together they form a short essay that may possibly hint at God's thinking: "My cattle and My herd were sacrificed fighting My battle." In other words, the victims of the Holocaust fought God's battle of good versus evil.

Message 25: "Graves" or "tombstones" (*Kiv-ray*), *The Complete Hebrew English Dictionary,* by Reuben Alcalay. The mass graves of the victims serve as monuments to remind us of the atrocities committed. Some of the graves are only being found today, and many may never be found at all. Nevertheless, these "tombstones" direct us to never permit such atrocities to recur.

LESSONS OF THE HOLOCAUST

The following eight messages refer to the importance of Holocaust study and to its lessons for us and all future generations. They explain why we will continue to examine and revisit this topic forever.

Message 26A: "Shall examine" or "shall inquire" (*Y'va-care*), Leviticus 27:33. Out of context, this message urges us to examine, study, and research the Holocaust so that nothing like it ever happens again.

A second interpretation of the previous message is as follows.

Message 26B: "Shall visit" (*Y'va-care*), an alternative translation of Leviticus 27:33. This tells us that we shall visit and revisit the topic of the Holocaust forever because it is the key lesson for all of humanity. And we shall visit the concentration camps, the Warsaw Ghetto, the monuments, and the many museums so that we finally learn that we must prevent all future genocides.

Message 27: "That this is" (*Sheh-who*), Ecclesiastes 2:22. This suggests that the Holocaust is the seminal event for humanity to study. The Hebrew word for "That this is" consists of the same letters as the Hebrew word for "Holocaust."

Message 28: "Increase wisdom and understanding" (*Ho-sefa Chachma Oo-binah*), from the *Gammatrikon,* a gematrial dictionary compiled by Shimshon Nesher. This tells us that we should increase wisdom and understanding in order to prevent all future Holocausts and genocides from occurring.

Message 29: "And instruction" or "And correction" (*Oo-moo-sar*), Job 5:17. This is a reminder that the key questions for us are: Will we ever learn the lessons of the Holocaust? And will we finally take instruction and make the necessary corrections to prevent any future Holocaust or genocide?

Message 30: "In high value" (*B'yokair* or *Be-kar*), Psalm 49:13. The key lesson of the Holocaust is that until Jews, women, minorities, homosexuals, immigrants, outsiders, and all people are held in high value, another Holocaust or genocide can occur. Sadly, most of us have the attitude that "it's just some Jews, or some Armenians, or some Cambodians, or some Bosnians, or some Rwandans, or some Darfurians who are being murdered." When we finally behave as if each human being has high value, we will have learned the lessons of the Holocaust. So that there can be no mistaking what we should hold in high value, Psalm 49:13 states: "A person in high value."

TO EMPHASIZE JUST HOW MUCH VALUE EACH PERSON HAS

Message 31: "Each a lovely tree" (*Kal Etz Nechmad*), Genesis 2:9. This message is metaphoric, that each of the murdered six million was a lovely tree that would have yielded much fruit. The metaphor "fruit" refers to the murdered six million victims, as well as their offspring, who never had the chance to be born. The victims and their offspring would have borne fruit in the form of contributions to humanity in all fields: science, art, literature, and medicine. Anne Frank was just one example of such a tree.

Message 32: "Each person is an entire world" (*Kol Adom Olam Maleh*), from the *Gammatrikon*. All the words of this phrase are found in Talmud Sanhedrin 4:5, but they are not consecutive. This section of the Talmud teaches that the life of each person is precious and equivalent to an entire world. The rabbis comment that the reason the Book of Genesis explains that we all descended from a single person, Adam, is to teach us two lessons: 1) That we are all related, and 2) That a single person can give rise to an entire world. From this, we are supposed to learn to value all human beings.

Message 33: "My heart is awake" (*Lee-be Air*), Song of Songs 5:2. This tells us that for eternity, in response to the Holocaust, our hearts will be awake with passionate feelings like those of sadness and anger.

Message 34: "Sadness" + "anger" (*Et-zev Ka-ahss*), nonconsecutive words found on the same page in Talmud Eruvin 65b. These are the feelings that will forever be connected to the Holocaust.

Message 35: "Without a friend" (*B'lee Ray-ah*), an anagram of Song of Songs 5:2 (see Message 33). This refers to a simple and powerful truth regarding the Jews trapped in Nazi Europe: They were without a friend in the world.

THE EUROPEAN INTELLECTUAL TRADITION EXPOSED

Message 36: "West" (*Ma-arav*), Daniel 8:5. Despite the great heights of refinement Western civilization had reached, including its classical philosophy, music, culture, and European intellectual tradition, the Holocaust occurred in Western Europe. "West" is an eternal reminder that our advanced culture was not enough to prevent the Holocaust.

Message 37: "And God was removed" or "And God has removed" (*V'E-L Hay-seer*), Job 34:5. This confirms that the Holocaust certainly seemed like a godless period of time. The full phrase in Job 34:5 states: "And God has removed justice from me."

Message 38: "Transition" (*Ma-ah-var*), from *The Complete Hebrew English Dictionary,* by Reuben Alcalay. In 70 C.E., after the Romans destroyed the Second Holy Temple in Jerusalem, most Jews who survived were exiled and scattered throughout the world. For the Jewish people, this began 1,900 years of exile, expulsion, and anti-Semitism. The Holocaust marked a major transition in Jewish and world history because, in 1948, Israel was again declared the Jewish homeland—thus ending almost two millennia of the Jews being a stateless people. The Holocaust also marked a further transition by making clear that anti-Semitism and all forms of racism were no longer acceptable but considered instead to be signs of ignorance. Sadly, the haters of Jews and others have found more acceptable ways of expressing their hatred.

Message 39: "Light for the Jews" (*Ohr La-Yehudim*), from the Sabbath evening song "Contentment and Gladness," written in 1545. This message seems to have prophesized that, after the Holocaust, there would again be light for the Jews. And, indeed, three years after the Holocaust, Israel was re-established as a Jewish state.

Message 40: "The good earth" (*Ah-retz Ha-tovah*), Deuteronomy 11:17. This phrase states: "The good earth that God provides for you." Out of context, it is as if God is shaking His head and sarcastically saying to humanity: "Upon this good earth that I provided, can't you do better than perpetrate and allow Holocausts?"

MESSAGES OF WARNING

The following messages seem to be directed at the perpetrators of the Holocaust and to the Holocaust deniers.

Message 41: "Speaking to Me [God]" (*Ay-lie Lay-more*), from Genesis 31:29. This implies that God's message to every evildoer is: You will be speaking to Me.

Message 42: "I shall make it equivalent" (*Ash-veh*), Lamentations 2:13. This Hebrew word consists of the identical letters as the Hebrew word for Holocaust, and the verse seems to directly refer to the Holocaust when it states: "O' daughter of Zion, your ruin is as vast as the sea; who can heal you?" But "I shall make it equivalent" is also a warning to the evildoers that their punishment shall be equivalent to their crime. (Actually, it seems that their punishment may be double their crime. See the chapter "What Happens After Death?")

The following messages apply if humanity does not learn from the events of the Holocaust.

Message 43: "Many will be slain by God" (*Ra-boo Cha-l'lay A-donai*), Isaiah 66:16. This chapter of Isaiah teaches us that all the nations of the world will eventually see the glory of God. However, there are two paths, to continue on the path of hatred—and many will die—or finally learn that hatred is unacceptable and witness God's glory in peace.

Message 44: "Shall rot" (*Yirkav*), from *The Complete Hebrew English Dictionary,* by Reuben Alcalay. This warns us that humanity shall rot if we continue to ignore the lessons of the Holocaust.

The following message consists of the same letters as the Hebrew word for Holocaust, *Shoah,* rearranged.

Message 45: "Shall it be in vain? (*Ha-shav*), Isaiah 5:18. It seems as if we have not learned from the Holocaust. Even today, the world is virtually ignoring the atrocities occurring in Darfur, the Congo, and throughout the world. After all of our research on the Holocaust, the 85,000 volumes, and all of the museums dedicated to the subject, the question we must ask is: Shall it be in vain?

HOW DID THE JEWS GO FROM THE HOLOCAUST TO RE-ESTABLISHING THE STATE OF ISRAEL?

How did the Jewish people go from the depths of the Holocaust in 1945 to re-establishing their ancient homeland of Israel only three years later in 1948?

In 1930, there was a theory, popularized by the British historian Arnold Toynbee, explaining that civilizations basically follow a cycle of rising and then declining to virtual extinction. Historians pointed out that all ancient civilizations and cultures have followed this pattern, including the ancient Egyptian, Greek, and Roman civilizations.

But one of the only ancient cultures to survive with its traditions intact has been the Jewish culture. In the first volume of *A Study of History,* published in 1934, Toynbee refers to the Jews as a "fossilized relic." And this was before the Holocaust! How much more so, after the murder of six million Jews, did it appear that Toynbee was correct, that the Jewish people were on their way to becoming a fossil. However, history proved him wrong. After the Holocaust, and after 1,900 years of exile, the Jewish people re-established their ancient homeland of Israel as a thriving Jewish state.

How did the Jewish people achieve this? Gematria can be used to reveal the answer. If we subtract the numerical value of the Hebrew word for Holocaust (*Shoah,* a 312 Gematria) from the numerical value of the Hebrew word for Israel (*Yisrael,* a 541 Gematria), the result is 229, because 541 – 312 = 229. Analyzing this number yields an explanation.

THE NUMBER 229 PROVIDES THE ANSWER

What follows are some examples of phrases with a Gematria of 229.

1. "The end has come to" (*Bah Ha-ketz El*), Amos 8:2. The full phrase states: "The end has come to My [God's] people Israel." Because "The end has come to" has a numerical value of 229, it can be interpreted to represent Toynbee's view of the Jewish people as a "fossilized relic," that the end had come for the Jews.
2. "Alone and suffering am I" (*Yachid V'ani Ani*), Psalm 25:16. This was the state of the Jewish people before and during the Holocaust.
3. "For the mourners of Zion" (*L'avalay Tzion*), Isaiah 61:3. As discussed in the Zion chapter, "Zion" is a term which can mean both Israel and the Jewish people. Therefore, this phrase seems to imply that, after the Holocaust, God will bring the Jewish people back to

Israel because of the mourners of the six million of Zion who were
murdered. The full sentence from the Book of Isaiah seems to prophet-
ically refer to the aftermath of the Holocaust, stating: "To place for the
mourners of Zion, to give them glory instead of ashes, oil of joy
instead of mourning, a mantle of fame instead of a feeble spirit."

4. "The voice of your brother's blood" (*Kol D'mai A-chi-cha*), Genesis
   4:10. The Hebrew word for "blood" can also be interpreted as the
   plural, "bloods." This suggests that when we murder one person we
   murder all their future progeny. When this principle is applied to the
   six million Jews who were murdered in the Holocaust, the loss is
   inconceivable.

5. "God shall fight for them" (*A-donai Nilcham Lahem*), Exodus 14: 25.
   This seems to explain Israel's re-establishment and its subsequent victory in the 1948 war, when, despite being vastly outnumbered, Israel
   prevailed over the invading Arab armies. Thus, this message suggests
   that the victory was due to divine intervention.

6. "Visible to the eyes" or "Revealed to the eyes" (*G'loo-ee Aynaim*),
   Numbers 24:4. The full sentence reads: "The words of one hearing the
   sayings of God, seeing the vision of God, while fallen, and visible to
   the eyes." "While fallen" could be interpreted as referring to the Jewish people after the Holocaust. The biblical prophets foretold that the
   Jews would return to Israel. Therefore, in 1948, after 1,900 years of
   exile and only three years after the Holocaust, many Christians and
   Jews considered the re-establishment of Israel a miraculous event, a
   sign that the biblical prophecy was being fulfilled, and that the event
   was equivalent to "seeing the vision of God . . . visible to the eyes."

7. "God created" (*A-donai Barah*), Jeremiah 31:21. This clearly explains
   the cause of the miraculous re-establishment of Israel after the Holocaust: God Himself. It is worth noting that the previous verse of Jeremiah 31:20 states: "Israel [the Jewish people] shall return to her cities."

8. "A Redeemer has come to Zion" (*Va L'Tzion Go-ale*), Isaiah 59:20
   and the daily prayers. This phrase explains that God, the Redeemer,
   has come to Zion to save Israel.

9. "Eternal life" (*Cha-yay Ha-Olamim*), from the Grace After Meals
   prayer recited on the Sabbath. In the context of the Holocaust, this
   refers to God fulfilling His promise that Israel shall be great (Genesis
   Chapter 12) and live for eternity. These promises were made because
   the Jewish people would later agree (Book of Exodus) to be God's
   partner in bringing the Torah to the world. In Book 1 of Samuel 15:29,
   the phrase "Eternal Israel" or "Eternal of Israel"(*Netzach Yisrael*) is
   used.

10. "This place is God's" (*Makom Ha-hoo A-donai*), a literal translation of Genesis 22:14. In the context of the re-creation of Israel out of the depths of the Holocaust, this could be understood as either "The realm of this event is God's" or "This place Israel is God's."

11. "Behold my enemies" (*R'eh Oy-vai*), Psalm 25:19. This verse refers to the many enemies of Israel. But in verse 25:22, the psalm states: "Thus may God redeem Israel from all its troubles." This suggests that the enemies of Israel will behold Israel's redemption.

12. "Understand clearly" (*Ba-air Hai-tev*), Deuteronomy 27:8. It is as if God were commenting: "Understand clearly the miracle that this is, that I God have performed."

13. "But a fool wouldn't understand" (*Oo-ch'seel Lo Yavin*), Psalm 92:7. Because of free will, each of us has the right to see, or not see, the Hand of God in history. "But a fool wouldn't understand" is directed at those who do not recognize the miraculous event of the Jewish people going from the ashes of the Holocaust to creating a vibrant and thriving Israel.

Chapter Sixteen

Peace

Make It or Cry Out

PEACE = 376

What are the divine messages directly embedded within the Hebrew word for peace (*Shalom*)? How important is peace? What is the connection between God and peace? What are the consequences for failing to make peace? What is the psychological reason why some people refuse to make it? How is peace connected to the coming of the Messiah? What are the components of peace? And what are the divine suggestions as to how we may better promote peace within ourselves and the world? This chapter discloses answers to all those questions.

Historically, much of the violence in the world has been caused by those who claim to speak in the Name of God. This includes the perpetrators of the Crusades, the Spanish Inquisition, the expulsion of the Jews from England in 1290 C.E., and countless pogroms. This chapter shows that only someone who comes in peace can speak for God, and that all those who have truly come in the Name of God have promoted peace. You cannot have one without the other.

The numerical value, or Gematria, of the Hebrew word for peace (*Shalom*) is 376. After researching all known Hebrew words and phrases with that numerical value I have found that each one refers to some aspect of peace. This chapter consists of a list of these words and phrases, referred to here as messages. While these messages may be literal or metaphorical, each has a value of 376.

If we were to ask a group of great poets, writers, philosophers, linguists, and biblical scholars to choose the most profound one- or two-word messages that could be associated with the word "peace," whatever profound answer they decided upon would not be as elegant or as beautiful as those generated by the simple mathematical techniques used in this book. This seems to suggest that the mathematically generated results presented here are not random but, rather, were deliberately embedded, possibly by God.

We said earlier that the Hebrew word for "peace" has a Gematria of 376. There are three unique and specific Hebrew letters that correspond exactly with 376 (שעו), and these three letters can be used to spell six words, listed here as the first six messages. All the other messages in this chapter also have numerical values of 376 but consist of a variety of different letters.

DIRECTLY EMBEDDED MESSAGES

Message 1: "Make" (*Asu*), *The Complete Hebrew English Dictionary,* by Reuben Alcalay. When "make" is joined with the word for "peace," it forms the directive "Make peace." This is interpreted as the primary divine message embedded within "peace," and the core message of this chapter. However, if you ignore this directive, then the three unique letters can also be rearranged to spell the warning of what will follow.

Message 2: "Cry out" (*Shiva*), *The Complete Hebrew English Dictionary,* by Reuben Alcalay. This tells us that the consequence of not making peace is that people will cry out.

Taken together, these first two messages seem to form an ultimatum: "Make peace or you shall cry out."

Message 3: "Rely" (*Shah-oo*), Isaiah 31:1. This verse speaks of those who trust in strong horses, chariots, and horsemen but do not rely on God. The hidden message and the literal one are the same: Trust in war and you don't trust in God, but if you trust in peace, you trust in God.

Message 4: "Hurry" or "Make haste" (*Oosh*), *The Complete Hebrew English Dictionary,* by Reuben Alcalay. This suggests that peace should be pursued and quickly.

Message 5: "Nobleman" or "rich" (*Show-ah*), *The Complete Hebrew English Dictionary,* by Reuben Alcalay. This teaches us that those with a higher economic status should use their position to promote peace. In addition, this reveals that the true nobleman is the person who makes peace.

Message 6: "Esau" (*Ay-sav*), Genesis 25:25. In the Book of Genesis, Jacob's brother, Esau, represents the opposite of peace. He is a man of war. As Isaac, Esau's father, said to him in Genesis 27:40: "By your sword you shall live."

MESSAGES OF WISDOM

The following two messages seem to list the components of peace.

Message 7: "Kindness and compassion" (*Chesed V'rachamim*), Psalm 103:4. That this phrase has the same numerical value as the Hebrew word for "peace" teaches us that kindness and compassion, together, add up to peace.

Message 8: "Responsible for each other" (*Ah-ray-vim Zeh La-zeh*), *The Complete Hebrew English Dictionary,* by Reuben Alcalay, and similar to Talmud Sanhedrin 27b. The acknowledgment that we are all responsible—not just for ourselves but for each other—will lead to peace.

Message 9: "For all of the earth" (*L'kol Ha-aretz*), Lamentations 2:15. The message is clear: Peace is for the entire earth. This verse in the Book of Lamentations describes the city of Jerusalem (in Hebrew, Jerusalem translates as "city of peace"). The verse states: "Could this be the city that was called Perfect in Beauty and Joy for All the Earth?" The hidden message is that peace itself is perfect in beauty and a joy for all the earth.

Message 10: "Request what?" or "Pray for what?" (*Sh'al Mah*), 1 Kings 3:5. This suggests that peace is always the answer.

Message 11: "Desire" or "wish" (*Mish-alah*), *The Complete Hebrew English Dictionary,* by Reuben Alcalay. This teaches us that peace should be our desire and our wish.

Message 12: "Urges" or "pleads" (*Po-tzair*), *The Complete Hebrew English Dictionary,* by Reuben Alcalay. That this word has the same numerical value as peace clearly reveals that God urges us to make it.

Message 13: "His essence," "His foundation," or "His origin" (*Ee-kah-row*), from *The Complete Hebrew English Dictionary,* by Reuben Alcalay. In this context, "His essence" refers to the divine essence, implying that each one of us should strive to make our essence and foundation one of peace.

Message 14: "Artery" or "vein" (*O-rake*), *The Complete Hebrew English Dictionary,* by Reuben Alcalay. This message leads us to understand that the desire to make peace is a vital part of our circulation and physical makeup. The commitment to it should flow through our veins to our thoughts, hearts, and muscles.

Message 15: "And with a precious stone" (*Oo-B'evan Y'karah*), Daniel 11:38. This appears to be a metaphor for the value of peace.

Message 16: "Your face to shine" (*Ee-ra Pa-necha*), Psalm 31:17. The verse states: "[God,] make Your face to shine upon Your servants." This suggests that in order to have God's face shine upon us, our focus and commitment must be to peace. When God's face shines upon us our faces also shine.

Message 17: "Your neighbor like yourself" (*Ray-acha Kamocha*), Leviticus 19:18. The full phrase states: "And you shall love your neighbor like yourself." The rabbis consider this to be the fundamental commandment of the entire Torah. The hidden message here is that promoting peace is the way to fulfill this commandment.

The following seven messages are formed by rearranging the Hebrew letters of the word peace (ש,ל,ו,ם). As you will see, each one seems to refer to an aspect of peace.

Message 18: The 36 are there (*Lamid Vuv Shom*). This phrase is formed by using only the letters in the Hebrew word *Shalom* to spell a short sentence. According to Jewish tradition, the "36" refers to the 36 righteous people on earth, upon whose merits the world exists. The hidden message here is that the 36 are committed to peace.

Message 19: "Ruler" or "rules" (*Mo-shale*), *The Complete Hebrew English Dictionary,* by Reuben Alcalay. This message suggests that whether we are a ruler of a household or of a great nation, our aim should be to make peace our priority and, as much as possible, have it rule our actions.

Message 20: "From kneading" (*Me-loosh*), *The Complete Hebrew English Dictionary,* by Reuben Alcalay. This may be metaphoric that, just as bread must be kneaded in order to fulfill its potential, peace requires some hands-on work as well.

Message 21: "Complete" (*Shah-loom*), *The Complete Hebrew English Dictionary,* by Reuben Alcalay. This reveals the hidden wisdom that peace is the key to being complete. This is in contrast to the common belief that wealth, success, fame, and power hold the key to feeling complete.

Message 22: "For its own sake" or "unselfishly" (*Lishmo*), alternative translation of Psalm 135:3. This suggests that we should promote peace for its own sake, because it is the right thing to do. But it is interesting that, invariably, we also personally benefit from it.

Message 23: "Reward" or "payment" (*She-loom*), *The Complete Hebrew English Dictionary,* by Reuben Alcalay. All of us ask the question: "What's in it for me?" This message reveals that peace itself is the reward.

Message 24: "To His Name" (*L'shmo*), Psalm 135:3. This phrase refers to praising God's Name. Usually, selfishness drives our behavior, and that rarely leads to peace. If we can shift our focus to God's Name and ask, "What would God want me to do?," then peace becomes a possibility.

THE CONNECTION BETWEEN PEACE AND GOD

Message 25: "God is there" (*Shahm Ha-E-L*), alternative reading and translation of a phrase in the daily prayers leading up to the recitation of the *Shema*. This reveals why we should work towards peace: Because God is there, within it.

While the next two phrases have the identical translation, each one uses a different term for God, yet they both have the same numerical value of 376.

This truly supports the thesis that these messages are not coincidental but that they have been deliberately embedded with meaning.

Message 26: "The Name of God" (*Shem Ha-E-l*), found in the daily Jewish prayers leading up to the recitation of the *Shema*. The implication here is that "Peace" is the Name of God. The Talmud in Tractate Shabbos 10a, agrees, explaining that "Peace" is actually one of God's holy names. This is based on a verse in Judges 6:24 which states: "God is Peace."

Message 27: "My Name is God" (*Sh'Me A-donai*), Exodus 6:3 and Jeremiah 16:21. This message further emphasizes the importance of peace to God.

Message 28: "Heavens of God" (*Sh-May A-donai*), Lamentations 3:66. The use of the plural "Heavens" may imply that there are multiple levels of Heaven, with the higher levels reserved for those who promote peace while on earth.

The following messages make it crystal clear that those who represent or dwell with God are peaceful and not violent.

Message 29: "He that comes in the Name of God" or "Brings with it the Name of God" (*Havah B'Shem A-donai*), Psalm 118:26. This message reminds those who claim to be speaking in the Name of God that only someone who comes in peace comes in the Name of God. Throughout history, many of those who have claimed to come in the Name of God have been violent.

Message 30: "Bidding of the King" (*Ma-amar Ha-Melech*), Esther 1:15. In the Book of Esther, the word "God" is never used. But some rabbis teach that when the term "the King" is used, it refers to God. With "Bidding of the King" valued at 376, we can read this injunction as a call to pursue peace, for it is the bidding of God, the Eternal King.

Message 31: "Intellect of God," "Intelligence of God," or "Divine wisdom" (*A-donai Say-chell*), Psalm 111:10. This seems to teach us that when we make peace, we move closer to the intellect of God.

Message 32: "And the mercies of God for all" (*A-donai La-kol V'rachamav*), Psalm 145:9. This appears to be a description of peace.

Message 33: "God shall be king for all eternity" (*A-donai Yimloch L'olam Va-ed*), Exodus 15:18. If God is described as a king, then God must have a kingdom or dominion: this is the realm of peace. When we behave as if we are God and that we alone can determine right from wrong, there is no peace. However, by accepting God as the one true king, peace may be possible.

Message 34: "He is the King that reigns over kings and works" (*Who Malkah Melech Malkaya O-vod*), from the Y-A-H Ribon prayer, recited each Friday night. When the prayer states, "He is the King that reigns over kings and works powerful and wondrous acts," the hidden meaning is: When we make and promote peace, then God will perform powerful and wondrous acts in return.

THE SECRET TO RECEIVING FAVOR FROM GOD

Message 35: "For favor" or "To the will" (*L'Rah-tzone*), Psalm 19:15 and Exodus 28:38. Psalm 19:15 states: "May the words of my mouth and the thoughts of my heart find favor before You, God, my Rock and Redeemer." This reveals that only peaceful words and thoughts will find favor before God.

Message 36: "He shall dwell" or "It shall dwell" (*V'Shoh-chan*), 2 Samuel 7:10. In the Bible, the verb "dwell" is always associated with peace. As this phrase states: "It [Israel] shall dwell in its place so that it shall be disturbed no more; iniquitous people will no longer afflict it." (Note: The Hebrew word for "dwell," *Shoh-chan,* is the root of the Hebrew word for God's Holy Spirit, *Sh'cheenah.*)

THE PSYCHOLOGICAL REASON
WHY SOME PEOPLE REFUSE TO MAKE PEACE

The following six messages explain why some people refuse to make peace. What is striking about these messages is that they seem to go directly to the heart of the matter.

Message 37: "To be inferior to" (*Naphal Me-plo-nee*), *The Complete Hebrew English Dictionary,* by Reuben Alcalay. The literal translation is "To fall beneath someone." This is what seems to always be present beneath the surface of the person who refuses to make peace: a feeling of inferiority. Feeling castrated is the perfect metaphor for inferiority. Sadly, just look at today's headlines, or at those people in your life who refuse to make peace, and see if this principle applies.

Message 38: "Eunuchs," "castrated," or "emasculated" (*Say-roo-sim*), *The Complete Hebrew English Dictionary,* by Reuben Alcalay. This can be read as a metaphor for those who feel powerless and weak and then compensate by promoting hatred or making war.

Message 39: "Castration," "emasculation," "sterilization," or "eunuch" (*E-koor* or *Awe-koor*), *The Complete Hebrew English Dictionary,* by Reuben Alcalay. This emphasizes the importance of the previous message. It is worth noting that although this is a different Hebrew word for "castration" than in the previous message, the Gematria is still 376.

Message 40: "To his eunuchs" (*L'saw-ree-sav*), 1 Samuel 8:15. This suggests, again, that those who refuse to make peace are compensating for feeling weak or emasculated.

Message 41: "The testicles" (*Ha-asha-chim*), *The Complete Hebrew English Dictionary,* by Reuben Alcalay. This is metaphoric, that it takes a person with testicles to make peace. This message unambiguously answers the question: What is the difference between the man of peace and the man of hatred?

Message 42: "And you shall be like the termite's chewings" (*V'hayah Kim-sos No-sase*), Isaiah 10:18. This is a clear insult to those who are obstacles to peace.

MESSAGES OF WARNING

Message 43: "Iniquitous people will no longer" or "Evil people shall not continue" (*V'lo Yosefoo B'nay Avla*), 2 Samuel 7:10. The phrase states: "Iniquitous people will no longer afflict." This suggests that when peace reigns, evil people will no longer afflict us, or, possibly, they simply will no longer be.

Message 44: "Book of Lamentations" (*Sefer Aicha*). The Book of Lamentations describes the destruction of Jerusalem and the First Holy Temple in 586 B.C.E. and is recited on the ninth day of the Jewish month of *Av,* the date the Temple was destroyed. The destruction of Jerusalem is an example of the warning "cry out" and a direct consequence of no peace. That this phrase has the same numerical value as peace teaches us that peace between ourselves and our neighbors, between us and God, and between all nations is essential, otherwise we will all lament and wail. This may also suggest that a hidden purpose of the city of Jerusalem is to serve as a divine test: Can the world make peace its primary objective, or will Jerusalem eternally be a source of conflict?

Message 45: "The sword comes to fight" (*Cherev Ba-im L'he-lachem*), nonconsecutive words found in Jeremiah 33:4–5. The literal meaning of this message is stated clearly so that there is no mistake: Violence in the Name of God does not represent God's desire for peace—the sword is for fighting, not for peace.

Message 46: "Tear" or "rip" (*Kow-ray-a*), *The Complete Hebrew English Dictionary,* by Reuben Alcalay. Traditionally, both in the Bible and in contemporary Jewish practice, the rending of garments is an indicator of deep mourning. This is similar to the earlier message "cry out," which reveals a consequence of not making peace.

Message 47: "Displace," "uproot," or "exterminate" (*O-kair*), *The Complete Hebrew English Dictionary,* by Reuben Alcalay. War is a consequence of not having peace and leads to people being uprooted or displaced.

Message 48: "Escape" (*O-rake*), *The Complete Hebrew English Dictionary,* by Reuben Alcalay. This continues the theme of the previous message, of being displaced or uprooted: Often those who are displaced need to flee.

Message 49: "Our affliction and our oppression" (*An-yay-noo V'la-chatz-anu*), Psalm 44:25. This reveals that a condition of no peace leads to affliction and oppression.

Message 50: "Towards other gods" (*El elohim Achay-rim*), Deuteronomy 31:18. As the verse states: "But I [God] will surely have concealed My face on that day because of all the evil that you did, because you turned towards other gods." This teaches us that when we refuse to make peace we are not worshipping the true God. The term "other gods" may also be metaphoric and refer to the worship of power, domination, and wealth.

The following six messages seem to refer to God's feelings and reactions to those who promote hatred and not peace.

Message 51: "He shall destroy" (*Who Yash-mid*), Deuteronomy 31:3. The literal text of Deuteronomy 31:3 states: "He [God] shall destroy these nations from before you." The inference is clear: God shall send destruction to those who do not make peace.

The next two messages both refer to the anger of God, and while they consist of different words, their numerical values are both 376, the same value as that of peace.

Message 52: "And the wrath of God flared greatly" (*Va-y'char Af A-donai M'ode*), Numbers 11:10. This suggests that when peace is not our primary objective, God gets angry.

Message 53: "The fury has gone forth" (*Yatzah Ha-ketzeff*), Numbers 17:11. As this verse states: "For the fury has gone forth from the presence of God, the plague has begun." This message reiterates that God gets angry when there is no peace. (This verse is from the section of the Bible that describes a rebellion against Moses led by Korach. God killed Korach and the other rebels but spared the lives of Korach's sons because they remained loyal to Moses. The following message takes note of their loyalty.)

Message 54: "The sons of Korach" (*B'nay Korach*), Numbers 26:11. This message is in honor of Korach's sons who did not join their father in rebelling against Moses but instead chose the path of peace.

WHAT IS THE CONNECTION
BETWEEN PEACE AND THE MESSIAH?

Message 55: "His Anointed One" (*Mi-she-cho Who*), Psalm 28:8. "His Anointed One" refers to the Messiah. While many of us wish for the Messiah's arrival or return, this message tells us that instead of waiting and hoping, we should be making peace, because peace will either bring about the Messiah or be the equivalent.

Message 56: "This World to the World to Come" (*Ha-Olam V'od Ha-Olam*), 1 Chronicles 16:36. The message here is obvious: Establish peace in this world and maintain it until the next one. However, this message may also be an answer to the question: What will bring about the Messiah? It seems that peace is the thing that will transform this world into the world to come. (It is worth noting that in the phrase "This World to the World to Come," the word "world" is spelled in two different ways even though they are in the same sentence. Many modern biblical scholars interpret variations in spelling as evidence that there were different authors of the Bible. This phrase, however, suggests that the reason for differences in spelling is to produce a specific numerical value. Had "world" been spelled identically in this phrase, the total value of the letters would not have added up to 376.)

Message 57: "In our Mouth and in the mouth of Your people" (*B'pheenu Oo-b'phee Om-cha*), from the daily Blessings of the Torah. This suggests that only by speaking peace can we be considered among God's people.

KEY BENEFITS OF CHOOSING PEACE

Message 58: "Fire at night" (*Aish Lai-lah*), Nehemiah 9:12. After the Exodus from Egypt, God created a pillar of fire at night to protect the Children of Israel in the desert. Metaphorically, this teaches us that peace is either a shining beacon in the darkness that lets us know what path to follow or peace is protective, just as the pillar of fire was.

Message 59: "For the victory of victories" or "For eternal victory" (*Le-netzach Netza-chim*), from the Kedushah prayer. The repetitive language suggests not just a victory but the pinnacle of all victories. This indicates the importance of peace, that it is the true victory of victories.

A single phrase from Genesis 17:19 yields the final two messages. This phrase can be read and translated two different ways: the first reveals divine coaching regarding the creation of peace, and the second reveals a divine warning.

Message 60A: "And God said nevertheless" (*Va-yo-mare Elokim Aval*), Genesis 17:19. This seems to be God's answer to any excuse we have for why peace is not possible. The verse states: "And God said nevertheless, Sarah your wife, shall give birth to a son." As unbelievable as it is that 90-year-old Sarah and her 100-year-old husband, Abraham, would bear a child, so too it may be unbelievable that peace is possible. But God says to make it nevertheless, no matter how difficult or how many excuses there are not to.

However, if we accept the excuses and do not make peace, then the following applies.

Message 60B: "And God said mourning" (*Va-yo-mare Elokim Ah-vale*), alternative translation of Genesis 17:19. This tells us that if we refuse to listen to the hidden directive "Nevertheless make peace," then mourning shall follow.

Chapter Seventeen

What Does Zion Represent?

ZION = 156

Zion is the name of the hill in Jerusalem where the City of David was built in approximately 1000 B.C.E. In 586 B.C.E., the Holy Temple in Jerusalem was destroyed by the Babylonians and the first exile of the Jewish people commenced. Over 600 years later, the Second Holy Temple in Jerusalem was destroyed by the Romans and the second exile began. These two exiles started the process that spread the Jewish people throughout the world. This is referred to as the Diaspora. Most of the Jews who were dispersed longed to return to Israel. Eventually, these Jews came to be referred to as Zionists.

According to the Bible, God has a special relationship with Zion, as stated in Psalm 132 verses 13–14: "For God has chosen Zion; He desires it for His habitation. This is [God's] resting place till the end of time; Here I [God] will dwell, for I desire it."

However, the name "Zion" has come to symbolize more than just the Land of Israel. It is also used in sacred literature to refer to the entire Jewish people, in Israel and elsewhere. Zion may ultimately represent all of God's people, both Jews and non-Jews.

This chapter discloses the messages that are directly embedded within the word "Zion" and which answer several important questions, including: What is the purpose of Zion? Is there a connection between Zion and God? What always happens to those who hate Zion? And what makes Zion invincible?

Zion (*Tzion*) has a Gematria of 156. When all known Hebrew words and phrases with the identical numerical value of 156 were studied and analyzed, each one was found to refer to some aspect of Zion. Three specific and unique Hebrew letters (ק, נ, ו) correspond exactly with the number 156. These letters can be rearranged to spell the first three messages. All other messages in this chapter also have Gematrias of 156 but consist of a variety of different letters.

DIRECTLY EMBEDDED MESSAGES

Message 1: "His nest" (*Key-no*), Deuteronomy 32:11. Moses describes God's relationship with the Jewish people as similar to that of an eagle protecting and feeding its eaglets. This validates Psalm 132:13-14, that God dwells in Zion, that it is "His nest."

Message 2: "Suckle" or "nurse" (*Nook*), from *The Complete Hebrew English Dictionary,* by Reuben Alcalay. This continues the metaphor of the previous message of God as protective mother, suggesting that Zion shall receive its physical and spiritual nourishment from God. As it states in Psalm 132:15: "I [God] will abundantly bless its [Zion's] sustenance."

Message 3. "Acquire" or "purchase" (*Kanu*), 2 Samuel 24:24. There are two hidden meanings here. The term "acquired" is used in the Talmud (Ethics of the Fathers) to teach us that God has acquired a special interest in certain elements of the world, including Israel, Zion, and the Bible. In addition, the word "purchase" in 2 Samuel 24:24 describes King David's purchase of the land upon which the Holy Temple in Jerusalem will be built, by his son Solomon. (Today, only the Western Wall of the Temple remains standing.) It is interesting that the Bible described in detail the purchase of this land. It is as if the Bible, although written or transcribed approximately 3,000 years ago, predicted that the same tract of land would still be the subject of fierce dispute today.

MESSAGES OF WISDOM

The following four messages reveal the purpose of Zion: the first two are from the "Song at the Sea," sung by the Israelites after the miracle of the splitting of the sea, following the Exodus from Egypt.

THE CONNECTION BETWEEN GOD AND ZION

Message 4: "God's right hand" (*Y'min-cha A-donai*), Exodus 15:6. The metaphor of "God's right hand" illuminates the purpose of the Jewish people. The full sentence states: "God's right hand is adorned in strength; God's right hand, smashes the enemy." When an enemy of God arises, God's right hand meets the blow whether it's Pharaoh, Amalek, the Roman Empire, the Spanish Inquisition, Nazi Germany, or Islamic extremism. It appears that world history often parallels Jewish history, that when the world faces a major challenge, God uses the Jewish people as His key chess piece to confront and destroy the enemy.

Message 5: "God's people" or "God Your people" (*Amcha-A-donai*), Exodus 15:16. This suggests that Zion and God's people are one and the same.

Message 6: "The people of God" (*Am Elokay*), Psalm 47:10. Although this phrase uses a different word for God than in the previous message, its numerical value is still 156. This reinforces the connection between Zion and God.

Message 7: "God is with you" (*A-donai Im-chah* or *A-donai Im-ach*), Genesis 26:28. The verse states: "We have indeed seen that God is with you." The hidden message here is clear: God is with Zion and with the supporters of Zion. This could explain the remarkable achievements of the Jews throughout the world in all fields, including science, art, medicine, law, finance, and in promoting civil rights and freedom.

CAN NON-JEWS ALSO BE PART OF ZION?

Message 8: "Evangel," "evangelist," or "gospel" (*Evangelion*), *The Complete Hebrew English Dictionary,* by Reuben Alcalay. Many of Israel's strongest supporters are Christian Evangelicals. That the numerical value of "evangel" is 156, the same as "Zion," suggests that evangels are also considered part of Zion.

The following four messages further reveal God's relationship with Zion.

Message 9: "Symbol of God" or "Emblem of God" (*Semel A-donai*), nonconsecutive words found in 2 Chronicles 33:15. "Symbol of God" is consistent with the earlier idea that the purpose of dispersing Jews throughout the world was to further spread the teachings of the Bible, the Ten Commandments, and God. As stated in Isaiah 2:3: "For from Zion the Torah shall come forth and the word of God from Jerusalem." Throughout history, it seems that God has used Zion as His tool to both spread the message of the Bible, *Tikkun Olam* ("Repairing the world"), and to confront the enemies of God, those who promote hatred.

Message 10: ["God] commands you" (*M'tzav-cha*), Exodus 34:11. This section of Exodus commands the Jews to conquer the land of Canaan and to remove all idolatry. This was a major purpose of Zion (meaning the Jewish people): to spread monotheism, the Bible, and the Ten Commandments. These are the tools that ultimately educate us on how to repair the world (*Tikkun Olam*), through the giving of charity and the performing of acts of kindness.

Message 11: "Work tools" *(Klay M'lacha)*, *The Complete Hebrew English Dictionary*, by Reuben Alcalay. This metaphor seems to confirm that the purpose of Zion is to perform God's work, like a divine tool.

Message 12: "Their blood as a tool" *(Daman B'klee)*, alternative translation of Mishnah *Zevachim*, Chapter 5:1. This phrase, taken out of context, seems to emphasize the idea that God uses Zion (the Jewish people) as a tool to fight His battles. "Their blood as a tool" can be understood literally, because throughout history Jewish blood has been spilled in these battles. In addition, one possible translation of the next two words of the text in Mishnah Zevachim is as follows: "Service in a hidden way" *(Shah-rate B'tza-foon)*. This appears to reveal the exact purpose of Zion: to serve God in a hidden way. The reason why it is "in a hidden way" is because if the world truly understood that Zion was serving God, no one would have the free will to hate Zion. And it seems that the whole point of creation was to give humans free will.

ZION AS A DIVINE TEST: SUPPORT IT OR HATE IT

The next message has two possible interpretations.

Message 13A: "Your voice" *(Ko-lecha)*, Proverbs 2:3. The Book of Proverbs teaches that wisdom is attained by honoring and fearing God, observing the commandments, and by performing acts of kindness. Proverbs 2:3 states: "For only if you proclaim understanding and give forth your voice to discernment [will you attain knowledge and wisdom]." This suggests that how you use your voice determines whether or not you have attained wisdom, and whether or not you are a member of Zion. If you use your voice to pray, help your neighbor, give charity, and speak up for the oppressed, then you are wise and a member of Zion. But if you do not use for voice to promote these principles, you are not. The choice is up to you.

Message 13B: "A measuring line for you" *(Kav Lecha)*, a different reading and interpretation of Proverbs 2:3. The letters comprising the Hebrew word for "Your voice" can be divided into two two-letter words, *Kav Lecha*, which translates to: "A measuring line for you." This suggests that God uses our voices as a measuring to determine whether we are or are not a part of His people. Gematria seems to reveal a recurring theme here: that God has certain measuring lines to determine whether we are His friend or His enemy. That "A measuring line for you" has the numerical value of 156 appears to suggest that support for Zion is one such measuring line for God.

Message 14: "Measuring lines" or "guidelines" *(Kavim)*, *The Complete Hebrew English Dictionary*, by Reuben Alcalay. Zion, in the sense of Israel, provokes strong opinions: it seems that every country in the world either strongly supports or condemns the country. This may not be a coincidence.

The hidden message here seems to be that God uses our support for Zion as a measuring line to judge each of us.

Message 15: "Eye of God" (*Ayin A-donai*), Psalm 33:18. The verse states: "The eye of God is towards those that have awe of Him." The eye of God, therefore, is towards Zion, suggesting that the exact issues that confront Zion, such as anti-Semitism and hatred, are the same issues that God takes note of. This seems to reveal that God may be looking at the world from the point of view of Zion.

Message 16: "God responds" (*Ya-an A-donai*), Job 38:1. Out of context, this implies that God ultimately protects and responds to Zion both in the sense of the people and the place.

Message 17: "Your God shall manifest His kingdom" (*Mah-lach El-o-ka-yich*), Isaiah 52:7. This verse states: "Saying unto Zion, your God shall manifest His kingdom." This section of Isaiah prophesizes that eventually God's kingdom will be visible to all. As it states in the next verse, Isaiah 52:8: "They will see that God returns to Zion." This is prophetic that eventually the world shall see the connection between God and Zion.

Message 18: "For God is above" or "for God is upon" (*La-donai Al*), Numbers 28:15. The meaning is clear: that God is above and watching over Zion.

Message 19: "The Lord God" or "Of God the Lord" (*Ha-Elokim Adon-oi*), Psalm 90:1. This verse states: "A prayer of Moses the man of the Lord God." Moses was the instrument through which Israel received the Bible and the Ten Commandments. The message here is that Zion follows in Moses' footsteps and continues God's work of repairing the world through the Bible and commandments.

Message 20 "Yes God" (*Elokim Kane*), Psalm 48:11. This phrase seems to confirm the strong connection between Zion and God. The end of the verse states: "Thy right hand is full of righteousness." "Right hand" may be a metaphor for Zion as was "God's right hand." In addition, each of the next two sentences in this Psalm: 48:12 and 48:13, contains a phrase that refers to Zion. They are: "Let Mount Zion be glad" and "Walk about Zion."

THREE BIBLICAL CHARACTERS
WHO REPRESENT ASPECTS OF ZION

Message 21: "Joseph" (*Yo-seff*), from the Book of Genesis. As the story goes, Joseph is sold into slavery, imprisoned, and exiled from his home before raising himself up to become the number-two person in Egypt. But Joseph always longed to return to the land of his ancestors. This is a lesson for Jews and anyone in exile: work and live peacefully in the country that you reside in, but never forget Zion or your roots. Through this lens, we can identify Joseph as the first Zionist, even if the term itself did not yet exist.

Message 22: "Ezekiel" (*Yechez-kel*), Ezekiel 1:3. The commentary of the *Artscroll* edition of the Book of Ezekiel states: "Ezekiel was the prophet whose primary mission was away from the Land of Israel." Ezekiel was a prophet in Babylonia at the time of the destruction of the First Temple in Jerusalem (586 B.C.E.). He prepared the exiled Jewish community for their return to Israel and Zion, and for the rebuilding of the Temple.

Message 23: "I am Daniel" (*Ani Daniel*), Daniel 8:1. Daniel was exiled to Babylonia after the destruction of the First Temple. The Book of Daniel portrays Jews living in exile while also adhering to the commandments. One of the lessons that we learn from this book is that Jews who live in exile but still keep the laws of the Torah will be rewarded with honors. This pattern has been repeated for the last 2,000 years, wherever Jews have lived. Daniel eventually returned to Israel in approximately 516 B.C.E., and the Holy Temple in Jerusalem was rebuilt.

A BIBLICAL AND A MODERN EXAMPLE OF ZION

Message 24: "Tent of Meeting" (*O-hel Mo-aid*), Exodus 28:43. This is the Holy Sanctuary where God met with Moses, a metaphor for the divine spirit watching over all of Zion.

Message 25: "Immigrants [to Israel]" (*Olim*), from *The Complete Hebrew English Dictionary,* by Reuben Alcalay. Those who immigrate or make *aliy-ah* to Israel are called *Olim*.

SECRETS TO ZION'S EXCELLENCE AND SURVIVAL

An example of the excellence of Zion is that, although Jews make up less than 1 percent of the population of the world, they have won approximately 20 percent of all Nobel Prizes.

Message 26: "The gold standard" (*Ha-bah-sis Ha-zahav*), from *The Com-plete Hebrew English Dictionary,* by Reuben Alcalay. This is a lovely meta-phor and symbol for the quality of those who dwell in, or support, Zion.

SPIRITUAL AND PHYSICAL PROTECTION OF ZION

The following three messages disclose three elements that have protected Zion.

Message 27: "The nation of the mother" or "With the mother" (*Am Ha-ame* or *Im Ha-ame*), alternative readings and translations of Talmud Tractate Chullin 114B. Both in the Bible and in the modern Jewish family, the Jewish mother is valued, honored, and treated as an equal partner with her husband to guide and shape the family. It could be said that the secret to the success of the Jewish people is the Jewish mother. Epidemiological studies have shown that the health of a family directly correlates with the health, education, and happiness of the mother. A healthier, smarter, and happier mother leads to a healthier family.

Message 28: "Know [and] understand" (*Yo-day-ah* + *Yah-vin*), from Psalm 92:7 (words not consecutive). These appear to be important abilities for all of us to have, but in the context of Zion, to "know and understand" suggests both an awareness and an honoring of national history and tradition. For example, wherever Jews have lived, they have honored and observed the Sabbath. According to Rabbi Asher Zvi Hirsch, better known as Ahad Ha'am (1856–1927), what allowed the Jewish people to survive for 1,900 years without a state of their own, enduring exile, expulsion, and persecution, was remembering the Sabbath Day. Ahad Ha'am said, "More than the Jewish people have kept the Sabbath, the Sabbath has kept the Jews."

Message 29: "Defense force" (*Tzava Hagana*), from the official name of the Israeli Army: the Israeli Defense Forces (IDF). It is perfect that "Defense force" has the same numerical value as "Zion," because this is the force that literally defends Zion.

THE ENEMIES OF ZION

Throughout history, every country that attacked or hated Zion (synonymous with Israel or the Jewish people) has either been defeated or receded from importance. The following three messages refer to the enemies of Zion and give us a glimpse of their future.

Message 30: "They sank" (*Tzalla-loo*), Exodus 15:10. This is part of the "Song at the Sea," sung by the Israelites after they safely crossed the Reed Sea during the Exodus from Egypt. In the context of Exodus 15:10, the enemies of Zion literally sank, but otherwise this phrase is metaphoric.

ARE THE ENEMIES OF ZION ACTUALLY ENEMIES OF GOD?

Message 31: "His [God's] enemies" (*Kah-mav*), Deuteronomy 33:11. This is consistent with the idea that Zion shall battle God's enemies. As the verse states: "And God shall crush the loins of His enemies."

(Note: the numerical value of "shall crush the loins of His enemies" (*M'chatz Mat-naim Ka-mav*) is 834. The Hebrew letters that correspond exactly with 834 can be used to spell the Hebrew word for "history" (*Toldot*). The phrase "Everlasting disgrace" (*Cherpot Olam*), from Jeremiah 23:40, also has a numerical value of 834. When you look at the history of the world, both ancient and modern, those who hate Jews, or any other people, always ultimately end up in disgrace.)

Message 32: "For behold Your enemies shall perish" (*Key He-nay Oy-vecha Yo-vaydo*), Psalm 92:10. The verse states: "For behold Your enemies O Lord, for behold Your enemies shall perish, all the workers of evil shall be scattered." This message here is referring to the enemies of Israel or of Zion, and clearly confirms what will be their ultimate fate. Additionally, because the full verse refers to the enemies as "Your enemies O God," we learn that the enemies of Zion are actually enemies of God, a concept that is verified in Numbers 10:35, which states: "When the Ark would travel, Moses would say, 'God arise, and let Your foes be scattered, and let those that hate You flee from You.'"

CHARACTERISTICS OF ZION

Message 33: "Daily study" or "Daily learning" (*Lee-mood Yomee* or *Lee-mooday Yomee*), a phrase used by countless organizations, synagogues, and groups. This message serves as a reminder that the daily learning of the Bible or Talmud is a common activity of Zion.

Message 34: "Glass of wine" (*Kose Yah-yin*), from the *Shulchan Aruch* (The Code of Jewish Law). When welcoming the Sabbath on Friday nights or when celebrating festival holidays, Jews throughout the world recite the *Kiddush* prayer and drink a glass of wine. This is a common practice of Jews residing both in and outside of Israel.

THREE MESSAGES: EACH CONSISTING OF TWO WORDS SPELLED WITH THE SAME THREE HEBREW LETTERS

Message 35: "Bread" and "Salt" (*Lech-em Meh-lach*), found separately in *The Complete Hebrew English Dictionary,* by Reuben Alcalay. This suggests that just as bread and salt are two fundamental and universal staples of life, so too is Zion.

Message 36: "Dream" and "Fight" (*Cha-lome + Lo-chame*), found separately in *The Complete Hebrew English Dictionary,* by Reuben Alcalay. This reminds us that, for the last 2,000 years, Zion has been both a dream and a fight.

Message 37: "Forgive" and "Pity" (*Ma-chole Cha-mole*), found separately in *The Complete Hebrew English Dictionary,* by Reuben Alcalay. This suggests that, although the people of Zion have encountered much pain and suffering, they should forgive and pity their oppressors.

THE MIRACULOUS AND ETERNAL NATURE OF ZION

It is incredible that Zion has survived intact through 3,800 years of turbulent history. Multiple empires and groups have conquered the Land of Israel, including the Romans, Byzantines, Arabs, Crusaders, Ottomans, and British. Meanwhile, the exiled Jews faced 1,900 years of expulsions, inquisitions, pogroms, blood libels, and the Holocaust. Then, in 1948, Jews re-established Israel as their national homeland. The following messages refer to Zion's eternal spiritual and physical survival.

Message 38: "It has no body" or "He has no body" (*Ay-no Goof*), from the daily *Yigdal* prayer, which summarizes the "Thirteen principles of faith," expounded on by Rabbi Moses Maimonides, also known as the *Rambam*. In context, both this phrase and the entire prayer refer to the greatness of God. Because "It has no body" has a 156 numerical value, it suggests that Zion, like God, is not a physical being but a spiritual one, existing in the hearts and souls of its supporters, whether they are held prisoner in a concentration camp, reside freely in a foreign country, or live in Israel itself.

Message 39: "Miracle" or "wonder" (*Miff-la-awe*), from *The Complete Hebrew English Dictionary,* by Reuben Alcalay. This refers to the miraculous indestructibility of Zion and, after 1,900 years of Jewish exile, the miracle of the re-establishment of Israel.

Message 40: "To perform wonders" (*L'hoff-lee*), Isaiah 29:14. This appears to emphasize the previous message.

Message 41: "Eternal" (*Oh-lamee*), from *The Complete Hebrew English Dictionary,* by Reuben Alcalay. This suggests that Zion will exist for all eternity, both as a country and as the Jewish people.

Message 42: "Existence" or "survival" (*Key-yoom*), from *The Complete Hebrew English Dictionary,* by Reuben Alcalay. These qualities are prophesized and promised to Zion throughout the Bible.

WHY IS ZION BLESSED AND PROTECTED BY GOD?

A Gematrial analysis of the first time the word "Zion" is used in the Bible reveals the answer. The word "Zion" first appears in Book 2 of Samuel 5:7: "David then captured the Fortress of Zion, it is the City of David." The phrase "the Fortress of Zion" (*Et M'tzudot Tzion*) has a Gematria of 1091. I have found that all text with a 1091 Gematria refers to "the study of Torah" (*Talmud Torah*). This suggests that because Zion honors and studies the Torah, Zion is like an invincible fortress. Here is a brief sample of words and phrases that have the identical numerical value of 1091.

1091 GEMATRIAS: "THE STUDY OF TORAH" (*TALMUD TORAH*)

1. "Beautiful of form" (*Y'phat Toar*), Deuteronomy 21:11.

2. "The Rose of Sharon" (*Cha-va-tzelet Ha-Sharon*), Song of Songs 2:1. A rose is an example of something extremely beautiful. "The Rose of Sharon," therefore, is a perfect metaphor for the study of Torah.

3. "Knowledge and awe" (*Da-ot V'yirot*), Isaiah 11:2.

4. "All of the living shall bless" (*Kal Chai T'vorech Et*), from the *Nishmat* prayer.

5. "Herald the power" (*Oo-Nisaneh Tokef*), from the High Holy Day prayer of the same name.

6. "My splendor" (*Tifartee*), Isaiah 46:13.

7. "Thoughts of a person" (*Mach-sh'votecha Eesh*), Psalm 92:6-7.

8. "Their great wealth they shall praise" (*Ashram Yit-ha-la-lu*), from Psalm 49:7. The hidden message here is that the study of Torah is itself great wealth.

9. "Shall understand charity and justice" (*Ta-vin Tzedek Oo-mishpat*), Proverbs 2:9. This emphasizes that the prime purpose of studying Torah is to understand and then perform acts of charity and justice in order to repair the world.

THE DIFFERENCE BETWEEN ZION AND ISRAEL

What is the difference between Zion and Israel? Gematria reveals that Israel has a numerical value of 541and that Zion has a value of 156. The difference between them is equal to 385 (541 − 156 = 385). The three specific and unique Hebrew letters that correspond exactly to 385 spell the word for "Language" (*Safah*). Therefore, those who love Zion can speak any language, but only by making Hebrew their primary language does Zion transform into Israel.

Chapter Eighteen

Anti-Semitism

Is It Hatred of Jews or of God Himself?

ANTI-SEMITISM = 826

The accepted definition of anti-Semitism is "hatred of Jews," but as the former chief rabbi of Great Britain Lord Jonathan Sacks has pointed out: "We do wrong to call it anti-Semitism; the hate that begins with Jews never ends with Jews." This is because hatred of Jews is really about hatred of God, which is measured by hatred towards His creations. Whether they be blacks, Hispanics, women, Christians, Chinese, Hindus, Armenians, immigrants, gays, Jews, or anyone else. For millennia, the primary litmus test for hatred has been that toward Jews. Approximately 3,800 years ago, Abraham, the first Jew, was hated because he introduced monotheism to a world that accepted only idolatry.

This chapter discloses the messages directly embedded within the Hebrew term for anti-Semitism, explains the true superficial and deeper causes of hatred, and reveals the consequences that always befall those who hate.

Evidence that anti-Semitism is actually hatred of God can be found in any dictionary. For example, *Merriam Webster's Collegiate Dictionary* (Tenth Edition) states that the word "Semite" is "from the Hebrew *Shem*." In Hebrew, *Shem* is defined as "name." In Jewish prayer, God is referred to as God (*A-donai* in Hebrew), but in conversation, out of respect, Jews do not call God "God," instead using the term *Hashem* (defined in English as "The Name"). Therefore, the literal definition of the term anti-Semitism is anti-*Shem* or anti-Name of God. (*Shem* was also the name of the son of Noah, from whom according to the Bible, the Jews descended.)

The notion that anti-Semitism is about hatred of God and not of the Jews is also supported by the Bible. Numbers 10:35 states: "When the Ark would travel, Moses would say, 'Arise God, and let Your foes be scattered, let those who hate You flee from You.'" Because Moses was referring to the haters of the Jewish people, he should have used the phrases: "our foes" and "those who hate us." But instead the phrases "Your foes" and "those who hate You" were used, with the words "Your" and "You" referring to God. Rashi (1040–1105), history's foremost commentator on the Bible, in his writings on Numbers 10:35, agrees that to be anti-Israel (Israel being synonymous with the entire Jewish people) is equivalent to being anti-God.

Thus, it seems that if you hate any person or any group it is a direct reflection and test of your own love for or hatred of God. These tests appear necessary because, if we were to ask anyone if they hated God, the answer would invariably be "No." In fact, haters often claim to, and even believe that, they love God. Therefore, hatred of God is not a function of what we say or believe but is expressed by how we behave in relationships with people that are different from us. Over 3,000 years ago, the Jewish people volunteered to be the primary litmus test for the hatred of God. Simply said: If you hate Jews or any person or any group, you hate God.

The numerical value of the Hebrew word for anti-Semitism (*Ante-Shem-ee-oot*) is 826. After studying all known Hebrew words and phrases with a value of 826, each has been found to refer to an aspect of anti-Semitism or anti-Israel sentiment. The four Hebrew letters that correspond exactly to 826 are תתכו, which have been used to spell the first four messages. All other messages in this chapter also have Gematrias of 826 but consist of a variety of different letters.

DIRECTLY EMBEDDED MESSAGES

Message 1: "Divide in the middle" (*Tee-vach-tah*), *The Complete Hebrew English Dictionary*, by Reuben Alcalay. This suggests that hatred of Jews is used as a divine test or measuring line to distinguish between those who hate God and those who are friends of God. The hatred of women, minorities, and anyone else can also be considered as measuring lines.

THE PSYCHOLOGICAL EXPLANATION
FOR ANTI-SEMITISM, RACISM, AND ALL HATRED

Message 2: "Crushed," "pounded," or "beaten" (*V'chee-tot*), 2 Kings 18:4. In context, "crushed" describes the destruction of idols, but in the context of anti-Semitism "crushed" seems to refer to a psychological or emotional state that gives rise to anti-Semitism, hatred, and bigotry. If we were to analyze anti-Semites or racists, we would find individuals who were beaten or crushed at some point in their lives. It may have been a physical, emotional, or even an intellectual beating at the hands of a parent, relative, teacher, or colleague. Not everyone who was beaten becomes an anti-Semite, but every anti-Semite and every racist feels crushed in some way. Thus, anti-Semitism and hatred can be interpreted as indicators or symptoms that the hater feels weak and insignificant and is projecting his or her shame and anger onto others.

Message 2A: "Crushed," "pounded," or "beaten" (*V'chee-tot*), an alternative interpretation of the above message. This may be a warning to anti-Semites, racists, Holocaust deniers, and all haters: If you do not change your ways, you will be beaten, crushed, and pounded. This seems true even if you are a famous celebrity or the leader of a great country. It is almost a law of physics: The ultimate fate of all those who hate is shame and humiliation.

Message 3: "Classes" or "schoolrooms" (*Key-tote*), *The Complete Hebrew English Dictionary,* by Reuben Alcalay. This appears to tell us that a good education that teaches children to respect all other people will help diminish anti-Semitism, racism, and hate.

MESSAGES OF WISDOM

Message 4: "Who shall grow poor and who shall prosper" (*Me Yay-ani Oo-me Yay-asher*), from the *Unesaneh Tokef* prayer, recited on the High Holy Days. This message is metaphoric and suggests that anyone who chooses hatred shall be impoverished, and that those who choose acceptance and peace shall grow rich. While some anti-Semites and haters may be financially wealthy right now, they may also be spiritually bankrupt, and their names will ultimately be associated with derision and humiliation. This illustrates one possible meaning of the earlier message "Divide in the middle."

Message 5: "Hatred of Jews" (*Sinot Yehudim*), used in multiple Hebrew articles and books. This reminds us that hatred of Jews is the conventional definition of anti-Semitism.

Message 6: "Envy" (*Tsa-root A-yin*), one of the litany of sins from the *Al Chet* confessional prayer, recited on Yom Kippur. This makes clear that envy is a root cause of anti-Semitism and probably the key explanation for most hatred, which is why the Tenth Commandment states: "Thou shall not covet" (Exodus 20:14).

Message 7: "Haughty" (*Ay-naim Ramote*), also from the *Al Chet* confessional prayer. This reminds us that describing Jews as haughty has a long history in anti-Semitism.

THE SOURCE OF ANTI-SEMITISM

The following phrase, recited every time the Torah is removed from the Ark, connects anti-Semitism with hatred of God and reveals that the major causes of anti-Semitism are envy that Israel received the Bible, and envy that Israel was chosen to receive the Bible over all others.

Message 8: "Your enemies and those who hate You flee from You, because." (*Oy-vecha V'yanusu M'san-echa Me-pa-necha Ki*), from the prayer recited when opening the Ark to remove the Torah. This phrase is from Numbers 10:35 except for the last word, "because," which is from Isaiah 2:3. What follows the word "because" (also from Isaiah 2:3) reveals the source of anti-Semitism. The prayer in full states: "Arise God, and let Your foes be scattered, let those who hate You flee from You, because: from Zion the Torah will come forth and the word of God from Jerusalem." This explains that the envious hatred of Jews resulted from God having given the Jewish people the Torah. It is as if the haters of Jews resent the morality and laws that the Torah brought to the world.

Message 9: "Behold Torah" (*Torah Ha-ray*), Mishnah Torah (Laws of the Study of Torah Chapter 3:A). This seems to be a divine directive to the world to behold Torah, with each of us having the free will to either embrace or reject it. Unfortunately, what seems to happen in practice is that, out of envy, some people choose to embrace anti-Semitism instead.

ANNE FRANK AGREES

To paraphrase Anne Frank, the reason that people hate Jews is because the Jews brought morality to the world by introducing the Bible. In her entry of April 11, 1944, Anne addresses the source of anti-Semitism, writing: "It might even be our religion from which the world and all peoples learn good." Anne was speaking about the purpose of the Torah, which is to repair the world, or *Tikkun Olam* in Hebrew. It seems that Jews remind the world to be conscious, to follow the laws of the Torah, and to heal the world. Because the world learned the Ten Commandments and the Bible from Zion (the Jewish people) the anti-Semites feel, consciously or unconsciously, that without Jews there would be no Ten Commandments and that any behavior, no matter how abhorrent, would be acceptable.

BIBLICAL EXPLANATION FOR WHY ANTI-SEMITISM
AND ALL HATE IS ACTUALLY HATRED OF GOD

The Book of Genesis explains that God created human beings in His own image. Therefore it is implied that hatred of any person is equivalent to hatred of God.

Message 10: "He [God] made the human being" (*Asah Et Ha-adam*), Genesis 9:6. The verse states: "For in the image of God He made the human being." The *Soncino Edition of the Pentateuch,* edited by Dr. J. H. Hertz (1970), comments on this verse: "We have here a declaration of the native dignity of man[kind], irrespective of his race or creed. Because man[kind] is created in the image of God, he can never be reduced to the level of a thing or chattel; he remains a person, with inalienable rights. To rob a man of these inalienable rights constitutes an outrage against God." Therefore, the hidden and literal meanings of "He made the human being" both refer to the same principle: Hatred of a Jew, or of any person, is an outrage against God.

Message 11: "Has fashioned the human with wisdom" (*Ya-tzar et Ha-Adam B'chachmah*), from the morning prayers. This reminds us that, while, God created humans with the capability of wisdom, we are guilty of widespread hatred. Hopefully, the day will come when wisdom triumphs over anti-Semitism, racism, and hate.

Message 12: "Doing any" or "Doing all" (*Asot Kol*), Isaiah 56:2. The phrase states: "Praiseworthy . . . Is the person who guards his hand against doing any evil." Because the Gematria of "Doing all" is identical to that of "anti-Semitism," it seems to equate the evil of hating Jews with all other forms of hatred. In addition, "Doing all" may reveal that engaging in anti-Semitism is a "gateway hatred," leading to other acts of evil.

PROVING THE CONNECTION
BETWEEN GOD'S NAME AND ANTI-SEMITISM

The following messages all relate to the holiness and greatness of God's Name, revealing the desecration that occurs when we hate any human being.

Message 13: "I shall sanctify Your Name [God]" (*Ah-nee Akadesh Shimcha*), from the Sephardic version of the *Aleinu* prayer. This tells us that sanctifying God's Name is the opposite of being against the Name of God and of being anti-Semitic.

Message 14: "May His [God's] great Name be blessed" (*Y'hay Shmay Rabah M'vorach*), from the Kaddish prayer. Keeping in mind that the literal translation of anti-Semitism is "against the Name of God," "May His great Name be blessed" seems to reveal that, when someone hates a Jew or any person or group, it is the opposite of blessing God. Therefore, this implies that the hater is actually cursing the Name of God.

Message 15: "And made for Yourself" (*Va-tah-as Lecha*), from Nehemiah 9:10. This refers to God when He took the enslaved Israelites out of Egypt by performing signs and wonders. The phrase states: "And made for Yourself a name." This again connects the word "name" with God, thus reinforcing that anti-Semitism is actually: Anti the Name of God.

Message 16: "Famous" (*M'for-sa-mote*), from *The Complete Hebrew English Dictionary* by Reuben Alcalay. This message emphasizes the idea that since biblical times, beginning with the nation of Amalek, anti-Semites have tried to gain fame by attacking Jews, God's people. Note: The word "famous" and the phrase "And made for Yourself [a name]" are not only synonymous but have the same numerical value of 826.

ANTI-SEMITISM AND HATRED AS DIVINE MEASURING LINES

Message 17: "To judge the" (*Lishpote Et*), from 1 Chronicles 16:33. As the full phrase states: "For God will have come to judge the earth." Because "To judge the" has the same numerical value as "anti-Semitism," it supports the idea that God uses anti-Semitism and hatred as His gauges for judgment.

Message 18: "Secret of the Most High" or "Secret of the Exalted" (*Sayter Elyone*), literal translation of Psalm 91:1. Out of context, this may suggest that, if anti-Semitism and hatred are indeed divine measuring lines for God's judgment, it must remain a secret, otherwise human beings will lose the free will to hate for fear of being divinely judged.

Message 19: "In order to test you" (*L'ba-ah-voor Nah-sote*), literal translation of Exodus 20:17. This may also refer to the idea that hatred of Jews is a litmus test. When the non-Jew can accept Jews without hatred or prejudice, he or she passes God's test and is elevated in some way. The more accepted definition of this phrase is "In order to elevate you," which will be discussed later in this chapter.

CONSEQUENCES OF ANTI-SEMITISM, RACISM, AND HATRED

Message 20: "What will You [God] do?" (*Oo-mah Ta'aseh*), Joshua 7:9. Threatened with defeat, Joshua, the leader of the Israelites after Moses, asks God: "What will You do for Your Great Name?" Joshua challenges God to prevent the desecration of God's own Name, by empowering the Israelites to defeat its enemies. This appears to reveal that God takes it personally when anyone hates Jews or Israel, and may explain why the enemies of Israel have always been defeated.

Message 21: "And God shall destroy them" (*V'tash-me-dame A-donai*), words are not consecutive but are found in same verse of Lamentations 3:66. This is a warning to anti-Semites and to all those who hate.

Message 22: "Their suffering shall increase" (*Yirboo Atz-vo-tam*), from Psalm 16:4. "Their suffering shall increase" seems to be a warning to anti-Semites and to all haters that, by hating others, they bring suffering unto themselves. This is true regardless of how wealthy or powerful the hater is. Inevitably, month in and month out, we witness on the news the shame and humiliation that befall people who hate. The full phrase states: "Those that chase after [other gods] their suffering shall increase." Here, "Those that chase after [other gods]" refers to the anti-Semites and the haters because "hatred" is actually a form of idolatry. How? Because when we hate, we are not obeying the Word of God, which teaches us that all people were created in His image, and are instead following our own religion of hate.

Message 23: "Destruction for all" (*Shah-mote L'kol*), alternative translation of Genesis 2:20. This seems to suggest that what begins as anti-Semitism ultimately leads to destruction for all. In addition, this may refer to the destruction of all anti-Semites and haters. The traditional definition of this Hebrew phrase is "Names for all" (*Shay-mote L'kol*), which in the context of anti-Semitism possibly refers to anti-Semitism as the name for all hate. As the former chief rabbi of Great Britain Lord Jonathan Sacks said: "The hate that begins with Jews never ends with Jews."

Message 24: "God has placed" or "God has delivered" (*Tate A-donai*), Joshua 10:12 and 1 Kings 5:17. This phrase is used in exactly the same way in both sources, that God has placed the enemies of Israel into Israel's hands, therefore suggesting that all anti-Semites and haters shall ultimately be defeated.

Message 25: "To the dust of death" (*La-afar Mavet*), Psalm 22:16. This reinforces the idea that the enemies of Jews shall end in the dust of death and defeat.

Message 26: "Your oppressors shall be downtrodden" (*L'mishisah Shosaich*), the *Lecha Dodi* prayer. This again emphasizes that the fate of those who hate is defeat.

Message 27: "I shall hear" or "I shall pay attention" (*V'sha-mah-tee*), Exodus 22:26. The full phrase states: "So it will be if he cries out to Me [God], I shall hear, for I am compassionate." This reaffirms that God hears the cries of the victims of anti-Semitism and hatred and will show compassion for them.

Message 28: "And they build eternal desolation" or "And they build ancient ruins" (*Oo-bah-nu Chur-vote Olam*), Isaiah 61:4. Out of context, this suggests that desolation and ruin are what anti-Semitism, racism, and hatred bring.

BIBLICAL EXAMPLE OF ANTI-SEMITISM

Message 29: "And it happened when Pharaoh stubbornly refused" (*Va-y'he Key Hikshaw Pharaoh*), Exodus 13:15. This suggests that hatred of Jews was behind Pharaoh's refusal to free the Israelite slaves.

HOW DOES ANTI-SEMITISM BENEFIT THE JEWISH PEOPLE?

Message 30: "Cohesion" (*Ta-a-chi-zute*), *The Complete English Hebrew Dictionary,* by Reuben Alcalay. This tells us that, while anti-Semitism is a destructive force in the world and a manifestation of hatred, it often creates unity among Jews.

Message 31: "This shall be upon your hearts and souls" (*Eleh Ahl L'vav-chem V'ahl Naf-sho-chem*), Deuteronomy 11:18. This phrase refers to the importance of embracing the commandments as part of our being, suggesting that the commandments should be upon our hearts and souls even when faced with anti-Semitism.

Message 32: "With Your abundant goodness guide Your congregation" (*B'rov tuv-cha na-hale a-datecha*), from the *Ana B'koach* prayer. The hidden wisdom here is that anti-Semitism may actually help guide the Jews in the right direction. For instance, when Jews assimilate into other cultures and stray from the commandments, anti-Semitism may help lead them back to Judaism.

Message 33: "God teach me Your paths" (*A-donai Hody-ainee Orcho-techa*), from Psalm 25:4. While anti-Semitism often reminds Jews that they are Jews, the larger impact is that its victims learn the importance of kindness and compassion, and may be inspired to advocate for others who are similarly oppressed. For example, many Jews were drawn to supporting the Reverend Dr. Martin Luther King Jr. and his fight for civil rights because of their own experiences with bigotry.

Message 34: "Raise our pride" (*Tag-be-a Kar-nanu*), from the "It was You before the world was created" prayer (*Atah Who*). This suggests that anti-Semitism raises the pride of the Jewish people. A study of world history and Jewish history reveals a striking pattern: Jews have basically thrived whether or not they faced discrimination, but all nations and individuals that have mistreated Jews have either descended into obscurity or been shamed and humiliated. This pattern seems to occur even today, maybe to a widely respected journalist at the end of his or her career, a famous Hollywood celebrity, or even the leader of a great country.

Message 35: "In order to elevate You (*L'ba-ah-voor Nah-sote*), Exodus 20:17. Again, this seems to suggest that anti-Semitism elevates the Jews, possibly because having enemies demands us to have greater wisdom and strength in order to survive. In addition, being hated also spiritually elevates the individual because fear and concern promote prayer, repentance, and observance. Furthermore, "In order to elevate you" may also provide the psychological explanation for all hatred: that people with envy and low self-esteem are attracted to anti-Semitism and other prejudices as an attempt to elevate themselves. It could be said that hatred of others is actually compensation for low self-esteem.

Message 36: "Candles before [God]" or "Lamps before [God]" (*Nay-rote Liphnay*), Leviticus 24:4. This is a directive to the Israelites to light the eternal lamp for God outside the holy Tent of Meeting and may be read metaphorically: that victims of anti-Semitism and other types of hatred bring light into the world by virtue of fighting against the forces of hate.

THE SYMBOL OF ANTI-SEMITISM

Message 37: "Sign of the Swastika" (*Shelet Tzlav Ha-keress*), from article in Ynetnews Yedioth Internet. This reminds us that the Swastika is the universal symbol of anti-Semitism and hatred.

DIVINE WISDOM FOR
VICTIMS OF ANTI-SEMITISM AND HATRED

Message 38: "Do not tremble before" (*Lo Ta-guru Mipnay*), Deuteronomy 1:17. The full phrase states: "Do not tremble before any man, for the judgment is God's." This reminds us that we should tremble only before God and not because of those who perpetrate hate against us.

Message 39: "And you shall perform them" (*Va-a-see-tem*), Numbers 15:39. The verse states: "Remember all the commandments of God and you shall perform them." This teaches us that, even when confronted with anti-Semitism or any form of hatred, we must continue to observe the commandments.

A DIVINE LESSON TO ANTI-SEMITES, RACISTS AND HATERS

In the Biblical story of Balak, the King of Moab, an enemy of Israel, hires Balaam, a non-Jewish prophet who also hates Israel, to curse Israel (Numbers Chapters 22–24). But when Balaam opens his mouth to articulate the curse, God allows Balaam to speak only words of praise and blessing toward Israel. Thus, the lesson to haters may be that their hatred is not only ineffective but may actually be transformed into blessings for those they choose to hate.

Message 40: "Balaam saw that it was good in the eyes of God to bless" (*Vayar Balaam Ki Tov B'ay-nay A-donai L'varech*), Numbers 24:1. This appears to be a divine promise that those who hate Israel will end up blessing Israel, and that those who bless Israel will also bring blessings upon themselves.

Message 41: "Crowns Israel" (*O-tare Yisrael*), from the morning blessings. As the full phrase states: "Crowns Israel with splendor." This reinforces the idea that Israel is actually rewarded for being hated.

Chapter Nineteen

Where Are the
Greats of the Generation?

GREATS OF THE GENERATION = 268

What makes one truly great? Ancient examples of great people include the matriarchs and patriarchs of the Bible, Moses, the Chinese and Greek philosophers, and Jesus. In more modern times, we can look to Dr. Martin Luther King, Mother Theresa, Dr. Elie Weisel, and Oprah Winfrey as having made huge contributions to society and the world.

To many of us, however, money is the measure of all greatness and achievement. We are quick to idolize celebrities, athletes, and those who have amassed great fortunes. Whether it is a C.E.O., a hedge-fund manager, or a movie star, we believe and behave as if they are great and worthy of our adulation. When the failings of these "greats" are exposed, we easily discard them and move on to the next one. The cycle continues as we confuse success, fortune, and fame with true greatness.

This chapter reveals examples of what true greatness consists of and provides guidance on how to direct our children towards it. The chapter also discloses messages that seem to answer questions such as: Where are the greats? What is God's opinion of those we idolize? What steps should we take to achieve greatness? Also revealed is the secret to becoming a true star.

The Hebrew phrase for "Greats of the generation" (*Gidolay Ha-dore*) was found in *The Complete Hebrew English Dictionary,* by Reuben Alcalay. It has a numerical value of 268; after studying all known Hebrew text with that specific numerical value, I discovered that each example could be interpreted as referring to an aspect of "Greats of the generation."

Three specific and unique Hebrew letters correspond exactly to 268: ר,ס,ח. These three letters can be used to spell four words, listed as the first four messages. They seem to reflect God's opinion and comments regarding whom we consider to be our greats today. All the other messages in this chapter also have the numerical value of 268, but they consist of a variety of different letters.

Message 1: "Lacking," "absent," or "missing" (*Cha-sair*), *The Complete Hebrew English Dictionary,* by Reuben Alcalay. This suggests that greats seem to be missing from this generation.

Message 2: "Business," "trade," or "commerce" (*Sa-char*), *The Complete Hebrew English Dictionary,* by Reuben Alcalay. This is a reference to those we mistakenly consider to be greats: those in business. It may be the entertainment business, finance, or even politics.

Message 3: "Stink," "stench," or "sin" (*Saw-rach*), *The Complete Hebrew English Dictionary,* by Reuben Alcalay. This appears to be a divine comment on our veneration of false greats.

Message 4: "Clay," "potsherd" or "fragments of pottery" (*Chee-race*), *The Complete Hebrew English Dictionary,* by Reuben Alcalay. "Clay" as a metaphor may have a positive or negative connotation. It may refer to the "clay" of the false idols that will soon shatter into fragments because the idols are insubstantial, or it may be a divine metaphor for how to have our children become truly great: mold them with solid values such as education and the importance of charity and kindness.

MESSAGES OF WISDOM

Message 5: "Like clay" (*Ka-cho-mare*), Job 10:9. This verse states: "Please remember that You [God] molded me like clay, and will return me to the dust." This verse serves to remind us of the importance of humility, as it exposes the truth about all of our "greats" and ourselves: that ultimately we are all but dust. It is worth noting that while the Hebrew terms for "Like clay," in this citation, and "clay" in the previous message are two entirely different words, incredibly they each have the same Gematria of 268.

REVEALING TRUE GREATNESS
AND MOCKING FALSE GREATNESS

Message 6: "Behold the Master of the Universe" (*Heno Adon Olam*), from the *Yigdal* prayer. The daily *Yigdal* (translated as the "He [God] is great") prayer states: "Behold the Master of the Universe to every creature, He demonstrates His greatness and His sovereignty." In this prayer, God is referred to as "the Master of the Universe." However, today, often the titans of finance are referred to as "masters of the universe." In the context of the prayer, this phrase acknowledges God as the greatest in each generation, but in the context of this chapter, "master of the universe" can be read as divine sarcasm towards the rich and famous.

BIBLICAL EXAMPLES OF TRUE GREATS OF THE GENERATION

Each of the following messages refers to a biblical character or place and possesses a numerical value of 268.

Message 7: "In Hebron" (*B'Hebron*), Genesis 13:18. The city of Hebron is the location of the Cave of the Patriarchs and Matriarchs (*M'arat HaMachpelah*). All of the Patriarchs and Matriarchs of the Bible: Abraham, Isaac, Jacob, Sarah, Rebecca, and Leah are buried there, except for Rachel. These are all examples of true greats of the generation.

Message 8: "To Rachel" (*L'Rachel*), Genesis 29:11. Since Rachel is the only matriarch not buried in Hebron (and therefore not included in the above message), the numerical value of "To Rachel" reminds us that we should also regard Rachel as a true great.

Message 9: "Aaron he is" (*Who Ah-haron*), Exodus 6:26. This acknowledges that Aaron, the high priest and brother of Moses, as well as his mouthpiece, was also a great.

Message 10: "Abraham His Beloved" (*Avraham O-hah-vo*), from the *Kol Mikadesh* prayer. This tells us that Abraham, God's beloved, who brought monotheism to the world, was a great as well.

NO LIMIT AS TO WHO CAN BECOME A GREAT OF THE GENERATION

Message 11: "The foreigners," "the aliens," or "the strangers" (*Ha-gay-rim*), 2 Chronicles 2:16. In the Bible, strangers or foreigners often become greats of the generation; for example, Jethro, the daughter of Pharaoh, and Ruth. This teaches us that foreigners and their children can also become greats. In addition, the term "The aliens" may be a metaphor for those we too often shun. Biblically, it is prophesized that the Messiah will arise from a descendent of someone masquerading as a prostitute (the story of Tamar and Judah). This reminds us to value and treat every human being like they have the potential to be great.

Message 12: "To all people in any manner" (*L'kol Ah-dam B'kol Ma-ah-chal*), Mishna Zevachim Chapter 5:6. Again, people, from any manner of life, have the potential to be a great of their generation.

Message 13: "Has no fixed limit" (*Ain La Kevah*), from Mishna 4:9. This emphasizes the previous message, that "greats" do not come from a limited section of society. Rather, the pool is limitless and includes all.

MESSAGES OF WARNING

The following messages may be directed to either the false greats or to those who venerate them.

Message 14: "Your donkey" or "Your ass" (*Cha-morcha*), Deuteronomy 28:31. In context, "Your donkey" admonishes Israel for disobeying God's commandments. Out of context, "Your ass" seems to be God's insult to the false greats of the generation and to us for idolizing them.

Message 15: "There shall not be light" (*Lo Yih-he-yeh Ohr*), Zechariah 14:6. This suggests that if we worship the false greats, or treat only certain people like they can become great, then, metaphorically, there will be no light, no hope.

Message 16: "God has a grievance" (*Riv LA-donai*), Micah 6:2. This phrase again suggests that God has a grievance with our embrace of false greats.

Message 17: "Then I shall be angry no more" (*V'lo Ech-oss Ode*), Ezekiel 16:42. In this section of Ezekiel, God is angry that the Israelites have strayed after superficial desires. Earlier in the chapter, verse 16:15 states: "But you trusted in your beauty, and you became licentious because of your fame." Beauty and fame are two of the superficial qualities of the false greats. The message here is that when we embrace the values of the true greats and stop imitating the false ones, God will be angry no more.

Message 18: "Facebook." When Facebook is spelled with Hebrew letters (פייסבוק), it has a numerical value of 268. Because Facebook measures popularity by recording the number of "likes," this message suggests that we may mistake this measure as an indicator of true greatness.

THE CONFUSION BETWEEN
STARS AND GREATS OF THE GENERATION

A great of the generation has the qualities of a star, but a star or a talented outstanding individual is not necessarily a great of the generation. The truly great Dr. Martin Luther King—his words, speeches, and actions—should be studied throughout all generations. There is less to study with a star, and when we mistake a "star" for a "great," problems arise. One distinction between them is that when a great makes a mistake they remain great, but when a star makes a mistake, they fall. The Bible tells countless stories of the mistakes of the truly great in order to teach us valuable lessons. From the mistakes of the stars (racism, anti-Semitism, abuse, fraud, etc.), there is also much to learn, but we should not confuse a star for a great.

STAR OR A FALLEN STAR?

Message 19: Star or fallen star? (*Kochav V'Kochav Nofale*), this phrase was found by translating the question: Star or fallen star? into Hebrew. It also has a numerical value of 268. When a star falls, it usually confirms that they were not truly a great of the generation.

QUALITIES OF A TRUE GREAT

Message 20: "Modest with all" (*Tza-noo-ah B'kol*), from the *Kitzur Shulchan Aruch* 3:1 (Condensed Code of Jewish Law). This tells us that modesty is an important virtue that a true great possesses.

Message 21: "Doer of good deeds" (*Go-mail Chasadim Tovim*), from the *Shemoneh Esreh* prayer. To perform good deeds is a primary commandment in the Bible and a quality present in all greats. In addition, through our doing of good deeds, our children learn by example.

WHAT ARE THE SECRETS TO BEING A STAR? STAR = 48

Obviously, the obsession with stars or with becoming a star is not going away. Therefore let us look at the messages directly embedded within the Hebrew word for "star" (*Kochav*).

AN ANALYSIS OF THE NUMERICAL VALUE OF "STAR": 48

Embedded within the Hebrew word for "star" (*Kochav*) are hidden messages that appear to be divine coaching on how to achieve stardom. The Hebrew word for "star" has a numerical value of 48. Two specific and unique Hebrew letters correspond exactly with 48 (מח), and they can be used to spell multiple words: two of these words are interpreted as the key ingredients to becoming a true star, and the third one reveals a superficial trait that many of us mistakenly use to measure value. These three words are listed as the first three messages. All the other messages in this section also have numerical values of 48, but they consist of a variety of different letters.

MESSAGES DIRECTLY EMBEDDED WITHIN
THE HEBREW WORD FOR "STAR"

Message A: "Brain," "intelligence," or "marrow" (*Mo-ach*), *The Complete Hebrew English Dictionary,* by Reuben Alcalay. Brains and intelligence are core to true greatness. However, what most people usually value are the more superficial "star" qualities, such as wealth, popularity, and appearance.

Message B: "Warmth" or "enthusiasm" (*Chom*), *The Complete Hebrew English Dictionary,* by Reuben Alcalay. This tells us that these are also important attributes for a star to have.

The following message is an example of a superficial trait that many of us consider extremely important. It is essential to recognize that this concern interferes with our ability to wisely judge ourselves and others.

Message C: "Fatness" (*May-ach*), *The Complete Hebrew English Dictionary,* by Reuben Alcalay. The superficial issue of weight consumes much of our attention. Obviously, to be overweight is a valid health concern, but too often we go beyond an interest in health to judging ourselves and others by their weight alone.

MESSAGES OF WISDOM

Message D: "Within you God" (*B'cha A-donai*), Psalm 31:2. As the verse states: "Within you God I have put my trust." This suggests that, to be a star, we must trust and value God instead of valuing superficial trends or people.

Message E: "Great" (*Gedolah*), Numbers 22:18. This verse states: "I cannot transgress the word of God, my Lord, to do anything small or great." This may imply that if your actions conflict with God's word, you will not be a star or achieve greatness.

Message F: "I shall merit glory" or "I shall merit greatness" (*Ezkeh Hod*), from the Sabbath evening song *Yom Zeh L'Yisrael*. This seems to emphasize that one may merit stardom if committed to intelligence, a trust in God, and observing the word of God.

MESSAGE OF WARNING

Message G: "To waste" (*L'vaz-bez*), *The Complete Hebrew English Dictionary,* by Reuben Alcalay. If you value the superficial over intelligence and brains, you are wasting your life.

Chapter Twenty

A Curse upon Corruption

CORRUPTION = 265

Almost weekly, some famous or successful person is brought down by a scandal of corruption. This person may be a journalist, money manager, renowned Hollywood director, actor, or even the leader of a great country. Corruption, whether based on words, actions, or both, can destroy individuals, corporations, families, and even entire communities. It both diverts assets to a few and invariably leads to bigger problems, like pollution. The term "corruption" is often assumed to mean financial misconduct, such as bribery, but it can also refer to hate speech in the form of racism, anti-Semitism, antigay attitudes, and all other expressions of prejudice and bigotry.

In this chapter, the messages directly embedded in, and having the same numerical value as, the Hebrew word for "corruption" are revealed. The messages seem to answer many questions, including: What is the connection between corruption and the Garden of Eden? What was the most famous biblical instance of corruption? And why is it that the corrupt eventually always fall? The consequences of participating in corrupt activities, as well as the rewards for resisting them, are disclosed. And a haunting answer is generated to the question: What happens to those who profit from corruption? While everyone knows that corruption is an immoral thing, in this chapter we learn God's specific opinion of it.

The Hebrew word for corruption (*Kal-kalah*) is found in *The Complete Hebrew English Dictionary,* by Reuben Alcalay, and it has a Gematria of 265. The three specific and unique Hebrew letters that correspond exactly with the numerical value of 265 are: רסה. These three letters can be used to spell four words, listed here as the first four messages. All other messages in this chapter have 265 Gematrias but consist of a variety of different letters that add up to 265.

DIRECTLY EMBEDDED MESSAGES

Message 1: "Destroy" (*Haw-ras*), Exodus 23:24. There are at least two levels of hidden wisdom here: The obvious one directs us to "destroy" corruption. However, when reading the full verse of Exodus 23:24, which warns against idolatry, a deeper meaning is uncovered. The verse states: "Do not prostrate yourself to their gods, do not worship them, and do not act according to their practices; rather you shall destroy them." Because the Hebrew word for "destroy" (with a numerical value of 265) is used in this verse, it reveals a connection between corruption and idolatry. Idolatry is not just the worship of physical idols but also of money, success, power, and influence, all of which, this message points out, can be very destructive.

Message 2: "Perversion" (*Saw-raw*), *The Complete Hebrew English Dictionary,* by Reuben Alcalay. This reminds us that corruption leads to perversion of the law and perversion of the values of society.

Message 3: "Prison" (*So-har*), *The Complete Hebrew English Dictionary,* by Reuben Alcalay. This suggests, while those who are corrupt are aware that they may end up serving actual jail time, what they do not know is that it is irrelevant whether or not they get away with their crimes because they are already spiritually imprisoned.

Message 4: "Remove" (*Ha-sare*), Genesis 30:32. The simple interpretation here is that we should remove corruption from our midst. But in addition, the word "remove" in Genesis 30:32 appears near the end of the story of Jacob and his uncle Laban. Jewish tradition considers Laban to be the biblical symbol of corruption and deceit because he exploited and cheated his son-in-law Jacob. The word "remove" is the key to Jacob's plan to get compensated for 20 years of unpaid labor at the hands of his uncle. The moral of this story is that corruption does not pay.

MESSAGES OF WARNING

Those who are corrupt often justify their behavior with some version of the excuse: "I am just trying to help my family." While it is completely understandable to want to take care of one's family, those who are corrupt are never truly happy, satisfied, or relaxed, even if they have achieved their goals. Most people will likely not believe this, but it is impossible to actually gain from corruption! The next message reveals why the fruits of corruption can never be truly enjoyed. It is formed by rearranging the letters of the Hebrew word for "corruption" (*Kal-kalah*).

Message 5: "The rotten," "the spoiled," or "the miserable" (*Ha-ki-lo-kale*), Numbers 21:5. Out of context, this verse describes corruption and its effects. It states: "There is no food and no water, and our soul is disgusted with the rotten food." This metaphorically explains that the "rotten food," or an ill-gotten gain from corrupt activity, is devoid of value and does not benefit the corrupt or their families. Notice that the verse uses the word "soul," as it states: "Our soul is disgusted with the rotten food." This reveals that, although we may physically consume the food, our souls will be disgusted. (Note: When the phrase "with the rotten food" (*Ba-lechem Ha-ki-lo-kale*) is analyzed, it is discovered to have a Gematria of 345. The three Hebrew letters that correspond exactly with 345 can be used to spell the following two words, which reveal why we can never actually profit from corruption.)

1. "The Name [of God]" (*Hashem*). This is a reminder that God knows all that we do and will make sure we do not ultimately profit from corruption.
2. "Destruction" (*Shamah*). This suggests that the end result of corruption will always be devastation and destruction.

Message 6: "Mighty ones" (*Ah-deerim*), Exodus 15:10. The term "Mighty ones" is found in the "Song at the Sea," sung by the Israelites after the Exodus from Egypt and the miracle of the Splitting of the Sea. "Mighty ones" refers to Pharaoh's chariots, which were chasing the Israelites: "The mighty ones sank like lead in the water." Here, the term "Mighty ones" is used sarcastically. The hidden wisdom is that arrogant people, such as those who profit from corruption, will also sink like lead, spiritually if not literally.

Message 7: "A curse upon" (*K'lalah Ahl*), Deuteronomy 11:29. This is a clear message to those who are corrupt. In this section of the Book of Deuteronomy, God speaks about the importance of the commandments and warns us of the consequences for not following them. The hidden wisdom here appears to be: No matter how observant we are of the commandments, if we are corrupt, we will be cursed.

Message 8: "On the gallows" (*Al Ha-atz*), Esther 9:13. The full phrase states: "Shall be hung on the gallows." This is a clear warning that if we are involved in corruption, we will end up on the gallows, either metaphorically or literally.

Message 9: "All those that fall" (*Kol Ha-noflim*), Psalm 145:14. Out of context, this is, again, a warning to those who are corrupt: literally or metaphorically, they shall fall.

Message 10: "What is the location" (*Ezeh-who M'komon*), Mishna Zevachim, Chapter 5:1. This section of the Mishna refers to the animal sacrifices that were performed in the courtyard of the Holy Temple in Jerusalem between approximately 1000 B.C.E. and 70 C.E. This sentence in the Mishna continues: "Their slaughter shall be in the north [of the courtyard]." However, the word for "north" in Hebrew (*Tzaphone*) can also be read as "hidden" (*Tzaphoon*). In the context of corruption, the full hidden meaning of this sentence can now be revealed: "Wherever the corrupt are located, they shall be slaughtered in a hidden way." This is an ominous warning to those who are complicit in corruption.

Message 11: "And many beasts" (*Oo-B'hay-mah Rabah*), Jonah 4:11. This seems to be a divine comment regarding those who have anything to do with corruption, that spiritually and morally they are no more than beasts.

Message 12: "The primitive man" (*Ha-ah-dahm Ha-kad-mo-nee*), *The Complete Hebrew English Dictionary,* by Reuben Alcalay. The primitive man was barely more evolved than the animals: he lived in trees and caves and was concerned only with survival. This message tells us that, when we choose to be corrupt, we are no more evolved than the primitive man. Hopefully, the day will come soon when we finally evolve and no longer engage in corruption, which stems from primitive survival instincts concerned only with the self and which ignore the costs to the community, the world, and even one's own family.

Message 13: "Physics" (*Physee-kah*), *The Complete Hebrew English Dictionary,* by Reuben Alcalay. In the context of this chapter, "physics" seems to suggest that engrained in the physical makeup of a human being is a tendency toward corruption. The challenge for each of us is to resist this intrinsic aspect of our nature.

Message 14: "Nations of your shame" (*Goyim Keelo-nech*), Jeremiah 46:12. The full phrase warns that "nations shall hear of your shame" if you continue your corrupt ways.

Message 15: "Unjustifiable" (*Lo Mootz-dak*), *The Complete Hebrew English Dictionary,* by Reuben Alcalay. As discussed earlier, all those who engage in corrupt behavior have their justifications for doing so. But this message makes clear that, despite any excuses, corruption is unjustifiable.

Message 16: "Bomb" (*P'tzah-tzah*), *The Complete Hebrew English Dictionary,* by Reuben Alcalay. This suggests that, just as a bomb destroys, kills, and causes unintended damage, so too does corruption.

Message 17: "Great expanse" or "Vastness of effect" (*Mare-chav-yah*), *The Complete Hebrew English Dictionary,* by Reuben Alcalay. This describes the wide-reaching effects of corruption.

Message 18: "Destroyer" (*Ma-cha-revah*), from *The Complete Hebrew English Dictionary,* by Reuben Alcalay. Clearly, this message describes anyone involved with corruption.

MESSAGES OF WISDOM

Message 19: "Until this place" (*Ahd HaMakom*), Deuteronomy 1:31. This verse states: "God carried you, as a man carries his child, on the entire way that you traveled, until this place." The hidden meaning here is that God shall carry and protect you on your path, as long as you do not cross the line into being corrupt.

Message 20: "To recognize" (*L'ha-keer*), *The Complete Hebrew English Dictionary,* by Reuben Alcalay. When we are corrupt, it is often difficult for us to recognize our own corruption because we always find some "reasonable" excuse for it. Nevertheless, recognizing our own wrongdoing is the essential first step in taking responsibility and changing bad behavior.

HOW CAN WE RESIST THE TEMPTATION OF CORRUPTION?

Message 21: "In the face of the King" or "In front of the King" (*Lif-nay Ha-Melech*), Esther 1:16. According to some commentators, in the Scroll of Esther, the Hebrew word for "the King" (*Ha-Melech*) can be understood on a deeper level to refer to God. Therefore, in the above phrase, "the King" refers to God, the Eternal King. This message reminds the corrupt that their behavior is in full view of God the King and will be recorded. In the Scroll of Esther, the entire story turned from tragedy to victory because the Persian king had recorded a good deed performed by Mordechai, Esther's uncle. This suggests that, just as our good deeds are recorded and can help us, so too our bad deeds are recorded and can hurt us.

Message 22: "Shall depart from Eden" (*Yatzah May-eden*), Genesis 2:10. This is a reminder that corruption was the cause of Adam and Eve's expulsion from the Garden of Eden. Although it sounds like a warning, we can infer that the end of corruption may be the path back to Eden.

Message 23: "In God's Garden of Eden" (*B'Ay-den Gan Elokim*), Ezekiel 28:13. Literally or metaphorically, if we forsake corruption, life may be as if we were back in God's Garden of Eden. This may also refer to the previously mentioned first instance of corruption: when Adam and Eve ate from the forbidden Tree of Knowledge of Good and Evil.

Message 24: "Filled with justice" (*Tzedek Ma-lay*), literal translation, taken from Psalm 48:11. This teaches us that, in spite of our tendency to be corrupt, we have the potential to create a world filled with justice. The choice is ours.

It is worth noting that, in Hebrew, the word for "provision" and "economics" (*Calcalah*) is pronounced exactly the same as the word for "corruption" (*Kalkalah*), but they are spelled differently. Therefore the two words have different numerical values: the word for "corruption" has a value of 265, and the word for "economics" or "provision" has a numerical value of 105. The difference between them is 160 (265 − 105 = 160). After studying all known Hebrew words and phrases with the numerical value of 160, I discovered that they all refer to our excessive focus on money, because the numerical value of the Hebrew word for money (*Kesef*) is 160. From this we learn that what begins as the natural human instinct of providing for the needs of one's family can become corrupted when we focus too much on the accumulation of money. This pursuit sets a person on a path evermore distant from the perfection of Eden.

Thus, the hidden purpose of the Hebrew word for "economics" sounding exactly the same as the Hebrew word for "corruption" is to serve as a warning, or reminder, that our economic endeavors, however well intended, can easily become corrupted.

V

Divine Wisdom and Coaching for a Great Life

Chapter Twenty-One

Feed the Hungry

HUNGRY = 277

To me, the existence and persistence of hunger and starvation reveal a sad truth: that human beings do not really care about each other. While everyone claims to feel badly about hunger, nothing substantive is ever done to change it. This is because we believe that hunger affects only those who are unfortunate enough to be hungry and does not touch the rest of us. But, as you read this chapter, you will see that nothing could be further from the truth.

This chapter lists the directives and warnings embedded within the Hebrew word for "hungry." In addition, you will learn the rewards for feeding the hungry and the consequences of not. Ending hunger is more than a moral issue—it is in our self-interest, because whether or not we work to end it appears to determine whether or not God responds to our prayers. It may even be that the solving of this problem could lead to messianic times.

A recurring theme in the Bible is that God is not impressed with our mere observance of the commandments unless it is also accompanied by our helping the poor, feeding the hungry, and being kind to the stranger, the widow, the orphan, and our neighbor. This work is called "repairing the world" (*Tikkun* in Hebrew), and feeding the hungry is *Tikkun* at its best—a measurement of whether or not we are truly honoring the commandments.

The Hebrew word for "hungry" (*R'ay-vah*) is found both in Psalm 107:9 and in the Book of Proverbs 27:7. In each instance the word refers to the soul, the complete phrase being "the hungry soul." The belief that hunger only affects those who lack food is false because almost all of us suffer from a spiritual hunger. In Psalm 107:9, "the hungry soul" is filled with good, and in Proverbs 27:7, "the hungry soul" mistakenly thinks that bitter is sweet.

Allowing hunger to persist, then, can warp our senses and prevent us from experiencing true sweetness or happiness. Today, we mistake standard of living for quality of life, and to compensate for our spiritual hunger we distract ourselves with technology, shopping, and overindulgence in food, alcohol, and drugs. Therefore, hunger actually affects all of us, either physically or spiritually. The question is: How can we determine whether our hungry soul is filled with good or is mistaking bitter for sweet? This chapter shows that feeding the physically hungry is the answer.

The Hebrew word for "hungry" (*R'ay-vah*) has a numerical value of 277. After studying all Hebrew words and phrases with a numerical value of 277, each one has been found to refer to an aspect of hunger. The three unique Hebrew letters that correspond exactly to 277 are: זער. These letters can be used to spell three words, which are listed as the first three messages. All other messages in this chapter also have 277 Gematrias but consist of a variety of different letters.

Message 1: "Plant," "seed," or "sow" (*Zaw-ra*), *The Complete Hebrew English Dictionary,* by Reuben Alcalay. This tells us that to plant, seed, and sow are the exact actions we must take to feed the hungry.

Message 2: "Help" or "aid" (*A-zor*), *The Complete Hebrew English Dictionary,* by Reuben Alcalay. This is a clear directive to help and aid the hungry.

Message 3: "Arm" is the literal translation, and the metaphorical one is "strength" or "might" (*Zro-ah*), from Daniel 11:6. This suggests that to merely talk about helping the hungry is not enough—we must physically exert our strength on their behalf.

MESSAGES OF WISDOM

Message 4: "Avert a disaster" (*Ma-no-ah Ah-sone*), *The Complete Hebrew English Dictionary,* by Reuben Alcalay. The numerical equivalence of this phrase to "hungry" serves to alert us to act immediately, before hunger leads to starvation, illness, or death.

By taking the Hebrew letters of the word "hungry" (רעבה), and rearranging them, we can spell the following ten messages, each of which refers to a positive result of feeding the hungry or warns of the consequences for failing to do so.

Message 5: "The evening" (*Ha-arev*), Leviticus 11:24. Just as evening delineates the brief time between day and night, the message here, metaphorically, directs us to act now, before the darkness comes, while there is still time to save the hungry. In addition, the full phrase in Leviticus states: "And you are contaminated until the evening." The hidden message here seems to be that we are contaminated until we take action to end hunger.

(Note: The Gematria of the Hebrew word for "starvation" (*R'avone*) is 328. 328 generates three specific Hebrew letters that spell "darkness" (*Choshech*). Starvation is a more serious, later stage of hunger, hence the metaphor of darkness. In addition, the exact letters that correspond to 328 also spell "denial" (*Ka-chosh*). This speaks to our psychological preference to live in denial rather than become actively aware that others—around the world, and even in our own neighborhood—are starving. These same letters also spell the word for "forgot" or "forsake" (*Sha-choch*), suggesting that those who are starving are the forgotten ones.)

Message 6: "To be kindled," "arson," or "damage done by careless burning" (*Hev-air* or *Havar*), *The Complete Hebrew English Dictionary,* by Reuben Alcalay. This warns that hunger can quickly devolve into the more serious state of starvation and become widespread, like a conflagration.

Message 7: "Fury," "sin," or "transgression" (*A-vay-rah* or *Evrah*), Psalm 78:49. "Fury" refers to God's anger at Pharaoh. Psalm 78 recounts the story of the Ten Plagues that God sent as a consequence of the Children of Israel being enslaved in Egypt. The hidden message here seems to be that, just as the plagues were a consequence to the sin of slavery, so too plagues will be a consequence for our refusal to feed the hungry.

Message 8: "The ignorant" (*Ha-ba-ar*), *The Complete Hebrew English Dictionary,* by Reuben Alcalay. It seems that the divine measuring line for intelligence is determined by our choice of whether or not to feed the hungry.

Message 9: "Remove" or "destroy" (*Be-ay-ra*), *The Complete Hebrew English Dictionary,* by Reuben Alcalay. This appears to be a directive: Remove and destroy the condition of hunger.

Message 10: "Guarantor" (*Ah-ray-va*), *The Complete Hebrew English Dictionary,* by Reuben Alcalay. This seems to suggest that each of us has the responsibility to guarantee that no one goes hungry.

Message 11: "The past" (*Ha-avar*), *The Complete Hebrew English Dictionary,* by Reuben Alcalay. This message urges us to make hunger a thing of the past.

Message 12: "Shall sweeten" or "Shall make pleasant" (*Ha-awe-reve*), from the daily blessings of the Torah. The full phrase states: "Please God, our Lord, sweeten the words of Your Torah in our mouths." This tells us that, if we act to feed the hungry, we can expect that God shall sweeten our life. It may also refer to the earlier concept of "the hungry soul," which cannot tell the difference between bitter and sweet.

Message 13: "In wickedness" (*B'ra-ah*), Genesis 44:29. This is a clear rebuke: Because we do not end hunger, we are acting wickedly. The full phrase seems to warn of the consequences for tolerating the condition of hunger; it states: "In wickedness to the grave."

(Note: The Gematria of "In wickedness to the grave" (*B'ra-ah Sheola*) is 613. This is also the total number of commandments in the Old Testament.

The hidden meaning is that, to honor the 613, you must feed the hungry, otherwise you are missing the purpose of the 613 commandments.)

Message 14: "Willow branch" (*Aravah*), Talmud Tractate *Sukkah*. The willow branch twigs make up one of the four species of the *Lulav* (palm branch), used on the festival of *Sukkot*. It is prophesized that when the Messiah comes the entire world will celebrate *Sukkot*. The hidden meaning here may be that each element of this holiday represents one universal condition to be repaired in order to bring about the Messiah. The willow branch would then represent feeding the hungry, because its numerical value is 277. Therefore, it is possible to infer that ending world hunger could lead to messianic times.

Message 15: "Way of life" or "lifestyle" (*O-rach Chaim*), Psalm 16:11. There are those who believe that hunger is inevitable and a normal way of life, as if it were a lifestyle choice. That is not true. While the true cause of hunger is beyond the scope of this book, scientists have shown that there is enough food on earth to feed everyone. The message "Way of life" instructs us that the appropriate way to conduct our lives is to help and aid the hungry.

Message 16: "Charity and kindness" (*Tzedakah Vah-Chessed*), from the *Avinu Malkeinu* prayer. It could be said that the purpose of the Torah, and of the entire Jewish tradition, is to perform charity and acts of kindness. The hidden message here is: Because "hungry" is mathematically equivalent to "charity and kindness," feeding the hungry is the perfect way to fulfill the commandment to give charity and be kind.

PERSONAL BENEFITS OF FEEDING THE HUNGRY

Message 17: "Though my father and mother have forsaken me, but God" (*Ki Avi V'imee A-za-vooni V'A-donai*), Psalm 27:10. The full verse states: "Though my father and mother have forsaken me, but God shall gather me in." The hidden message here is that, when we feed the hungry, God shall embrace us.

Message 18: "Your children upon the earth" (*B'nay-chem Ahl Ha-ada-mah*), Deuteronomy 11:21. This phrase is part of the holiest and most popular Jewish prayer, the *Shema,* which summarizes the entire Bible and underlines the major principles of life: to believe in and to love the one true God, and to observe and teach God's commandments. Deuteronomy 11:21 states the reason to observe the commandments: "In order to prolong your days and the days of your children upon the earth." The hidden message here suggests that feeding the hungry may influence God's blessings upon our children.

Message 19: "Measuring line" "of trouble" (*Kav Akah*), each of these two words (the first one Hebrew, the second Aramaic) was found separately in *The Complete Hebrew English Dictionary,* by Reuben Alcalay, and together they add up to 277. A recurring theme in this book is the idea that God measures certain actions we take, or choices we make, as indicators of who we are and our holiness. This message tells us that, at the very least, the persistence of hunger and starvation is an indicator of some massive failure on the part of all humanity.

Message 20: "At every season and time" (*Kal Ziman V'edan*), from the Sabbath prayer *Yekum Purkan*. The Bible tells us that at all times we must consider the well-being of our fellow human beings. Therefore, this message emphasizes that at every season and time we should feed the hungry.

MESSAGES OF WARNING

If we fail to feed the hungry then the following messages apply.

Message 21: "I shall be angry" (*Eck-tzoff*), Isaiah 57:17. Isaiah Chapter 57 warns that God shall be angry and not come to our aid if we are wicked. The hidden message here, again, is that not feeding the hungry angers God. Chapter 58 of Isaiah, which is recited on Yom Kippur, the holiest day of the Jewish calendar, describes God's rebuke of those who fast on this holiday but did not feed the hungry or perform acts of kindness during the previous year.

Message 22: "Shall no longer" or "Shall not continue anymore" (*Lo Yo-sif Ode*), Isaiah 10:20. This verse in Isaiah explains that, "On that day," you shall not rely on God's enemies anymore but on God. The hidden message here is that, on the day we all commit to ending hunger, we will be allied with God and not allied with His enemies: greed, hatred, apathy, and corruption.

Message 23: "Desert" or "Dry land" (*A-ravah*), *The Complete Hebrew English Dictionary,* by Reuben Alcalay. The meaning here may be literal but also metaphoric—for what our lives will be like if we continue to tolerate the persistence of hunger. The quality of our lives will be like dry land, incapable of providing nourishment. In other words, if we allow others to suffer, then we shall suffer, too.

Message 24: "To a desert" (*El Midbar*), Exodus 15:22. This repeats the warning of the previous message. It is worth noting that, even though "To a desert" uses a different Hebrew word for "desert," than Message 23, it has the identical numerical value of 277.

Message 25: "The swarms of wild beasts" or "The swarms of flies" (*Ha-Awe-rove*), Exodus 8:20. This was the fourth of the Ten Plagues in Egypt. Whether this message is metaphoric or literal, it is a warning of what may befall us if we ignore the plight of the hungry.

Message 26: "A severe plague" or "A severe epidemic" (*Deh-vair Kah-ved Mih-ode*), Exodus 9:3. This is from the story of the fifth plague in Egypt, and, again, whether this message is metaphoric or literal, it reveals another possible consequence of our selfish choices.

Message 27: "He shall be last" (*Who Acha-rone*), from the morning prayers. Out of context and metaphorically, this tells us that whoever does not help the hungry shall be "last" in God's eyes.

Message 28: "Rude," "haughty," or "vulgar" (*Gahss Ruach*), *The Complete Hebrew English Dictionary,* by Reuben Alcalay. This describes someone who fails to help the hungry.

THE CONNECTION BETWEEN
GOD AND FEEDING THE HUNGRY

Message 29: "Since God has spoken" (*N'oom A-donai Ki Ya-an*), Genesis 22:16. This is a reminder that to feed the hungry is a requirement—since God has thusly spoken. What follows this phrase in the text are blessings, teaching us that the way to receive blessings is by doing acts of kindness, such as feeding the hungry.

Message 30: "Says the Lord" (*Yomare A-donai*), Numbers 15:37. This phrase is also found in the most important Jewish prayer, the *Shema,* which is a declaration of love for God and a vow to follow His commandments. The hidden message here is that the manifestation of loving God and following His commandments is to feed the hungry.

Message 31: "He shall respond to His people" (*Oneh L'amo*), from The Helper of Our Forefathers prayer. This prayer promises that God shall respond to His people when they cry out to Him. This establishes the connection between feeding the hungry and God responding to us and considering us among His people.

Message 32: "I am before You God" (*Ah-nee Li-pha-necha A-donai*), from the daily prayer My God, the Soul. Metaphorically, this translates to: "I stand before You God." In this prayer we thank God for restoring our souls. This message suggests that when we feed the hungry, we can stand before God with merit.

Message 33: "Measuring line" "of the Most High" (*Kav Ha-Elyone*), both Hebrew words were found separately in the Bible but together they add up to 277. In Jewish liturgy, the term "Most High" refers to God. Therefore, as in the earlier "Measuring line of trouble," this also seems to refer to a divine accounting of the actions of human beings. Two behaviors are being measured here: learning what is important and acting on what is important.

While the final two messages are exact opposites—one a warning and the other a blessing—they have the identical numerical value of 277.

Message 34: "And God shall not be with me" (*V'ain Elokim E-mah-dee*), Deuteronomy 32:39. Here, Moses warns Israel of the consequences for violating its covenant with God. If they worship other gods, including the gods of money, fame, and power, terrible consequences will follow, such as the heavens withholding rain. This seems to be a warning to us all for failing to feed the hungry.

Message 35: "Behold I [God] am with you" (*V'Henay Anochi Eemach*), Genesis 28:15. In this phrase, God promises Jacob that He, God, shall be with him and protect him. We learn from this that, to earn God's protection, we must protect the most vulnerable, those who do not even have food to eat. And if we work to feed the hungry, God shall be with us and protect us.

Chapter Twenty-Two

Honor Mothers . . . but Not Daughters?

MOTHERS = 452

While most everyone professes to love their mother, mistreatment of women persists in our society, whether it takes the more subtle forms of verbal abuse and workplace inequality or extends into physical violence, such as rape and sex slavery. But what is truly remarkable is that, despite a universal belief in loving and respecting one's mother, there continue to be unspeakable abuses and crimes committed against daughters, the future mothers of the world. These abuses include female-genital mutilation, honor killings, acid throwing, and the selective aborting of female fetuses. Through the use of Gematria, this hypocrisy is exposed.

This chapter examines the messages directly embedded in, and having the same numerical value as, the Hebrew word for "mothers." The messages seem to answer questions such as: What is the purpose of mothers? What are their special qualities? And what is God's opinion of and instructions regarding mothers and daughters?

The Hebrew word for "mothers" (*Ema-hote*) is found in *The Complete English Hebrew Dictionary,* by Reuben Alcalay, and has a Gematria of 452. The three specific and unique Hebrew letters that correspond exactly with the numerical value of 452 are: תנב. These three letters can be used to spell three words which are listed as the first three messages. All other messages in this chapter also have 452 Gematrias but consist of a variety of different letters.

DIRECTLY EMBEDDED MESSAGES

Message 1: "Understand" or "grasp" (*Ban-ta*), *The Complete Hebrew English Dictionary,* by Reuben Alcalay. This message reminds us that the ability to be understanding is a primary quality of a mother.

Message 2: "Build" (*Tee-ven*), Zechariah 9:3 and 1 Chonicles 7:24. "Build" is an appropriate metaphor for describing the purpose and contributions of mothers to their children, husbands, communities, and the world. While men are often associated with war and destruction, the contributions of women, as mothers and nurturers, are more closely tied to images of creation and building for the future.

REVEALING THE HYPOCRISY
OF HONORING MOTHERS BUT NOT DAUGHTERS

Message 3: "Daughters" (*Ba-note*), from the commentator known as Onkelos (second century C.E.) on Genesis 6:1. This section of Genesis tells of divine beings recognizing the greatness of daughters. An accepted variation of the spelling of the Hebrew word for "daughters" has the same numerical value as the Hebrew word for "mothers," thus reminding us that daughters are the future mothers and deserve the appropriate respect. Therefore, this numerical equivalence suggests that when we mistreat daughters we actually mistreat mothers.

Message 4: "Whose daughter?" (*Baht Me*), Genesis 24:47. This section of Genesis describes the kindness and understanding of Rebecca (one of the Four Matriarchs of the Bible), qualities which were interpreted as signs that she was an appropriate wife for Isaac. The numerical equivalence of the phrase "Whose daughter" to the value of the Hebrew word for "mothers" reveals and emphasizes that all mothers were once daughters, and implies, once again, that mistreatment of a daughter is equivalent to mistreatment of a mother.

Message 5: "To your daughter" (*L'vitcha*), Deuteronomy 22:17. Out of context, this again emphasizes the connection between daughters and mothers. In addition, it is worth noting that this section of Deuteronomy lists laws protecting married women and girls against rape and false accusations.

Message 6: "I accuse" (*Ani Ma-ashim*), Hebrew title of "J'accuse," the 1898 front-page article regarding the Dreyfus Affair by the French journalist Emile Zola, in which he accuses the French military of gross injustice, hatred, and lies. "J'accuse" has since become an expression of anger and accusation against hypocrisy, but in the context of mothers it may be interpreted as a divine statement regarding them: God's accusation that mankind is guilty of hypocrisy and hatred toward women.

MESSAGES OF WISDOM

Message 7: "The human race" (*Geza Ha-enoshi*), *The Complete Hebrew English Dictionary,* by Reuben Alcalay. This is a reminder that all of humanity is descended from mothers.

Message 8: "Who shall enjoy tranquility and who shall?" (*Me Y'shalev Oo-me*), from the *Unisaneh Tokef* prayer, recited on the High Holy Days. This prayer beseeches God to inscribe us for a good and healthy year. The complete verse states: "Who shall enjoy tranquility and who shall suffer?" This suggests that our relationships to mothers, to daughters, and to all women appear to determine the quality of our life: treat them well and have tranquility or mistreat them and suffer.

Message 9: "God [said]: Peace to you" (*A-donai Shalom Lecha*), Judges 6:23. The full verse states: "God said to him, Peace to you, do not be afraid, you will not die." In the context of mothers, daughters, and women, this verse seems like a divine recommendation: Don't be afraid to treat women well, you won't die and you will have peace. In addition, "God [said]: Peace to you" may reveal a secret purpose of mothers: to promote the divine agenda of peace, thus disclosing that mothers serve as divine agents.

Message 10: "Elders of the city" (*Ziknay Ha-eer*), Deuteronomy 22:17. If the "elders of the city" are the city's leaders and wise counsel, then the fact that this phrase is numerically equivalent to "mothers" may indicate that the wisdom of mothers should be equally valued. A deeper meaning also seems to emerge from an inquiry into this section of Deuteronomy, which describes young, newly married women appearing before a legal proceeding of the "elders of the city" to defend themselves against accusations of promiscuity and infidelity. The numerical equivalence may reveal that this legal proceeding of "elders" literally consisted of a group of mothers, thus ensuring a sympathetic hearing for the young bride.

ARE MOTHERS DIVINE AGENTS?

Message 11: "Make marriages" or, literally, "Sits and makes couples" (*Yoshav Oo-mezug Zugim*), from the ancient commentary of *Midrash Rabbah.* The full phrase, "Marriages are made in Heaven," implies that when a mother arranges marriages for her children, she acts as a divine agent.

Message 12: "[God] continue Your loving kindness" (*M'shoch Chasdecha*), Psalm 36:11. The numerical equivalence of this phrase to "mothers" suggests that the ability to promote the divine agenda of loving kindness is a quality inherent to mothers.

Message 13: "God help for" (*Hoshea A-donai Key*), Psalm 12:2. The full verse states: "God help, for the devout one is no more, for truthful people have vanished from among mankind." This may refer to the hypocrisy of those who claim to honor and love their mothers, or it may suggest that God's help often takes the form of a mother's help.

Message 14: "For help is with God" (*LA-donai Ha-yeshua*), Psalm 3:9. As the full verse states: "For help is with God, Your blessing upon the people Selah." The hidden message here appears to be that mothers are God's blessing and help to humankind.

Message 15: "God our Creator" (*A-donai Asanu*), Psalm 95:6. Because of the numerical equivalence of this phrase to the value of "Mothers," it seems to refer to God as a metaphorical mother, thus connecting the holiness of God to that of mothers.

Message 16: "With me is God" (*Iti-E-L*), literal translation of a proper name in Nehemiah 11:7. This may imply that when we treat mothers, daughters, and women with dignity and respect, God will be with us. In addition, another hidden meaning may be that, because God is with mothers, we should empower them and embrace their opinions.

MOTHERS: SOURCE OF DYNASTIES

Message 17: "Dynasties," literally "houses" (*Batim*), Exodus 1:21. This section of Exodus describes the two Hebrew midwives who defied Pharaoh's decree to drown all the Jewish male newborns. The Bible states that in the merit of the midwives' courageous acts, their families were established into "dynasties," or "houses." (Note: the numerical value of the phrase "And He [God] established them as houses" is 913. All Hebrew text of a 913 numerical value refers to the first word of the Bible, "In the beginning" (*Berashis*), thus suggesting that the midwives both metaphorically and literally gave birth to the Jewish people.)

MESSAGES OF WARNING

The following messages seem to describe the consequences for not respecting or valuing mothers, daughters, or any woman.

Message 18: "In sackcloth" (*Ba-sakim*), 2 Kings 19:2. Sackcloth is a biblical symbol for mourning, thus revealing both a metaphoric and literal consequence of not valuing women. Some of the other consequences appear to be listed in the following verse of 2 Kings 19:3, which states: "Today is a day of distress, rebuke, and sacrilege. [We are like babies] who have entered the birth canal, but [the mother] has no strength to give birth." Distress, rebuke, and sacrilege appear to describe the consequences for disempowering a mother in particular and women in general.

Message 19: "In the sin of" (*B'pesha*), Proverbs 12:13. The full phrase states: "In the sin of the lips lies the snare of evil." This appears to alert us to be mindful of how we speak to and about women: not to slander, lie, insult, or gossip about them.

Message 20: "Contamination of" (*B'toomot*), Leviticus 5:3. This section of Leviticus describes some of the prohibitions associated with unkosher food. In our context, "Contamination of" may reveal that not valuing women is as serious a sin as being unkosher and, metaphorically, constitutes an ingestion of contaminated values.

THE TRUTH ABOUT MOTHERS

The final message is spelled by rearranging the letters of the Hebrew word for "mothers."

Message 21: "And the truth" (*V'Ha-emet*), 2 Chronicles 31:20. This verse states: "Doing what was good and proper and the truth before God," suggesting that valuing mothers and our future mothers, as well as all women, is good, proper, and true.

Epilogue

What Does God Say about Gematria?

As this book has shown, Gematria is a wonderful technique for uncovering hidden wisdom and beautiful associations. But what is God's opinion of it? In an attempt to solve this question, I decided to analyze the word itself.

There are two legitimate spellings of "Gematria" and, therefore, two different numerical values. The first spelling found in *The Complete Hebrew English Dictionary,* by Reuben Alcalay, has a numerical value of 277. The three specific and unique Hebrew letters that correspond exactly with 277 (רעז) spell the word for "help" *(Ozer)*. This suggests that a purpose of Gematria is to help us interpret the Bible and reveal its hidden wisdom. These letters can also spell the Hebrew word for "seed," "sow," or "plant" (*Za-ra*), further suggesting that Gematria helps to sow the seeds of divine wisdom.

However, the second spelling of "Gematria," found in the commentary of the *Baal HaTurim* (1269–1343), has a value of 273, and suggests a different view. The three specific and unique letters that correspond exactly to 273 (רעג) can be used to spell the Hebrew word for "scold" or "rebuke" (*Ga-ar*), implying that too great a focus on numerical values may lead us to ignore the value of the actual texts themselves, meriting God's disapproval or "rebuke." For example, if we spend too much time analyzing and discussing the numerical value of the word "charity" instead of actually giving charity, it could merit a divine scolding. These same letters can also be arranged to spell the Hebrew word for "moment" or "minute" (*Reh-ga*), suggesting that it is all right to use Gematria occasionally. And the same letters that correspond to 273 can also spell the word for "yearns" (*Aw-rog*), as Psalm 42:2 states: "So yearns my soul for You, God." This speaks to the yearning for greater meaning that many seek, including myself. It led me to search, uncover, and develop this system and to spend so many hours in pursuit of understanding and explaining these ideas in the pages you have just read. For those of us who yearn to become closer to God, and to understand God's expectations for us in this world, Gematria is a useful tool. In addition, a phrase from Psalm 126:6 also has a value of 273, and it states: "Shall surely bring joy" (*Bo Yavo B'renah*). It is worth noting that the word preceding this phrase is "seed" (*Za-ra*), with a value of 277, thus connecting both Hebrew spellings of "Gematria." This suggests that Gematria, when used appropriately, can bring joy to the world and help create a rewarding connection to God.

Let us also look at the related question: What is God's opinion of numbers? When the Hebrew word for "numbers" is analyzed it tells a similar story. The numerical value of "numbers" (*Misparim*) is 430, and the two specific unique letters that correspond exactly to 430 (תל) can be used to spell the word "tell" (in Hebrew *Tel*): an archeological term defined as a mound of earth consisting of layers of civilizations and societies, as one town or city fades into history and a new one rises on its ruins. Thus, just as analyzing a mound of earth reveals layers of stories, using numerical values to examine scriptures and text reveals deeper and hidden meanings. When all words and phrases with a 430 value were studied, each was found to refer to an aspect of "numbers." Many of the examples show that numbers are God's language, such as: "Holiness of God" (*Kodesh A-donai*), Psalm 93:5 and "Blessed be God forever" (*Baruch A-donai L'olam*), Psalm 89:53. However, one phrase with a numerical value of 430 was particularly intriguing: "Bread for the hungry" (*Lechem La-re-evim*), Psalm 146:7. This phrase reminds us of the true purpose of the Bible, and of virtually all religions: to encourage us to perform acts of kindness and compassion. Additionally, a metaphoric interpretation of "Bread for the hungry" is that the insights from Gematria are like nourishment for our hungry souls.

Index